Medaka Kuroiwa is Impervious to My Charms

Ran Kuze

CONTENTS

Chapter 29 ★
That Jerk and "Ya Big Dummy"

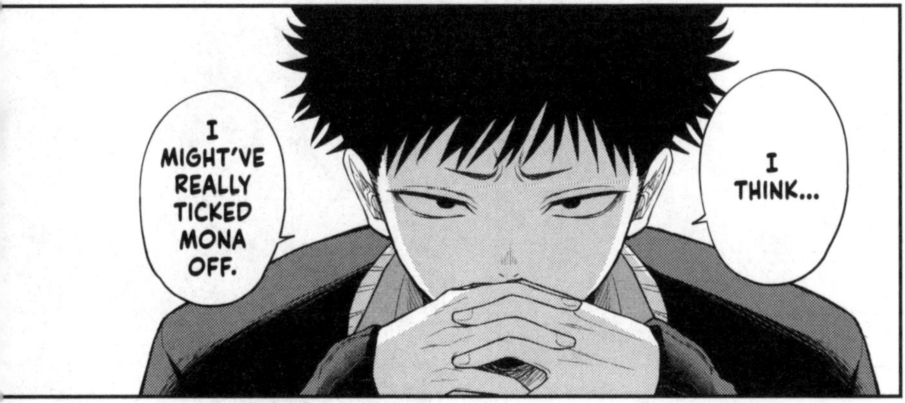
I THINK...
I MIGHT'VE REALLY TICKED MONA OFF.

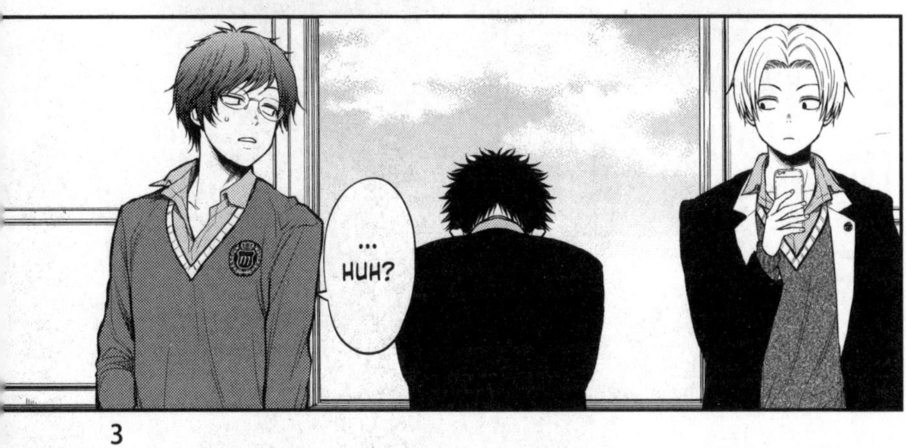
... HUH?

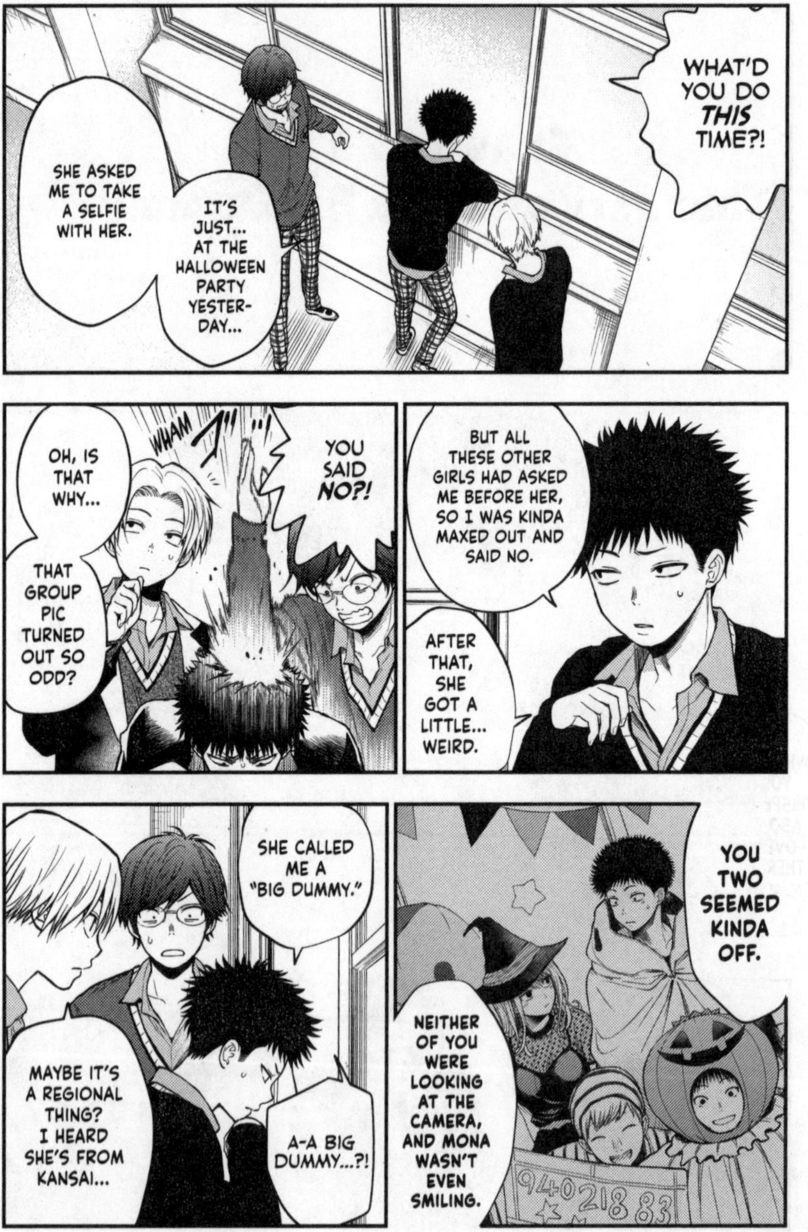
WHAT'D YOU DO *THIS* TIME?!
IT'S JUST... AT THE HALLOWEEN PARTY YESTER-DAY...
SHE ASKED ME TO TAKE A SELFIE WITH HER.
BUT ALL THESE OTHER GIRLS HAD ASKED ME BEFORE HER, SO I WAS KINDA MAXED OUT AND SAID NO.
AFTER THAT, SHE GOT A LITTLE... WEIRD.
YOU SAID *NO?!*
WHAM
OH, IS THAT WHY...
THAT GROUP PIC TURNED OUT SO ODD?
YOU TWO SEEMED KINDA OFF.
NEITHER OF YOU WERE LOOKING AT THE CAMERA, AND MONA WASN'T EVEN SMILING.
SHE CALLED ME A "BIG DUMMY."
A-A BIG DUMMY...?!
MAYBE IT'S A REGIONAL THING? I HEARD SHE'S FROM KANSAI...

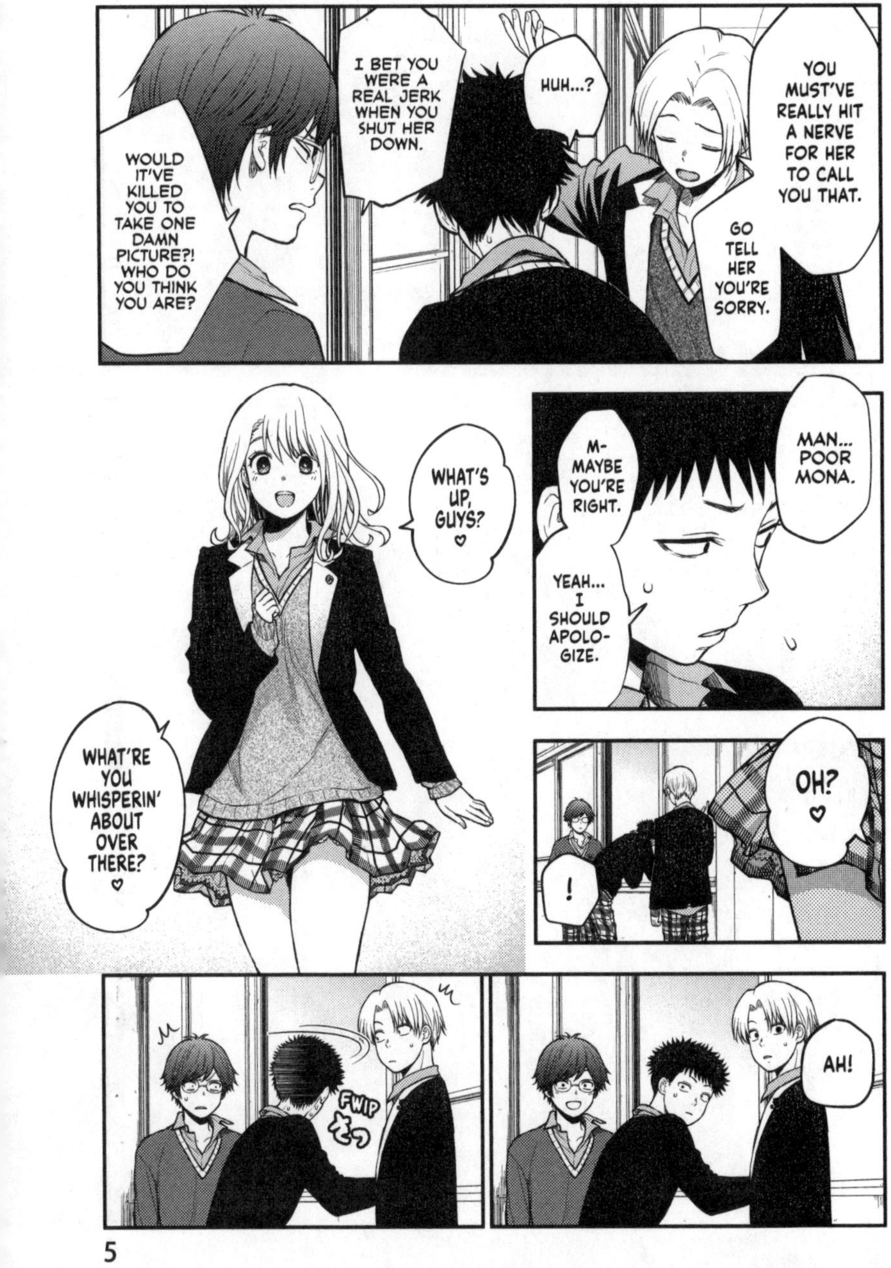
YOU MUST'VE REALLY HIT A NERVE FOR HER TO CALL YOU THAT.
GO TELL HER YOU'RE SORRY.
HUH...?
I BET YOU WERE A REAL JERK WHEN YOU SHUT HER DOWN.
WOULD IT'VE KILLED YOU TO TAKE ONE DAMN PICTURE?! WHO DO YOU THINK YOU ARE?
MAN... POOR MONA.
M-MAYBE YOU'RE RIGHT.
YEAH... I SHOULD APOLO-GIZE.
OH? ♡
!
WHAT'S UP, GUYS? ♡
WHAT'RE YOU WHISPERIN' ABOUT OVER THERE? ♡
AH!
FWIP
そっ

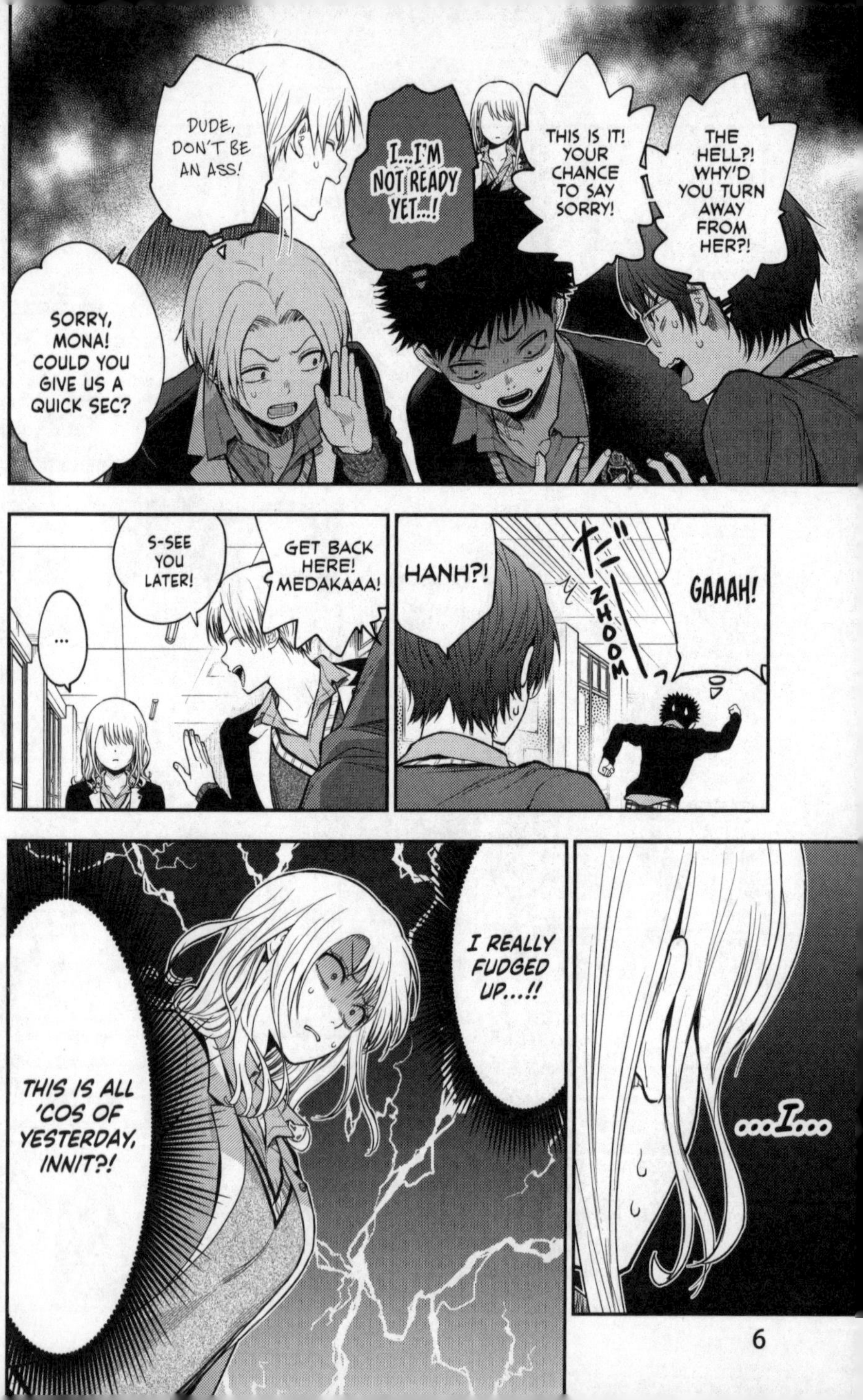
THE HELL?! WHY'D YOU TURN AWAY FROM HER?!
THIS IS IT! YOUR CHANCE TO SAY SORRY!
I...I'M NOT READY YET...!
DUDE, DON'T BE AN ASS!
SORRY, MONA! COULD YOU GIVE US A QUICK SEC?
GAAAH!
ZHOOM
HANH?!
GET BACK HERE! MEDAKAAA!
S-SEE YOU LATER!
...
...I...
I REALLY FUDGED UP...!!
THIS IS ALL 'COS OF YESTERDAY, INNIT?!

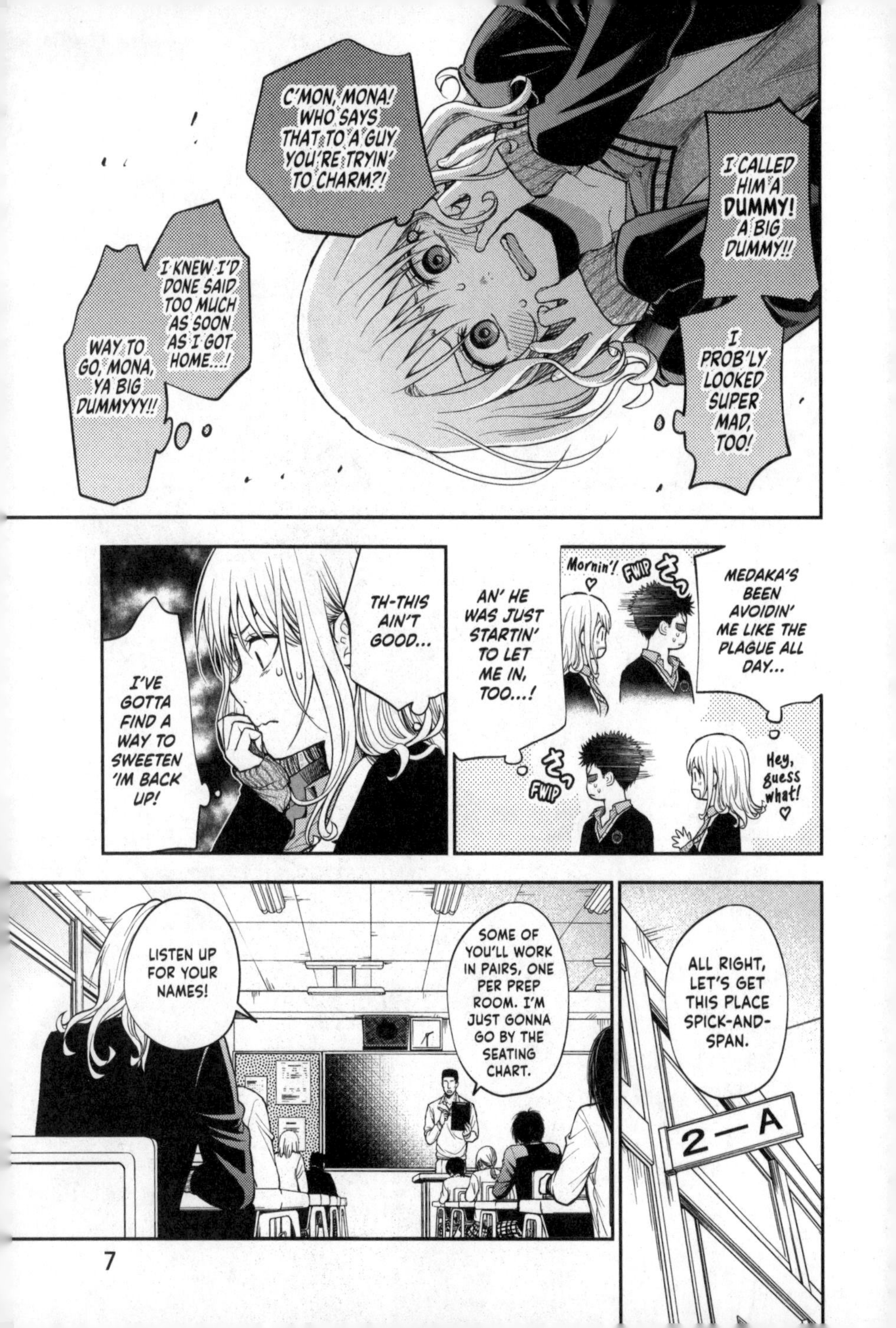

I CALLED HIM A DUMMY! A BIG DUMMY!!
I PROB'LY LOOKED SUPER MAD, TOO!
C'MON, MONA! WHO SAYS THAT TO A GUY YOU'RE TRYIN' TO CHARM?!
I KNEW I'D DONE SAID TOO MUCH AS SOON AS I GOT HOME...!
WAY TO GO, MONA, YA BIG DUMMYYY!!
MEDAKA'S BEEN AVOIDIN' ME LIKE THE PLAGUE ALL DAY...
Mornin'! ♡
FWIP さっ
Hey, guess what! ♡
FWIP さっ
AN' HE WAS JUST STARTIN' TO LET ME IN, TOO...!
TH-THIS AIN'T GOOD...
I'VE GOTTA FIND A WAY TO SWEETEN 'IM BACK UP!
2—A
ALL RIGHT, LET'S GET THIS PLACE SPICK-AND-SPAN.
SOME OF YOU'LL WORK IN PAIRS, ONE PER PREP ROOM. I'M JUST GONNA GO BY THE SEATING CHART.
LISTEN UP FOR YOUR NAMES!

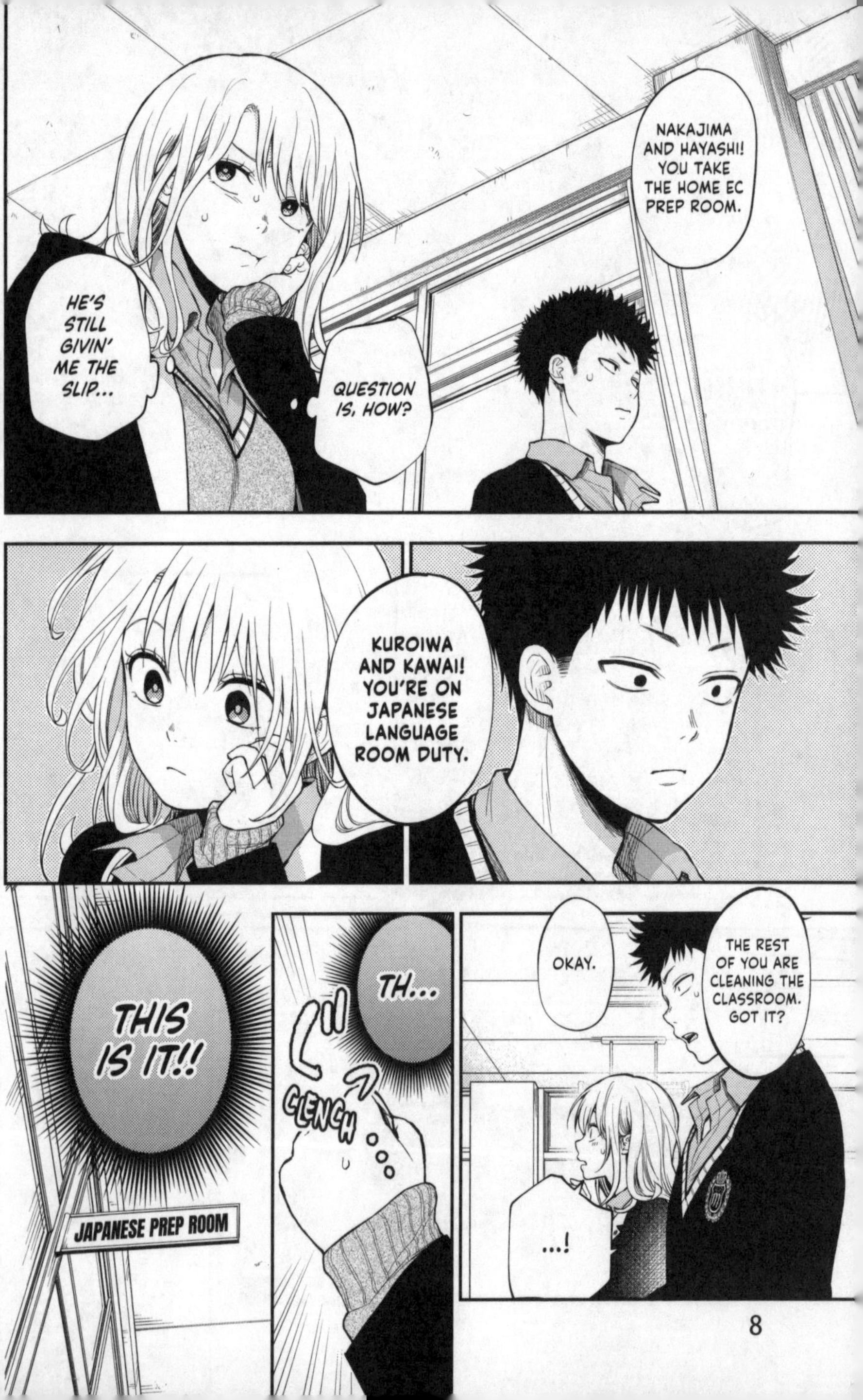
NAKAJIMA AND HAYASHI! YOU TAKE THE HOME EC PREP ROOM.
QUESTION IS, HOW?
HE'S STILL GIVIN' ME THE SLIP...
KUROIWA AND KAWAI! YOU'RE ON JAPANESE LANGUAGE ROOM DUTY.
THE REST OF YOU ARE CLEANING THE CLASSROOM. GOT IT?
OKAY.
...!
TH...
CLENCH
THIS IS IT!!
JAPANESE PREP ROOM

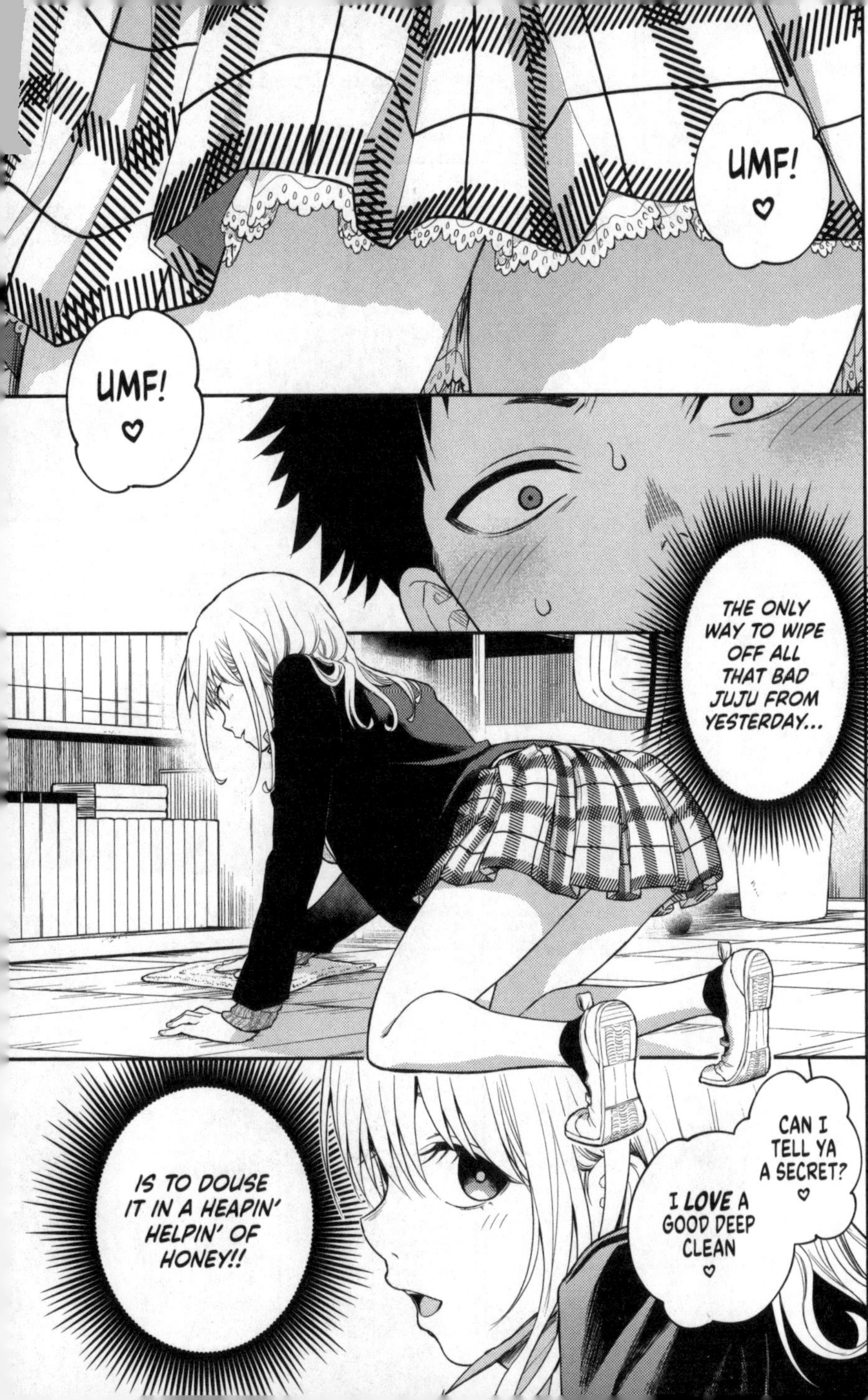
UMF! ♡
UMF! ♡
THE ONLY WAY TO WIPE OFF ALL THAT BAD JUJU FROM YESTERDAY...
CAN I TELL YA A SECRET? ♡
I **LOVE** A GOOD DEEP CLEAN ♡
IS TO DOUSE IT IN A HEAPIN' HELPIN' OF HONEY!!

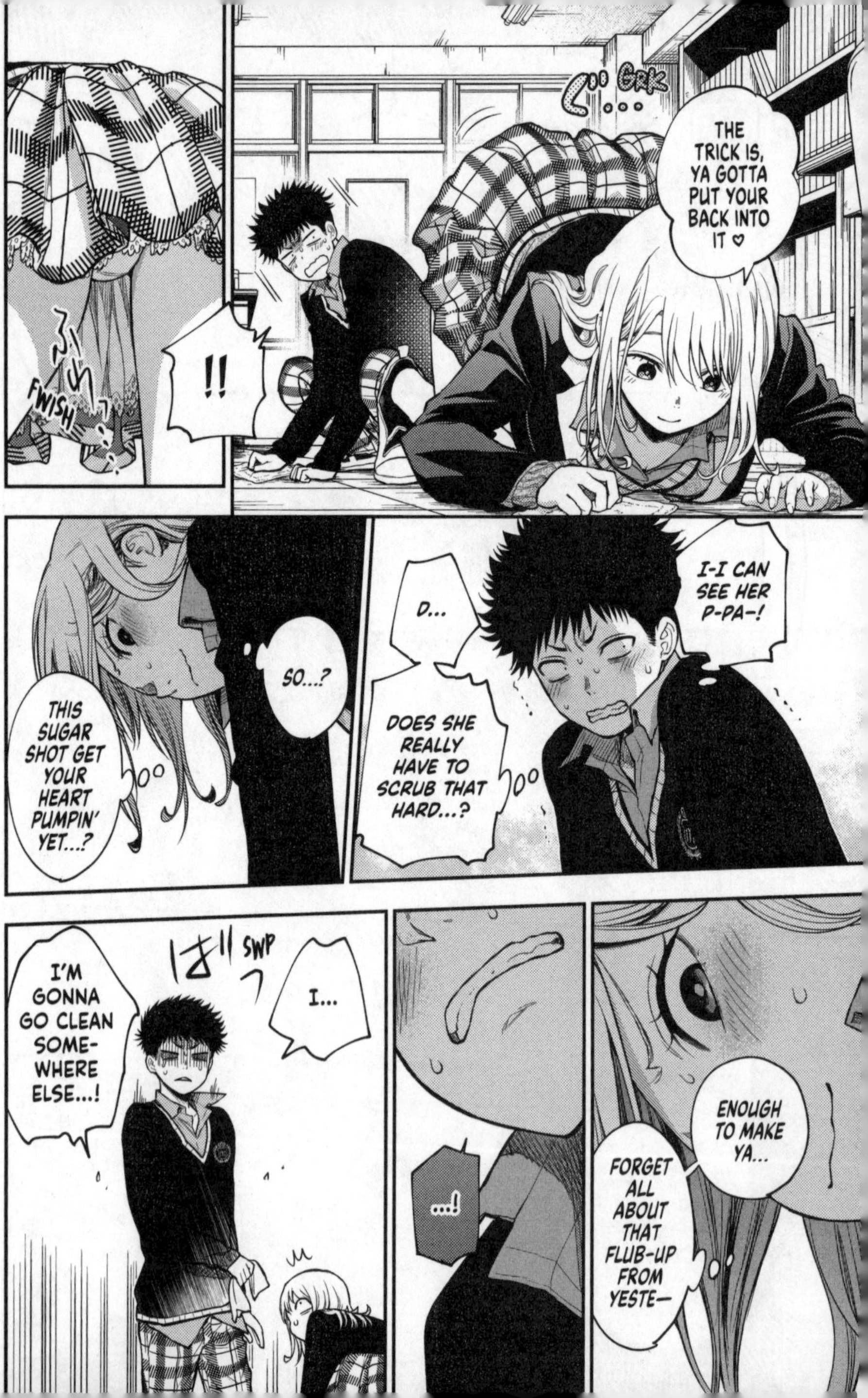
THE TRICK IS, YA GOTTA PUT YOUR BACK INTO IT ♡
GRK
...
!!
FWISH
I-I CAN SEE HER P-PA-!
D...
DOES SHE REALLY HAVE TO SCRUB THAT HARD...?
SO...?
THIS SUGAR SHOT GET YOUR HEART PUMPIN' YET...?
ENOUGH TO MAKE YA...
FORGET ALL ABOUT THAT FLUB-UP FROM YESTE—
...!
I...
SWP
I'M GONNA GO CLEAN SOMEWHERE ELSE...!

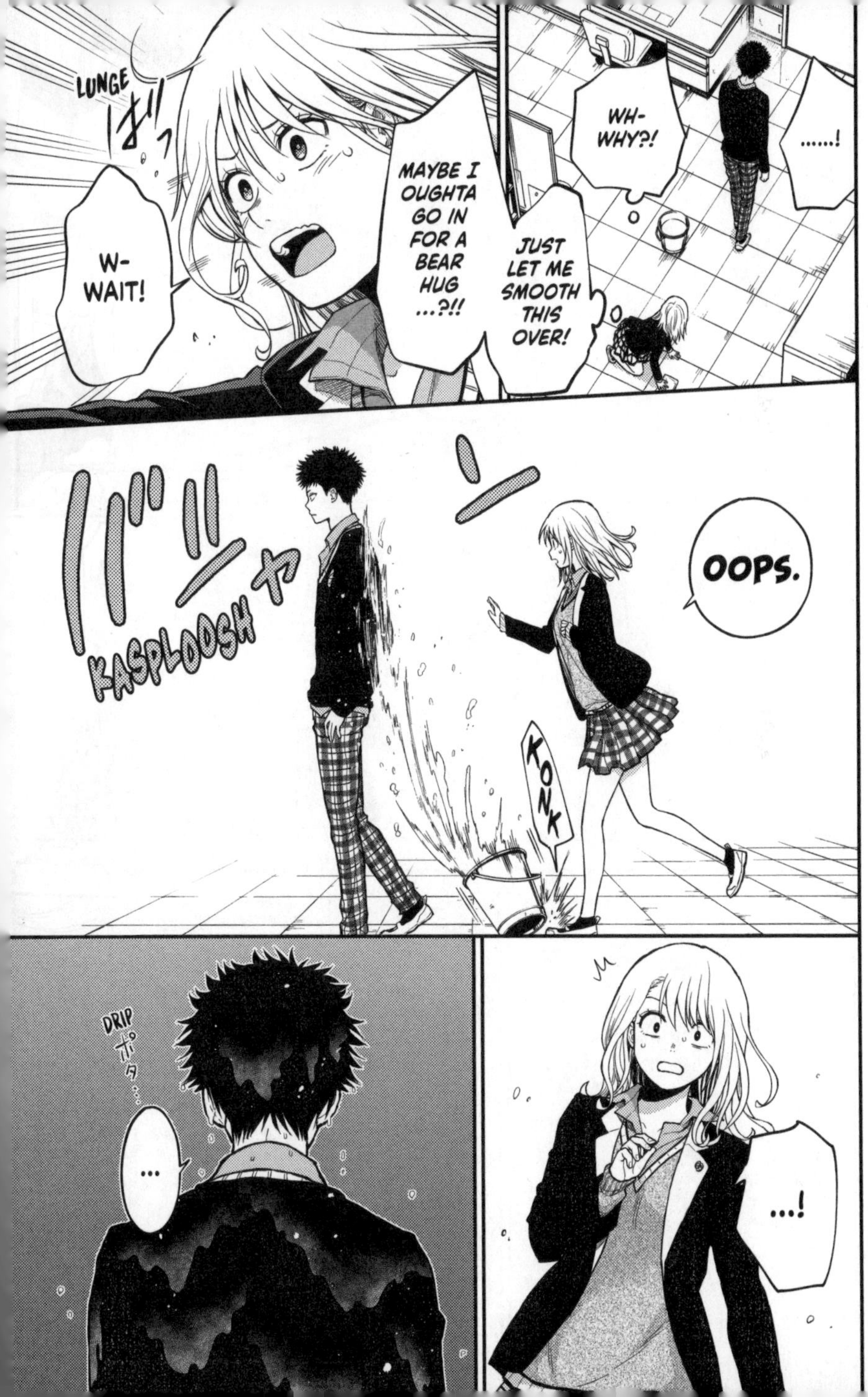
......!
WH-WHY?!
JUST LET ME SMOOTH THIS OVER!
MAYBE I OUGHTA GO IN FOR A BEAR HUG ...?!!
LUNGE
W-WAIT!
OOPS.
KONK
KASPLOOSH
...!
DRIP
...

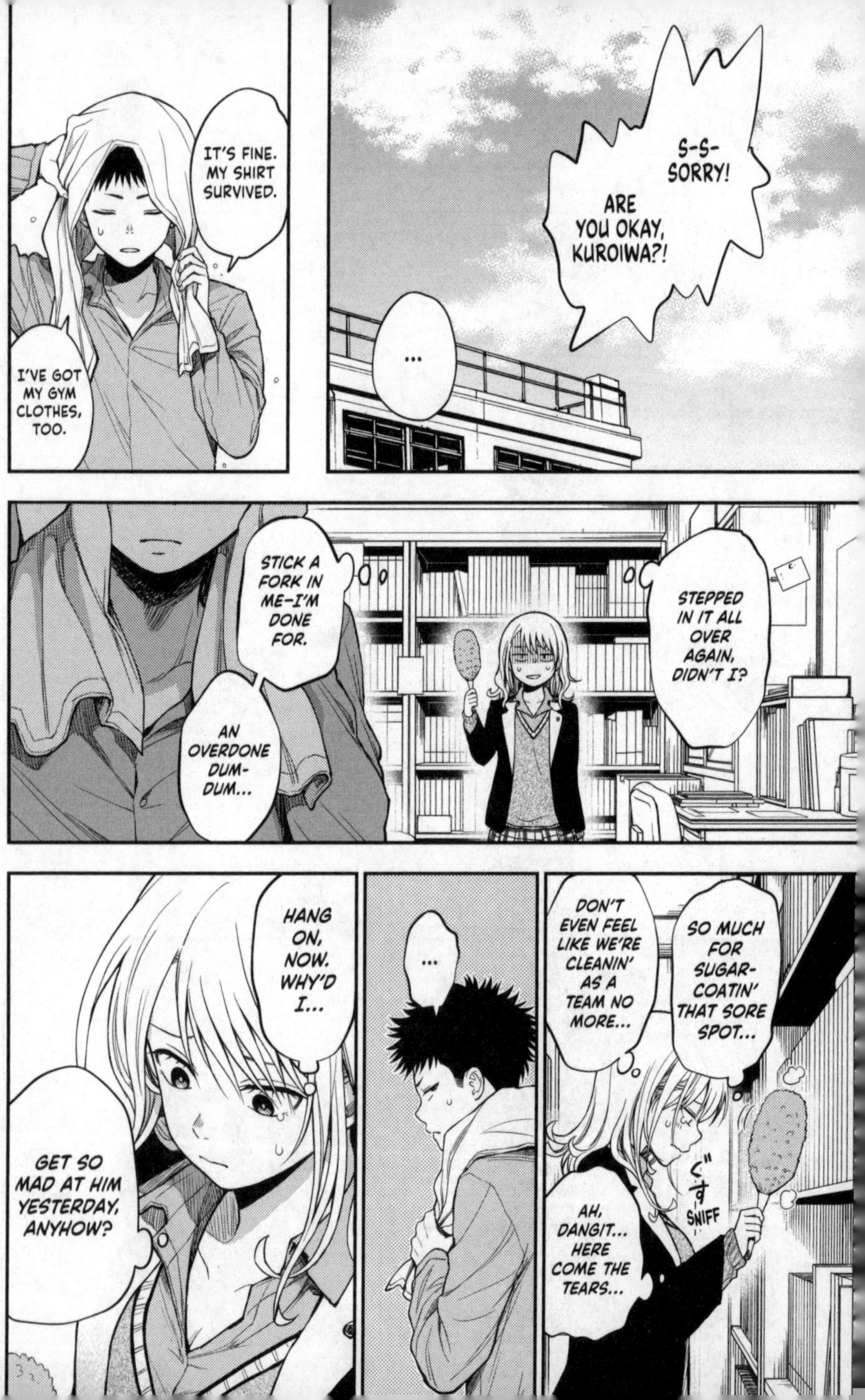
S-S-SORRY!
ARE YOU OKAY, KUROIWA?!
...
IT'S FINE. MY SHIRT SURVIVED.
I'VE GOT MY GYM CLOTHES, TOO.
STEPPED IN IT ALL OVER AGAIN, DIDN'T I?
STICK A FORK IN ME—I'M DONE FOR.
AN OVERDONE DUM-DUM...
SO MUCH FOR SUGAR-COATIN' THAT SORE SPOT...
DON'T EVEN FEEL LIKE WE'RE CLEANIN' AS A TEAM NO MORE...
ぐす
SNIFF
AH, DANGIT... HERE COME THE TEARS...
...
HANG ON, NOW. WHY'D I...
GET SO MAD AT HIM YESTERDAY, ANYHOW?

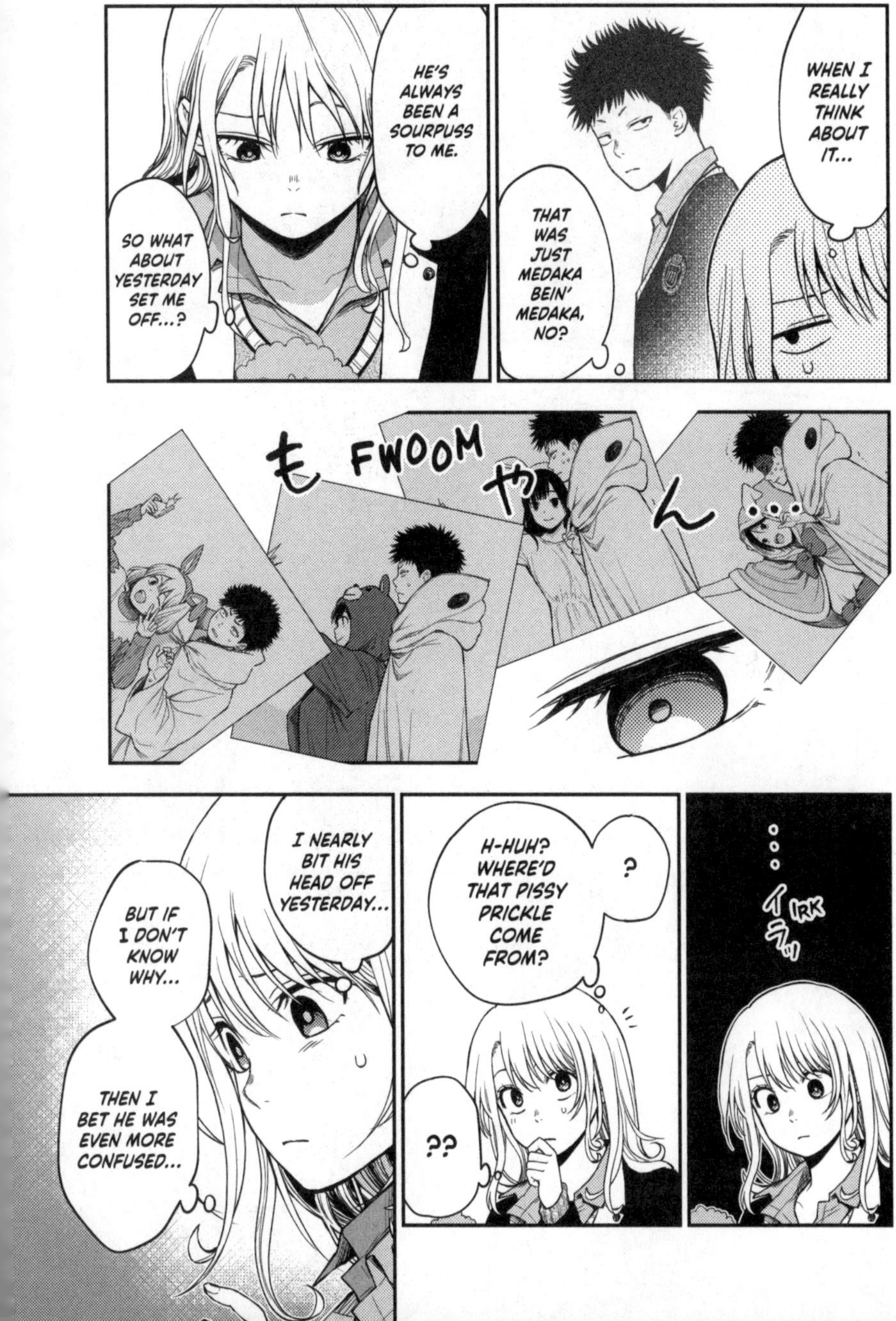
WHEN I REALLY THINK ABOUT IT...
THAT WAS JUST MEDAKA BEIN' MEDAKA, NO?
HE'S ALWAYS BEEN A SOURPUSS TO ME.
SO WHAT ABOUT YESTERDAY SET ME OFF...?
もやん FWOOM
...
...イラッ IRK
?
H-HUH? WHERE'D THAT PISSY PRICKLE COME FROM?
??
I NEARLY BIT HIS HEAD OFF YESTERDAY...
BUT IF I DON'T KNOW WHY...
THEN I BET HE WAS EVEN MORE CONFUSED...

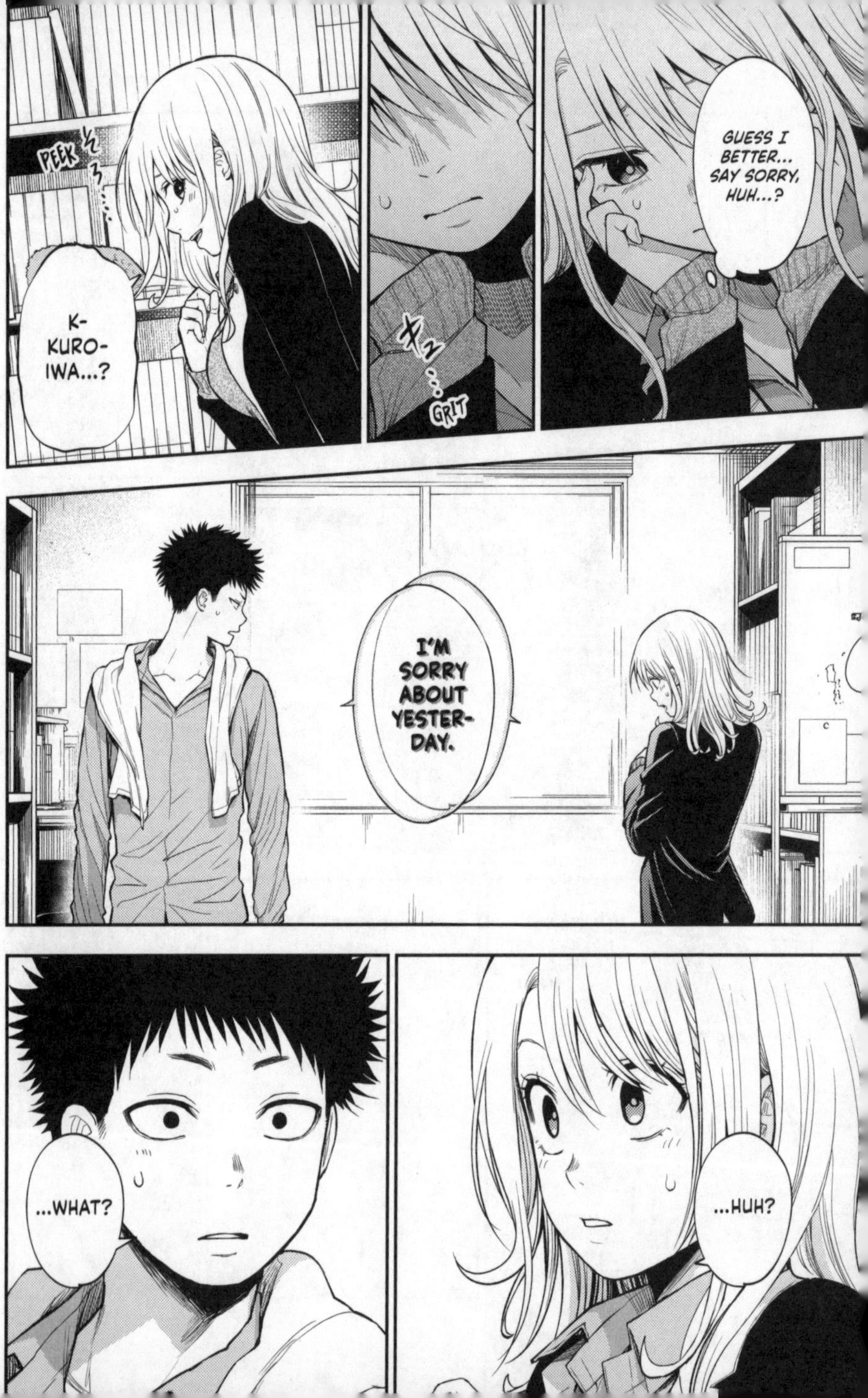
GUESS I BETTER... SAY SORRY, HUH...?
GRIT
PEEK
K-KURO-IWA...?
I'M SORRY ABOUT YESTER-DAY.
...HUH?
...WHAT?

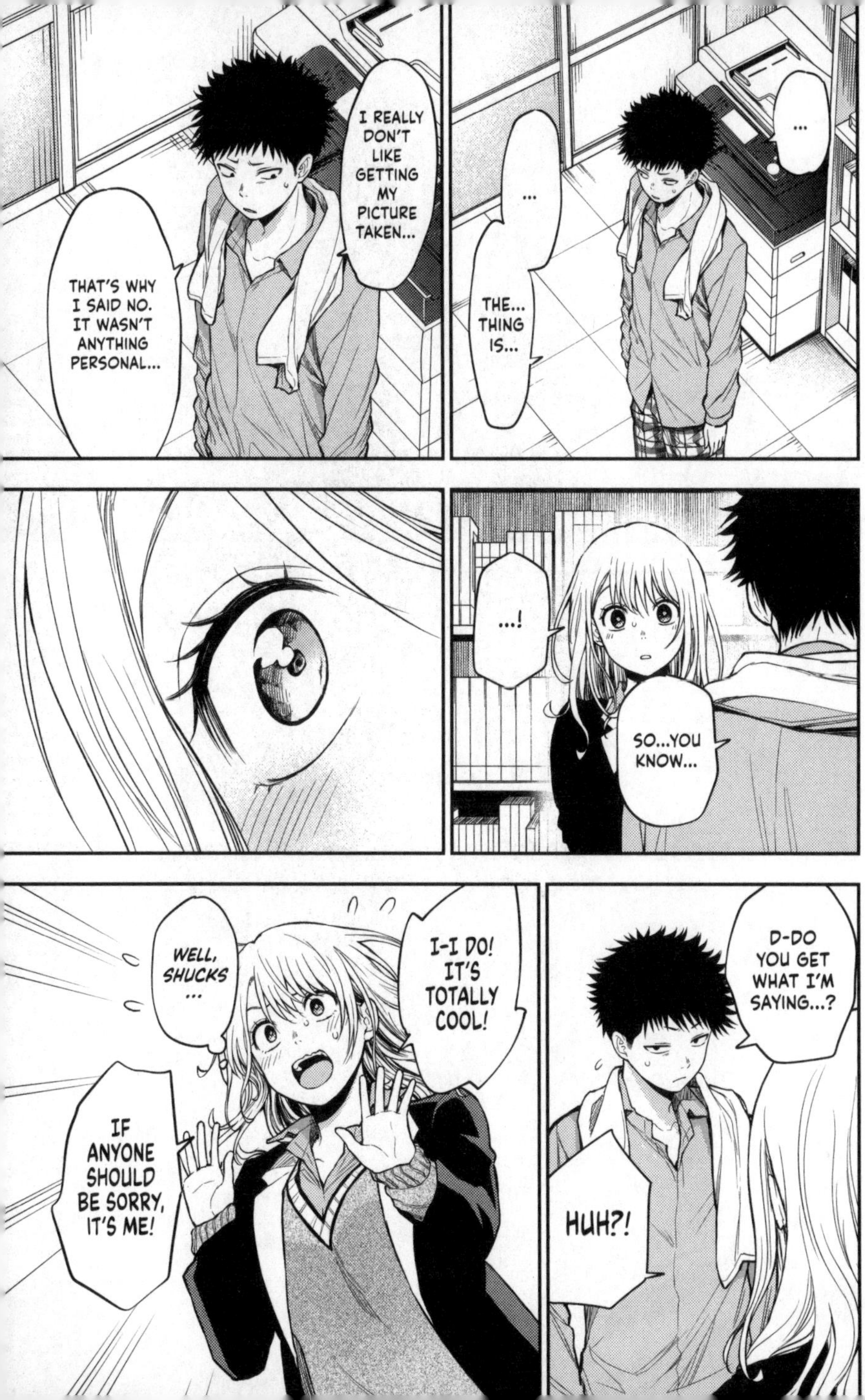
...
...
THE... THING IS...
I REALLY DON'T LIKE GETTING MY PICTURE TAKEN...
THAT'S WHY I SAID NO. IT WASN'T ANYTHING PERSONAL...
...!
SO...YOU KNOW...
D-DO YOU GET WHAT I'M SAYING...?
HUH?!
I-I DO! IT'S TOTALLY COOL!
WELL, SHUCKS...
IF ANYONE SHOULD BE SORRY, IT'S ME!

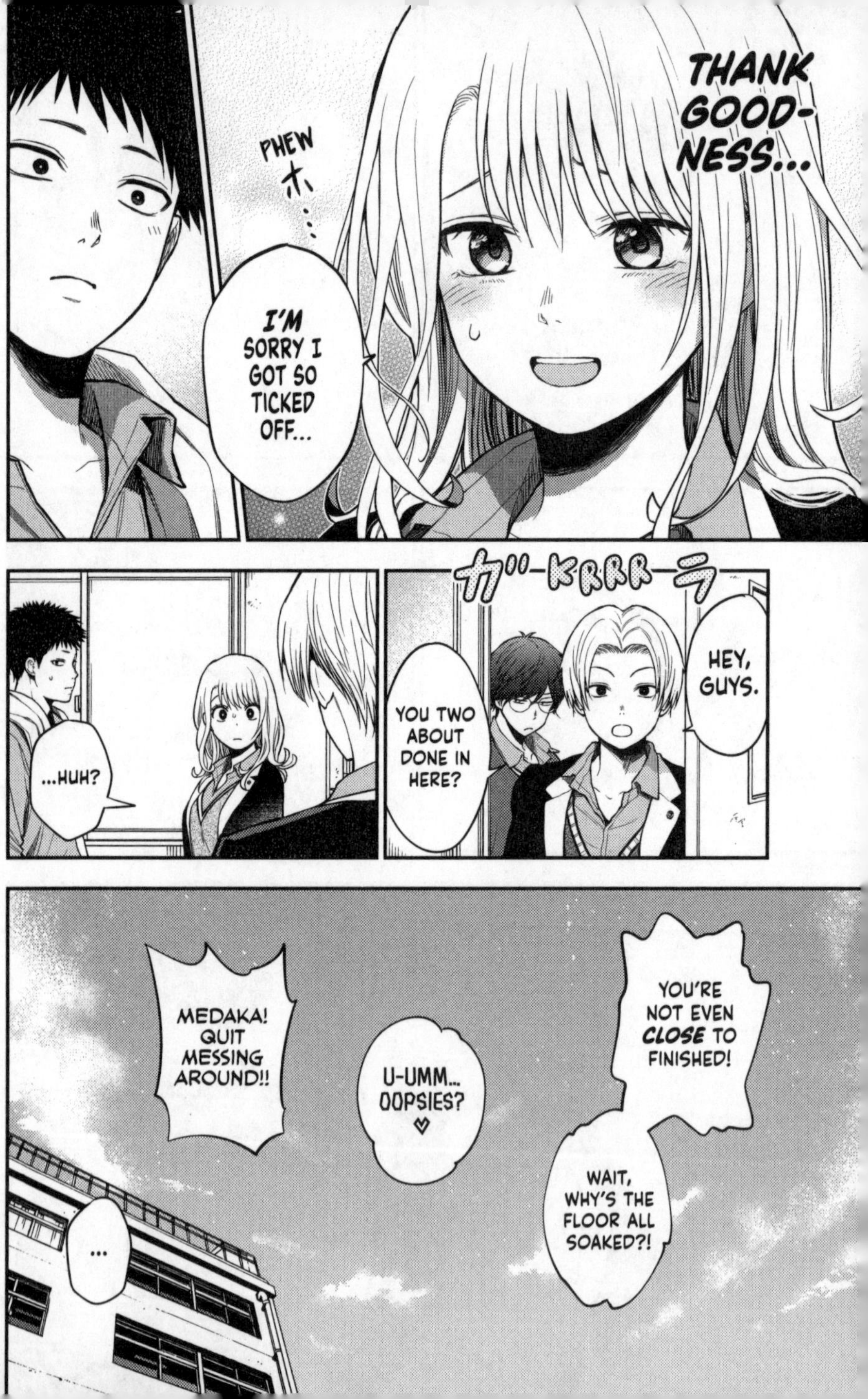
THANK GOODNESS...
PHEW ホ...
I'M SORRY I GOT SO TICKED OFF...
ガー KRRR ラ
HEY, GUYS.
YOU TWO ABOUT DONE IN HERE?
...HUH?
YOU'RE NOT EVEN *CLOSE* TO FINISHED!
WAIT, WHY'S THE FLOOR ALL SOAKED?!
U-UMM... OOPSIES?
MEDAKA! QUIT MESSING AROUND!!
...

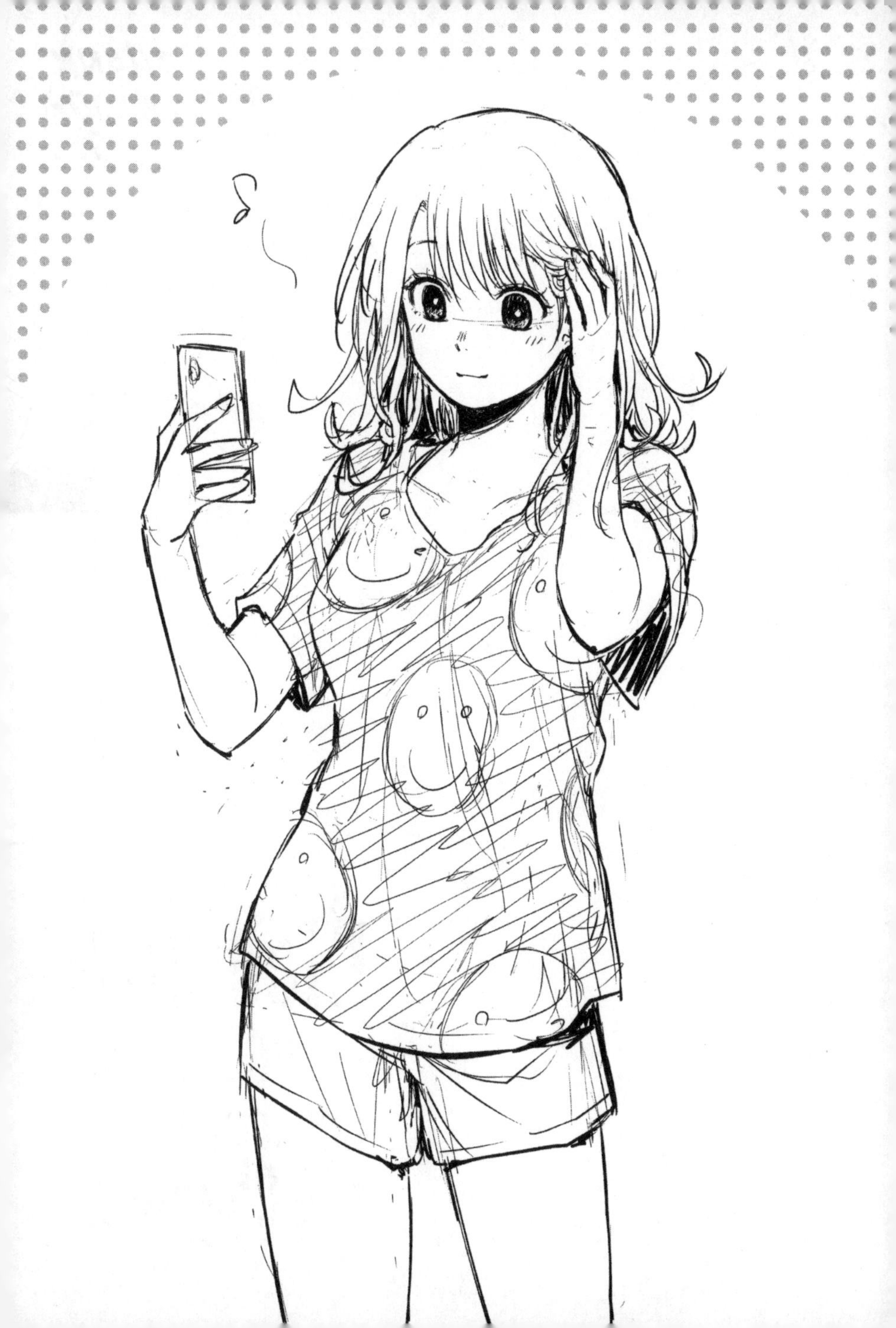

Medaka Kuroiwa is Impervious to My Charms

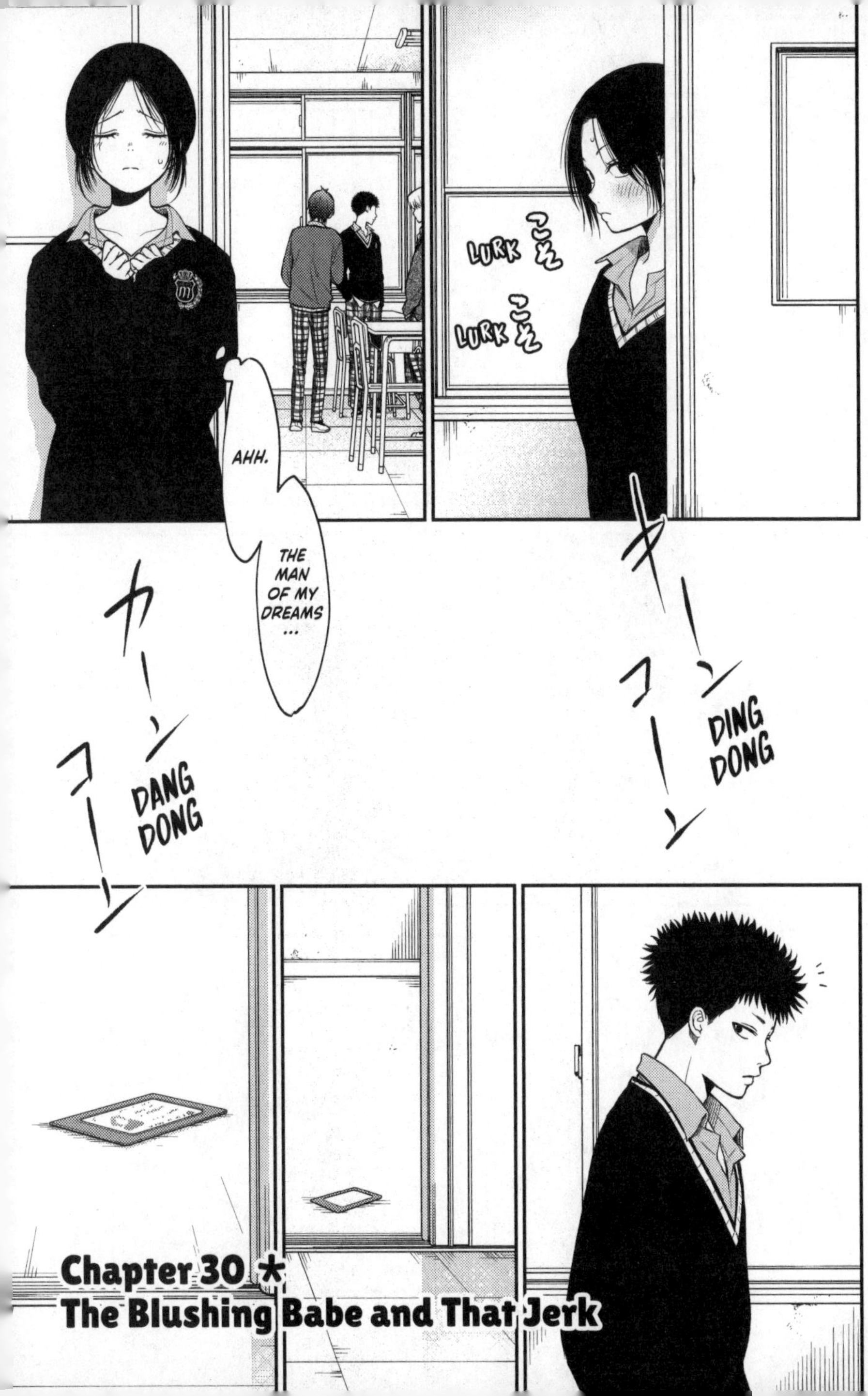
LURK こそ
LURK こそ
AHH.
THE MAN OF MY DREAMS...
キーンコーン
DING DONG
カーンコーン
DANG DONG

Chapter 30 ★ The Blushing Babe and That Jerk

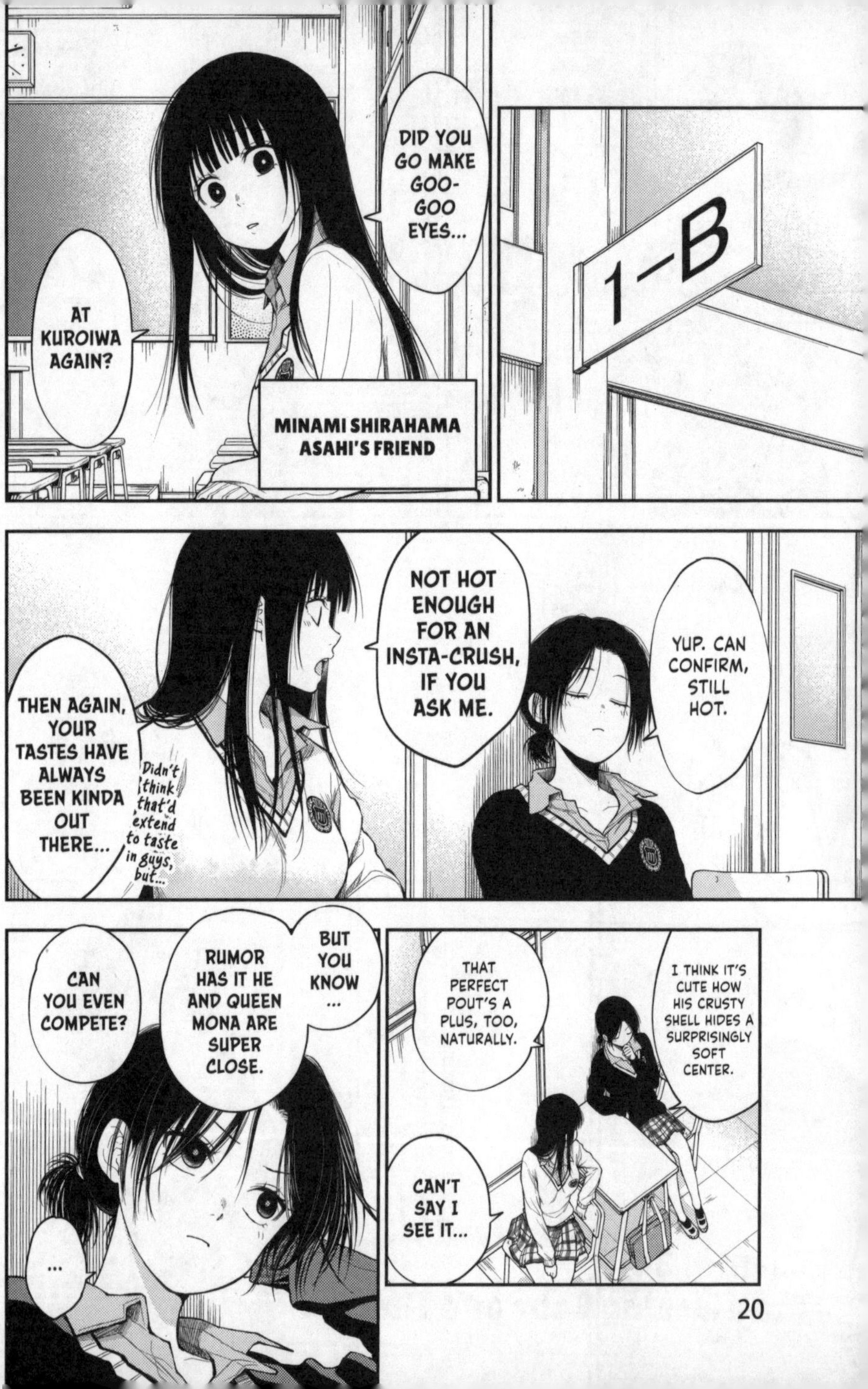
DID YOU GO MAKE GOO-GOO EYES...
AT KUROIWA AGAIN?
MINAMI SHIRAHAMA
ASAHI'S FRIEND
YUP. CAN CONFIRM, STILL HOT.
NOT HOT ENOUGH FOR AN INSTA-CRUSH, IF YOU ASK ME.
THEN AGAIN, YOUR TASTES HAVE ALWAYS BEEN KINDA OUT THERE...
Didn't think that'd extend to taste in guys, but...
I THINK IT'S CUTE HOW HIS CRUSTY SHELL HIDES A SURPRISINGLY SOFT CENTER.
THAT PERFECT POUT'S A PLUS, TOO, NATURALLY.
CAN'T SAY I SEE IT...
BUT YOU KNOW...
RUMOR HAS IT HE AND QUEEN MONA ARE SUPER CLOSE.
CAN YOU EVEN COMPETE?
...

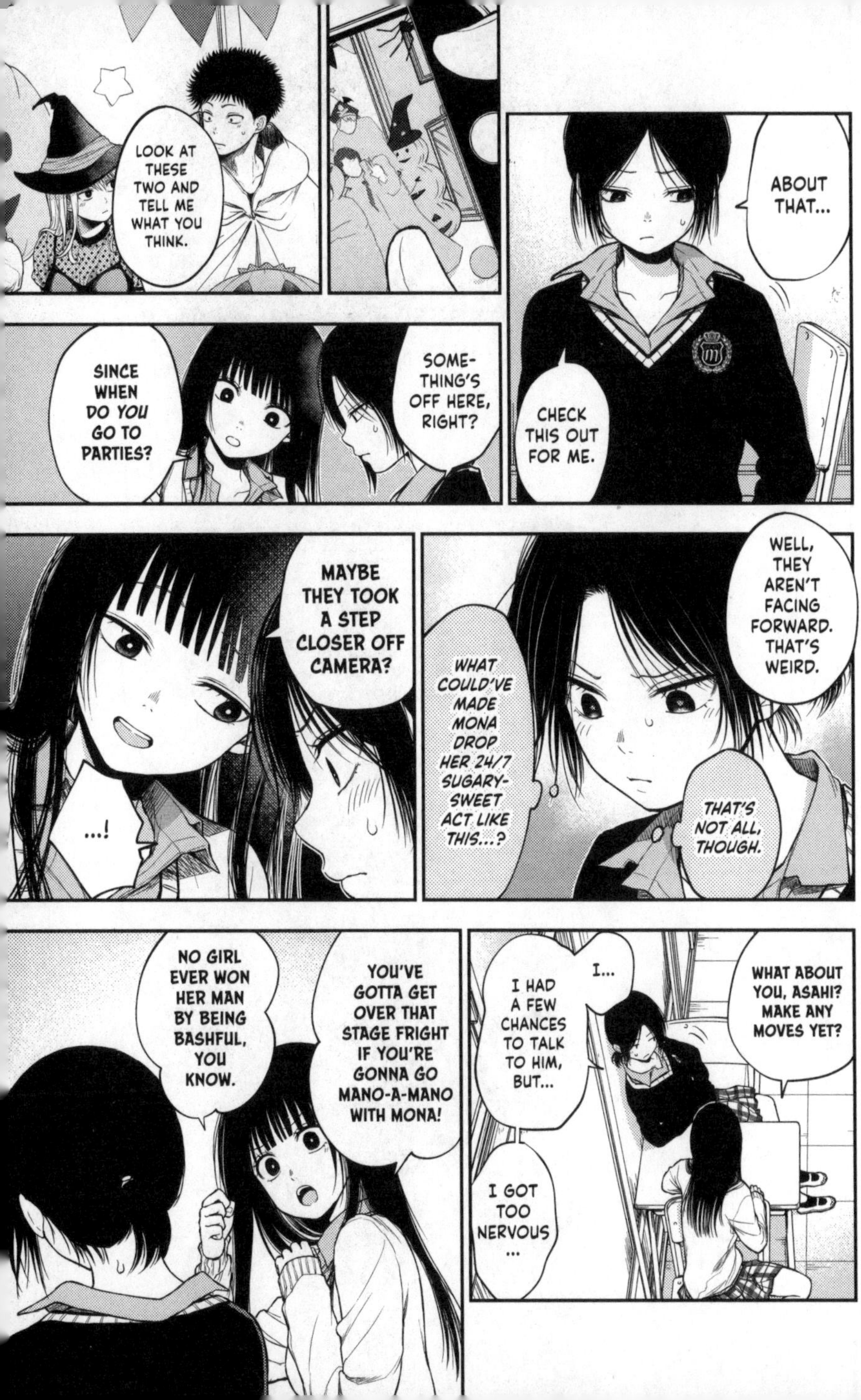
ABOUT THAT...
CHECK THIS OUT FOR ME.
LOOK AT THESE TWO AND TELL ME WHAT YOU THINK.
SOME-THING'S OFF HERE, RIGHT?
SINCE WHEN DO *YOU* GO TO PARTIES?
WELL, THEY AREN'T FACING FORWARD. THAT'S WEIRD.
WHAT COULD'VE MADE MONA DROP HER 24/7 SUGARY-SWEET ACT LIKE THIS...?
THAT'S NOT ALL, THOUGH.
MAYBE THEY TOOK A STEP CLOSER OFF CAMERA?
...!
WHAT ABOUT YOU, ASAHI? MAKE ANY MOVES YET?
I...
I HAD A FEW CHANCES TO TALK TO HIM, BUT...
I GOT TOO NERVOUS...
YOU'VE GOTTA GET OVER THAT STAGE FRIGHT IF YOU'RE GONNA GO MANO-A-MANO WITH MONA!
NO GIRL EVER WON HER MAN BY BEING BASHFUL, YOU KNOW.

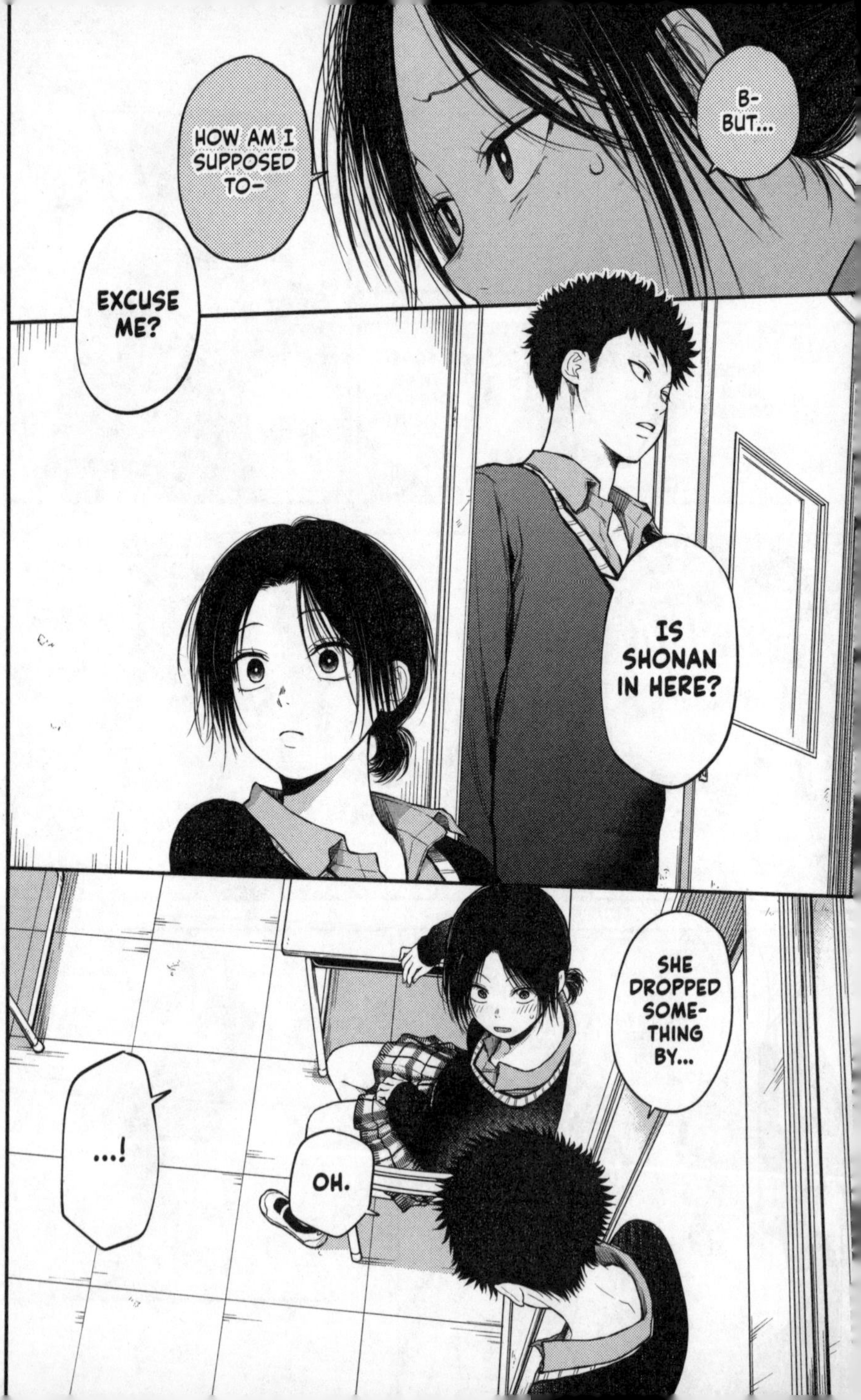
B- BUT...
HOW AM I SUPPOSED TO-
EXCUSE ME?
IS SHONAN IN HERE?
SHE DROPPED SOME-THING BY...
OH.
...!

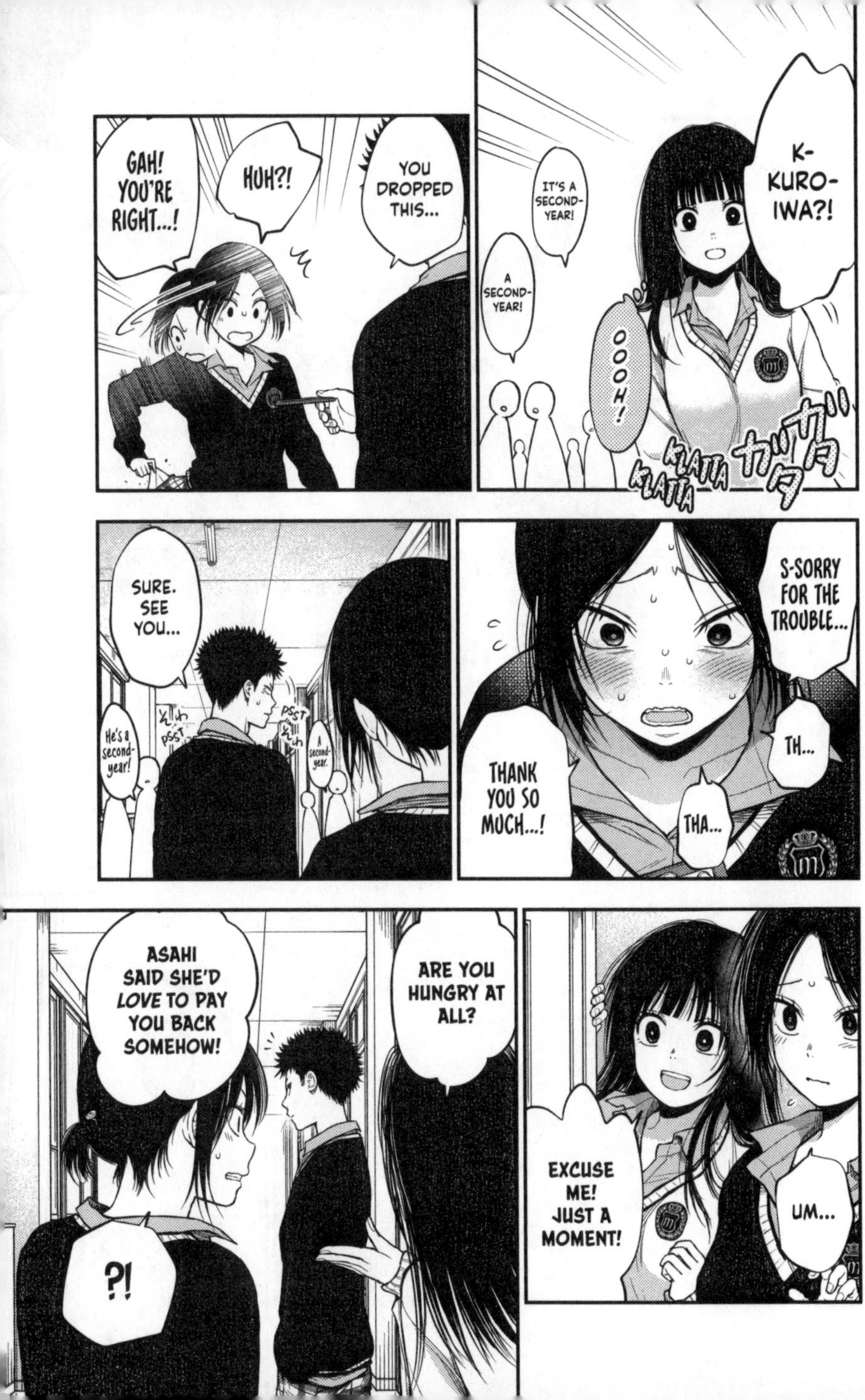
K-
KURO-
IWA?!
IT'S A SECOND-YEAR!
A SECOND-YEAR!
OOOH!
KLATTA KLATTA
YOU DROPPED THIS...
HUH?!
GAH! YOU'RE RIGHT...!
S-SORRY FOR THE TROUBLE...
TH...
THA...
THANK YOU SO MUCH...!
SURE. SEE YOU...
PSST PSST
A second-year.
He's a second-year!
EXCUSE ME! JUST A MOMENT!
UM...
ARE YOU HUNGRY AT ALL?
ASAHI SAID SHE'D *LOVE* TO PAY YOU BACK SOMEHOW!
?!

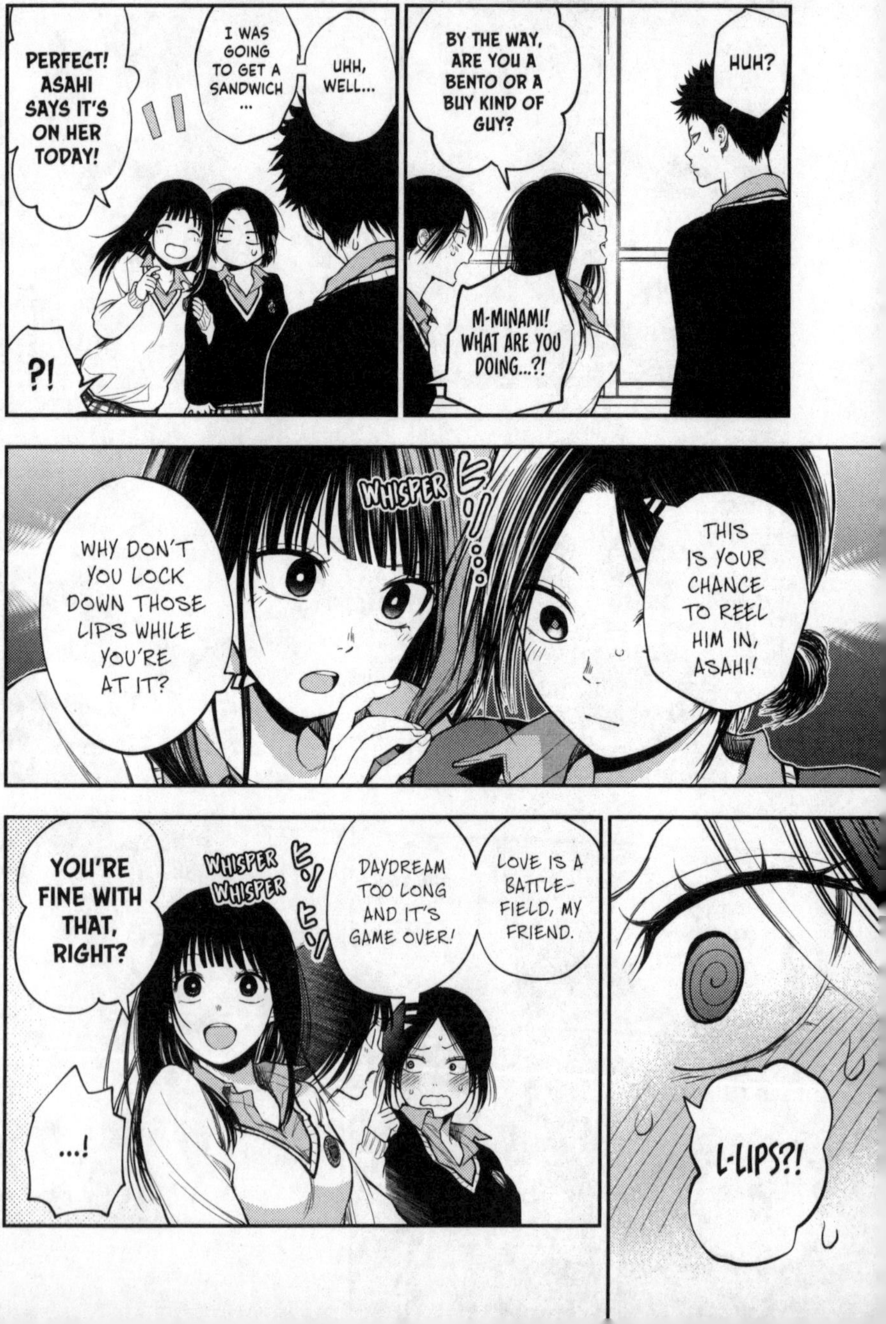
HUH?
BY THE WAY, ARE YOU A BENTO OR A BUY KIND OF GUY?
M-MINAMI! WHAT ARE YOU DOING...?!
UHH, WELL...
I WAS GOING TO GET A SANDWICH ...
PERFECT! ASAHI SAYS IT'S ON HER TODAY!
?!
THIS IS YOUR CHANCE TO REEL HIM IN, ASAHI!
WHISPER
WHY DON'T YOU LOCK DOWN THOSE LIPS WHILE YOU'RE AT IT?
L-LIPS?!
LOVE IS A BATTLE-FIELD, MY FRIEND.
DAYDREAM TOO LONG AND IT'S GAME OVER!
WHISPER WHISPER
YOU'RE FINE WITH THAT, RIGHT?
...!

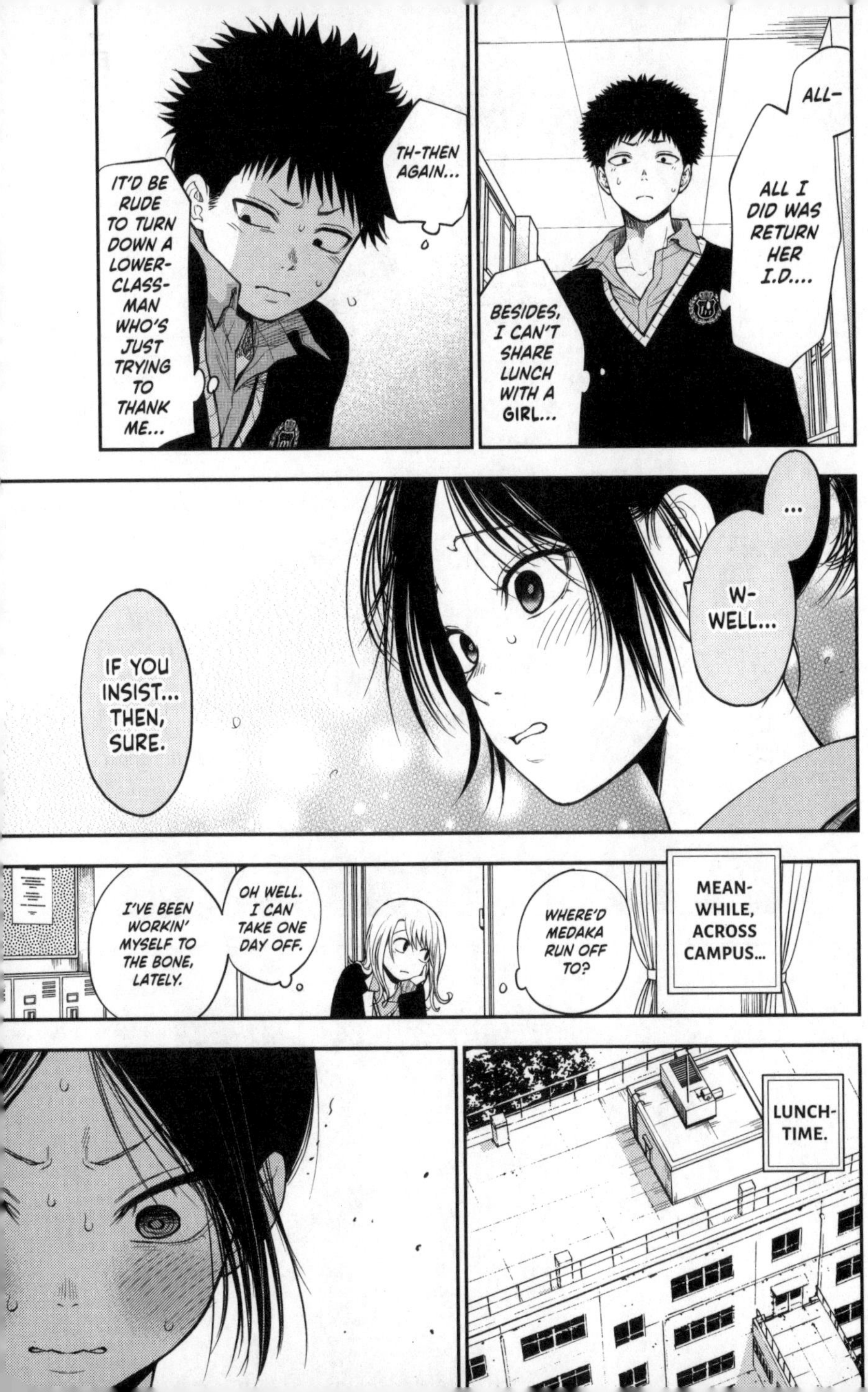
ALL-
ALL I DID WAS RETURN HER I.D....
BESIDES, I CAN'T SHARE LUNCH WITH A GIRL...
TH-THEN AGAIN...
IT'D BE RUDE TO TURN DOWN A LOWER-CLASSMAN WHO'S JUST TRYING TO THANK ME...
...
W-WELL...
IF YOU INSIST... THEN, SURE.
MEAN-WHILE, ACROSS CAMPUS...
WHERE'D MEDAKA RUN OFF TO?
OH WELL. I CAN TAKE ONE DAY OFF.
I'VE BEEN WORKIN' MYSELF TO THE BONE, LATELY.
LUNCH-TIME.

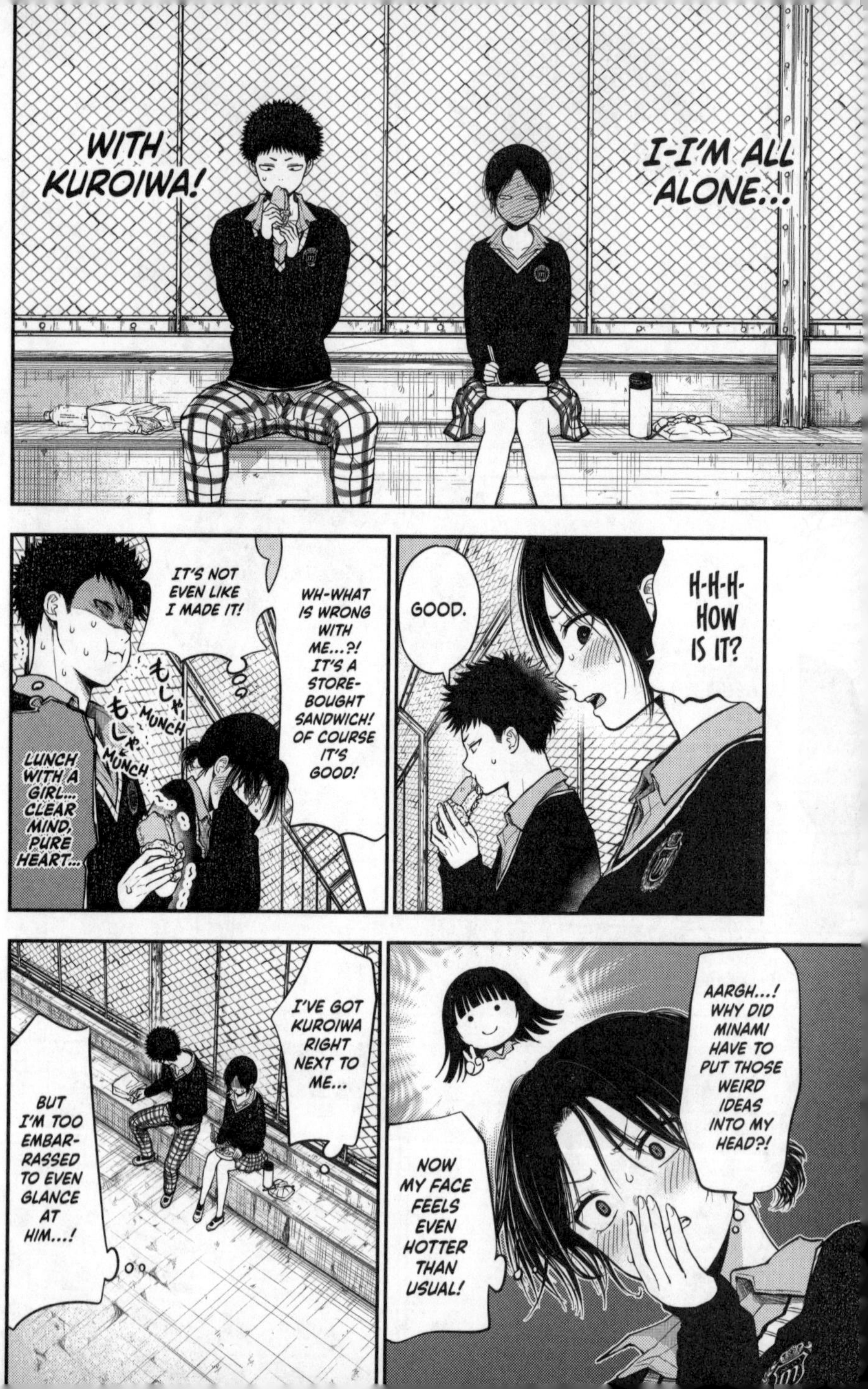
I-I'M ALL ALONE...
WITH KUROIWA!
H-H-H-HOW IS IT?
GOOD.
WH-WHAT IS WRONG WITH ME...?! IT'S A STORE-BOUGHT SANDWICH! OF COURSE IT'S GOOD!
IT'S NOT EVEN LIKE I MADE IT!
もしゃ MUNCH
もしゃ MUNCH
LUNCH WITH A GIRL... CLEAR MIND, PURE HEART...
AARGH...! WHY DID MINAMI HAVE TO PUT THOSE WEIRD IDEAS INTO MY HEAD?!
NOW MY FACE FEELS EVEN HOTTER THAN USUAL!
I'VE GOT KUROIWA RIGHT NEXT TO ME...
BUT I'M TOO EMBARRASSED TO EVEN GLANCE AT HIM...!

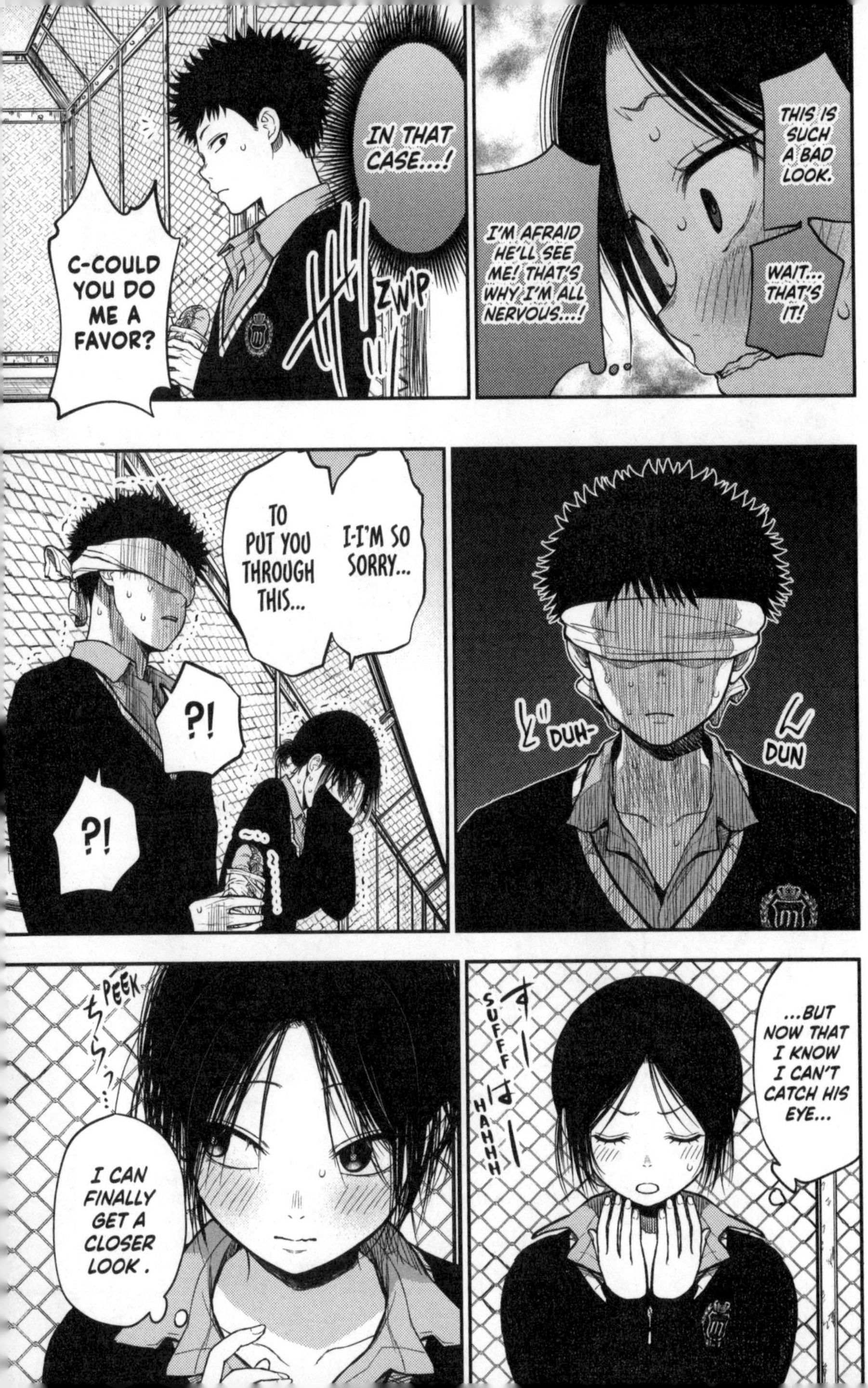

THIS IS SUCH A BAD LOOK.
I'M AFRAID HE'LL SEE ME! THAT'S WHY I'M ALL NERVOUS...!
WAIT... THAT'S IT!
IN THAT CASE...!
ZWIP
C-COULD YOU DO ME A FAVOR?
ど DUH-
ん DUN
I-I'M SO SORRY...
TO PUT YOU THROUGH THIS...
?!
?!
...BUT NOW THAT I KNOW I CAN'T CATCH HIS EYE...
すー SUFFF
はー HAHHH
PEEK
I CAN FINALLY GET A CLOSER LOOK.

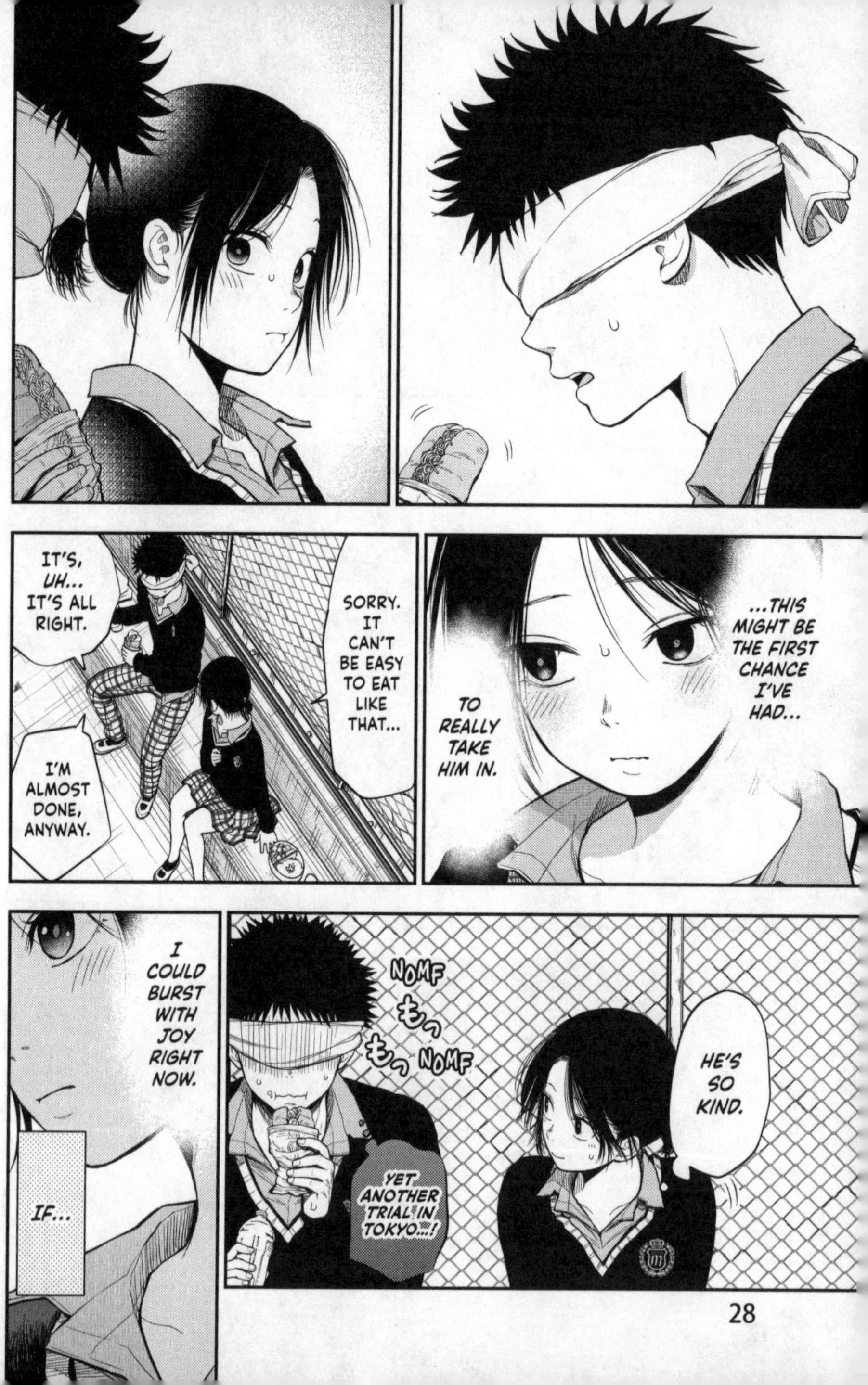
...THIS MIGHT BE THE FIRST CHANCE I'VE HAD...
TO REALLY TAKE HIM IN.
SORRY. IT CAN'T BE EASY TO EAT LIKE THAT...
IT'S, UH... IT'S ALL RIGHT.
I'M ALMOST DONE, ANYWAY.
HE'S SO KIND.
NOMF
もっ
もっ
NOMF
YET ANOTHER TRIAL IN TOKYO...!
I COULD BURST WITH JOY RIGHT NOW.
IF...

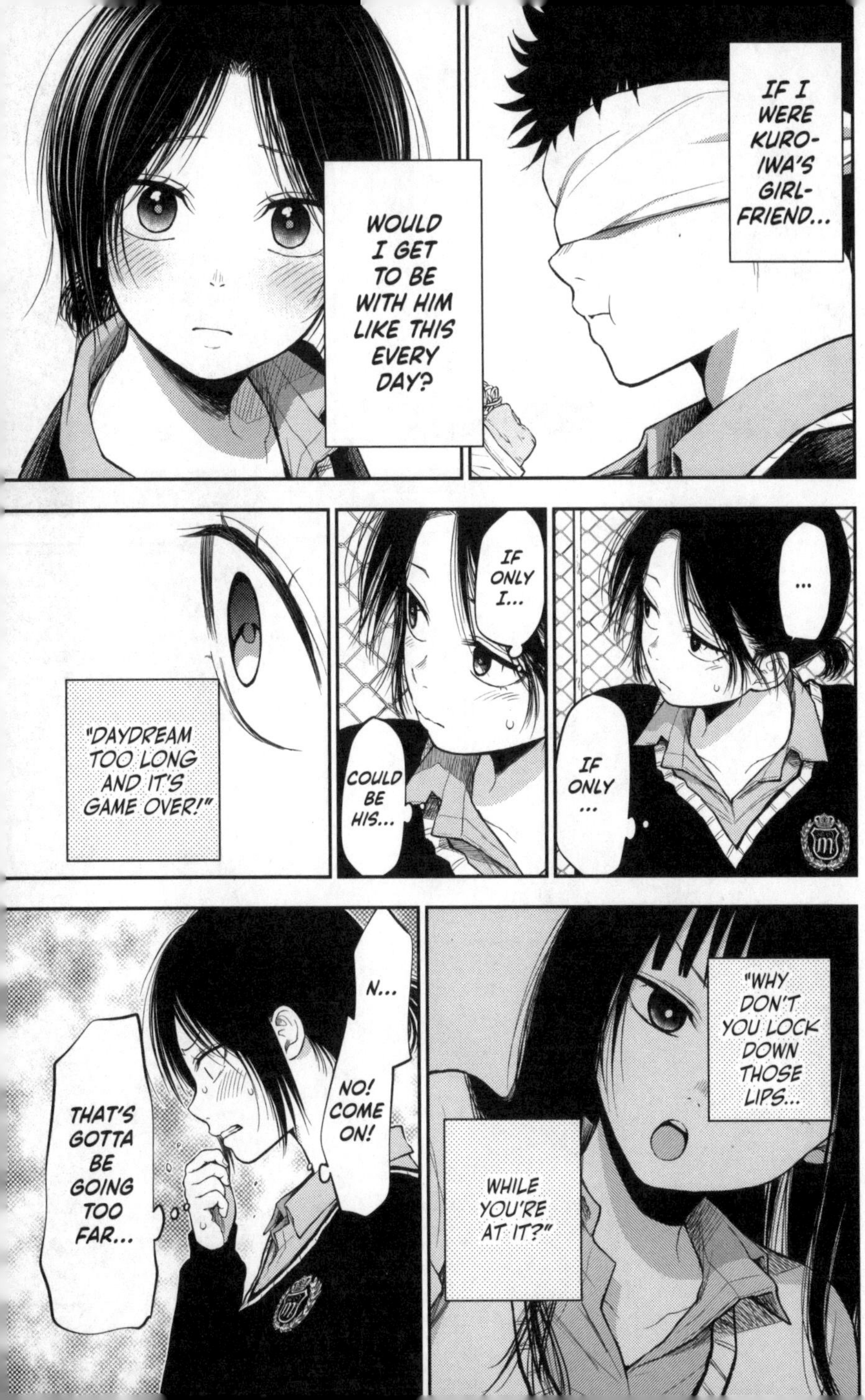
IF I WERE KURO-IWA'S GIRL-FRIEND...
WOULD I GET TO BE WITH HIM LIKE THIS EVERY DAY?
...
IF ONLY ...
IF ONLY I...
COULD BE HIS...
"DAYDREAM TOO LONG AND IT'S GAME OVER!"
"WHY DON'T YOU LOCK DOWN THOSE LIPS...
WHILE YOU'RE AT IT?"
N...
NO! COME ON!
THAT'S GOTTA BE GOING TOO FAR...

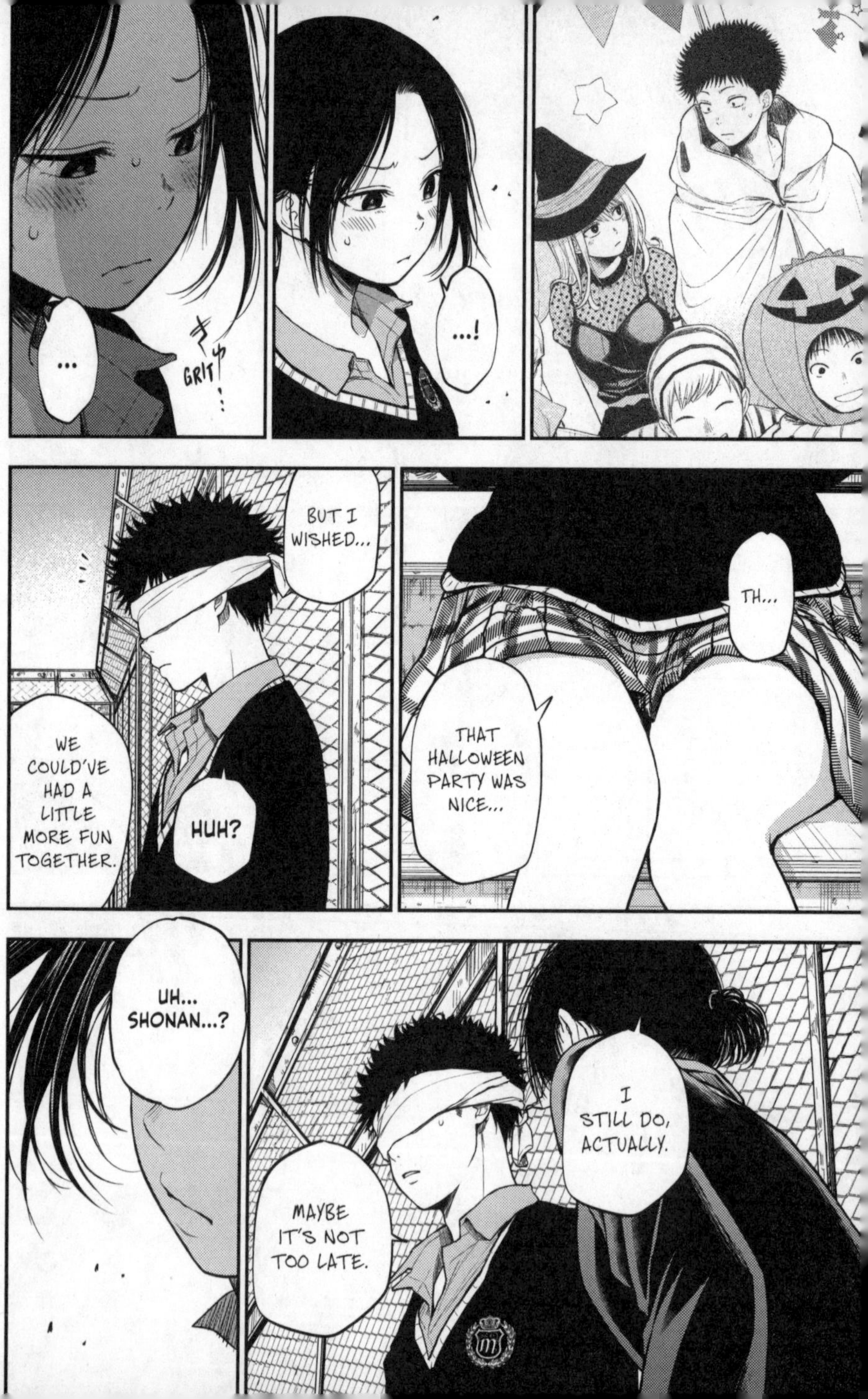
...!
...
GRIT
TH...
THAT HALLOWEEN PARTY WAS NICE...
BUT I WISHED...
WE COULD'VE HAD A LITTLE MORE FUN TOGETHER.
HUH?
I STILL DO, ACTUALLY.
MAYBE IT'S NOT TOO LATE.
UH... SHONAN...?

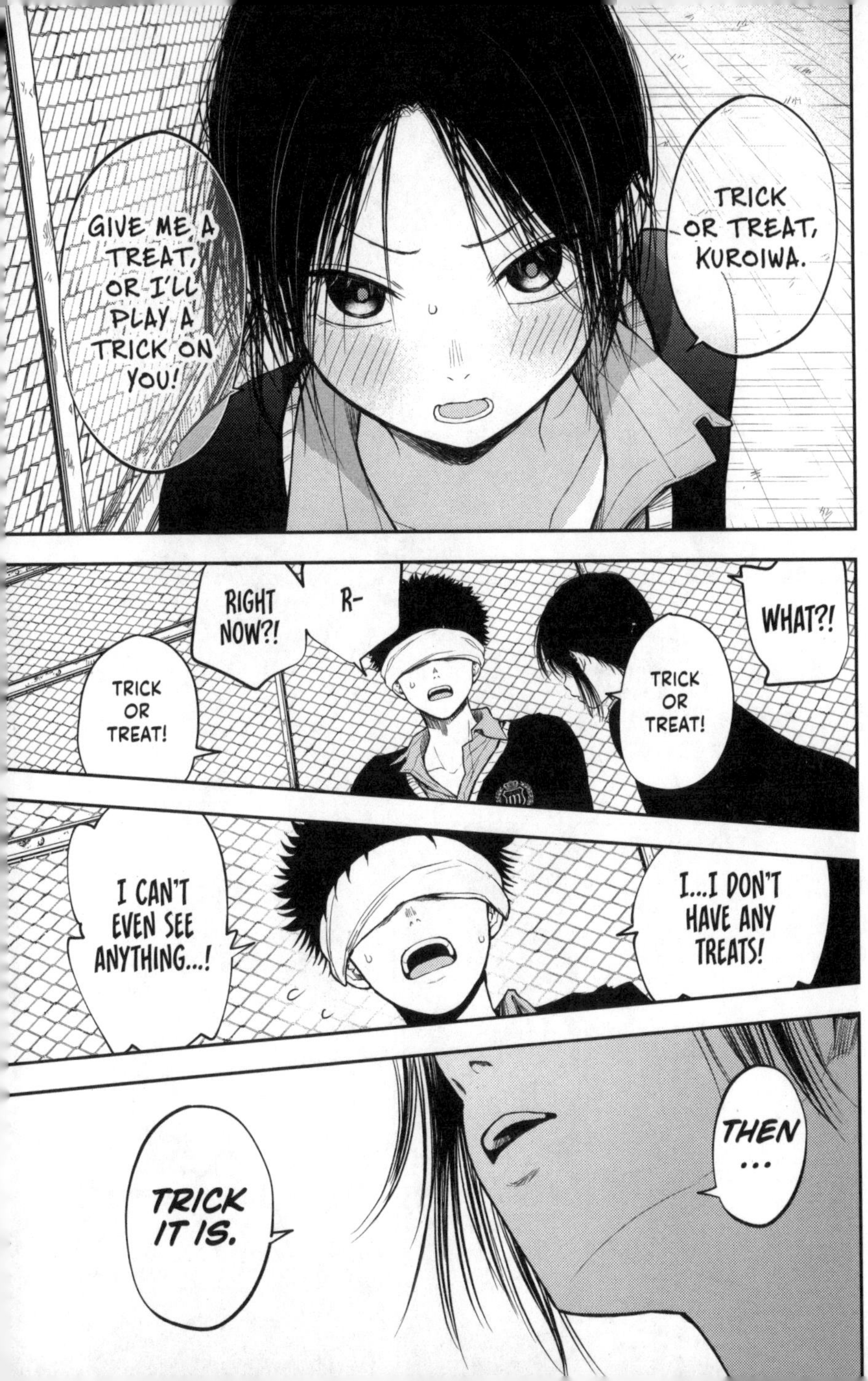
TRICK OR TREAT, KUROIWA.
GIVE ME A TREAT, OR I'LL PLAY A TRICK ON YOU!
WHAT?!
TRICK OR TREAT!
R-
RIGHT NOW?!
TRICK OR TREAT!
I...I DON'T HAVE ANY TREATS!
I CAN'T EVEN SEE ANYTHING...!
THEN...
TRICK IT IS.

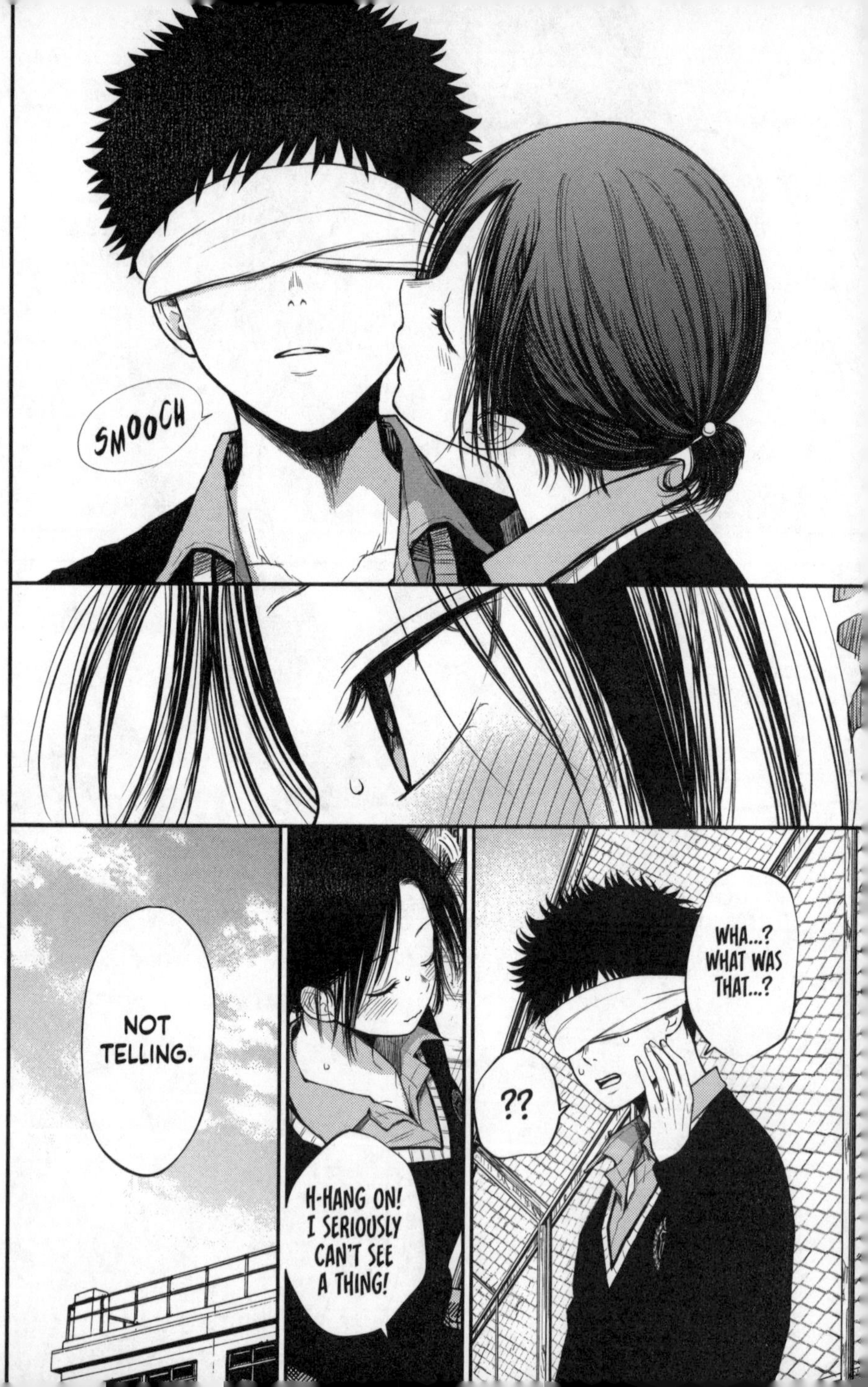
SMOOCH
WHA...? WHAT WAS THAT...?
??
H-HANG ON! I SERIOUSLY CAN'T SEE A THING!
NOT TELLING.

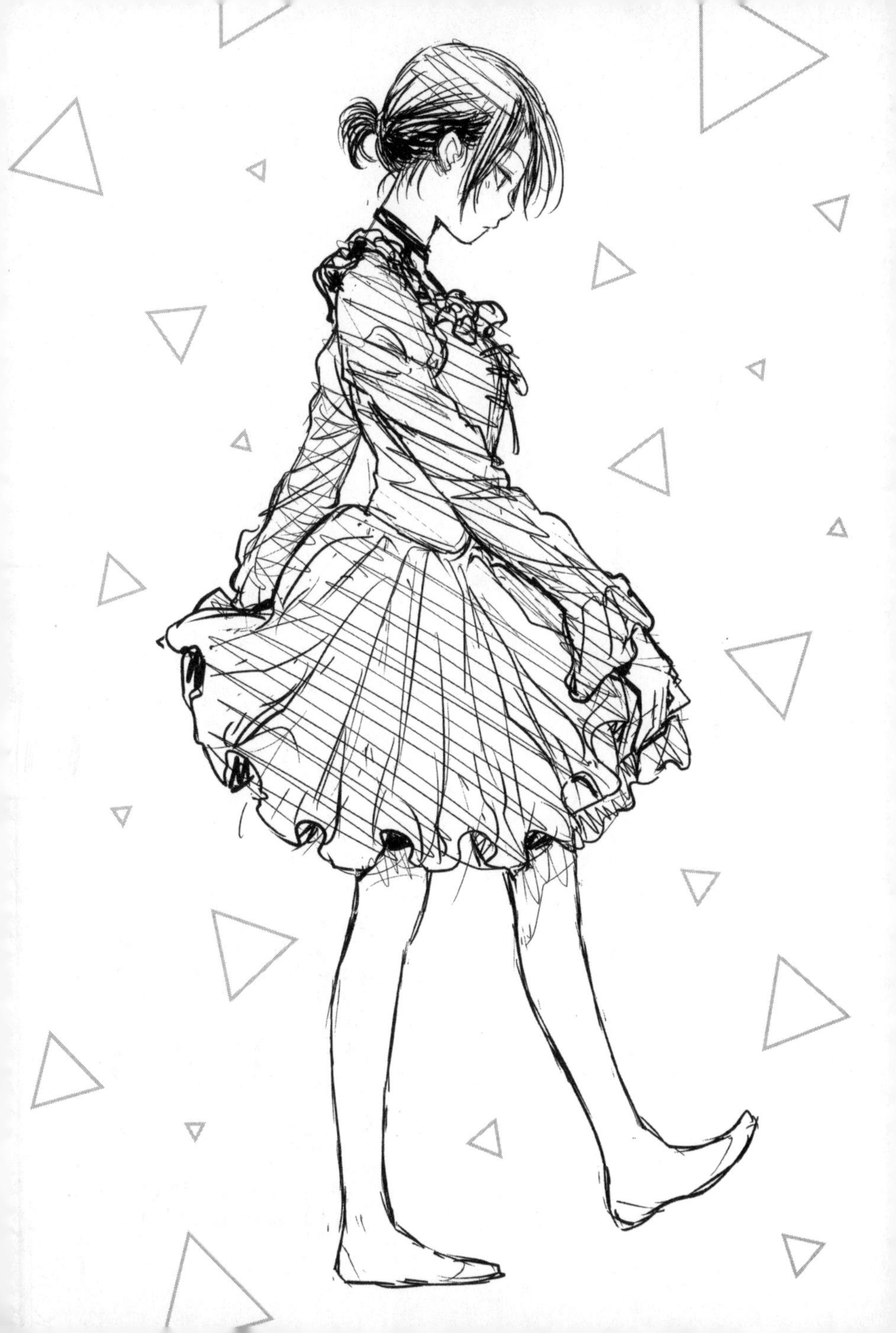

Medaka Kuroiwa is Impervious to My Charms

Chapter 31 ★ Besties and That Jerk

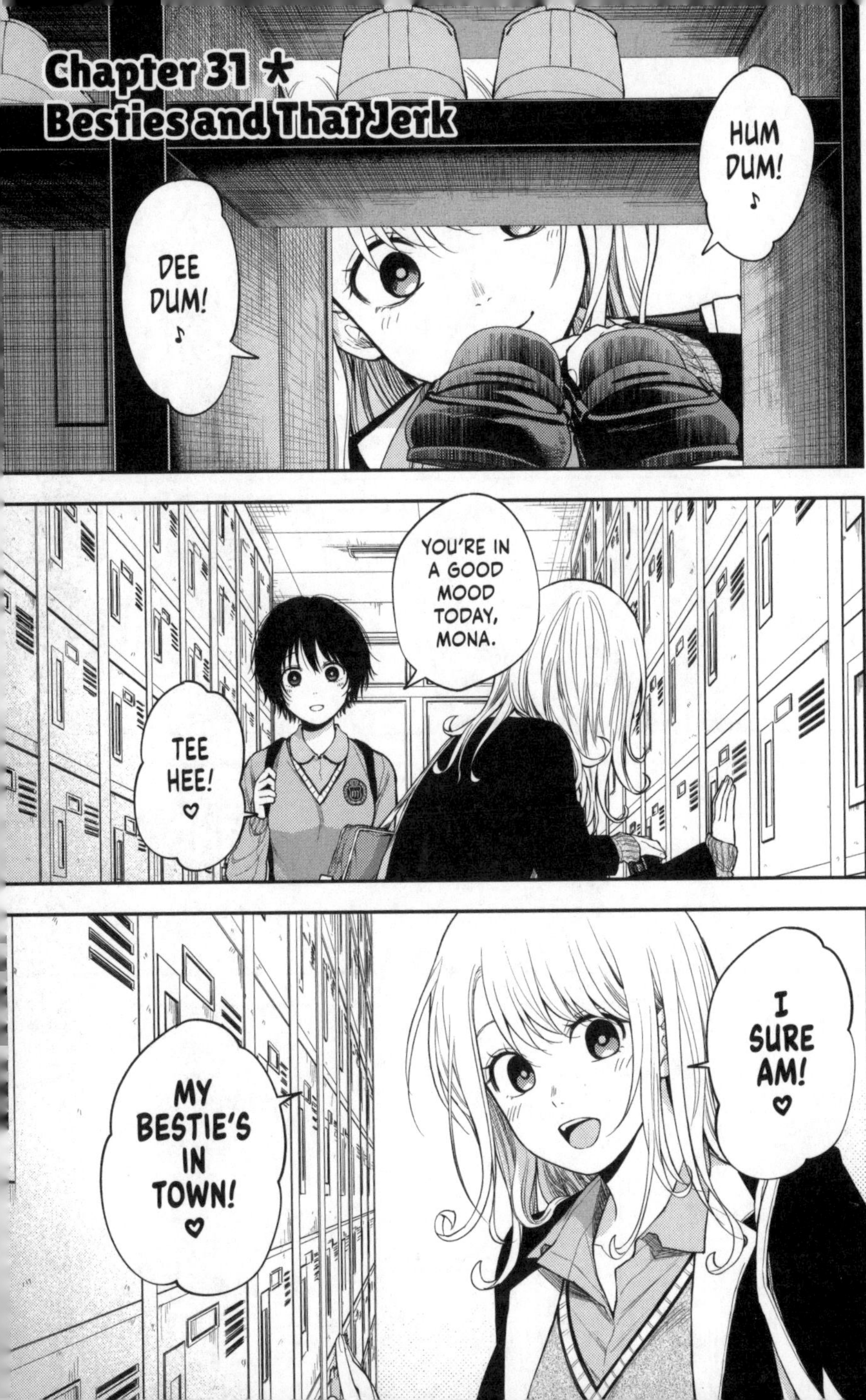
HUM DUM! ♪
DEE DUM! ♪
YOU'RE IN A GOOD MOOD TODAY, MONA.
TEE HEE! ♡
I SURE AM! ♡
MY BESTIE'S IN TOWN! ♡

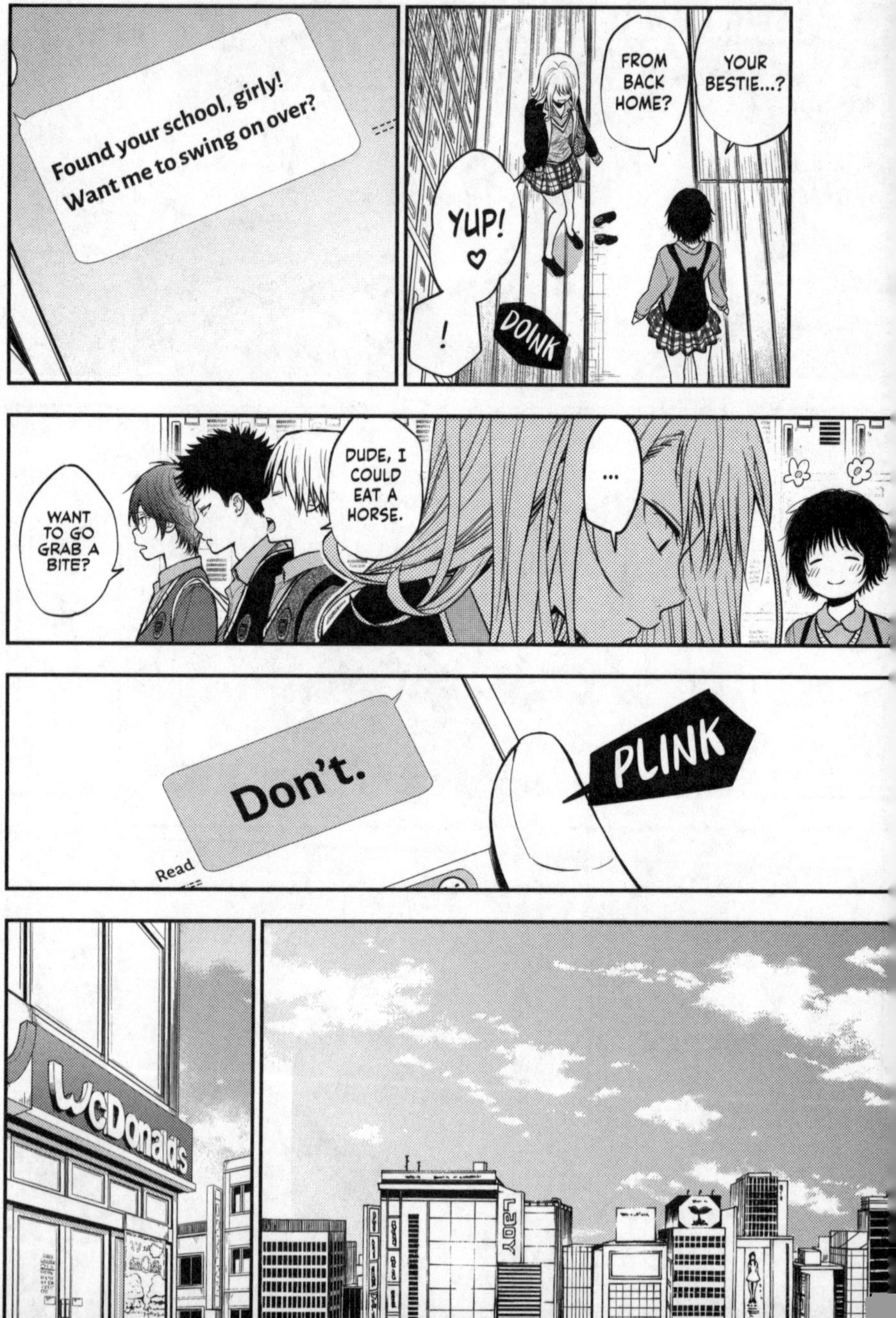
YOUR BESTIE...?
FROM BACK HOME?
YUP! ♡
!
DOINK
Found your school, girly! Want me to swing on over?
...
DUDE, I COULD EAT A HORSE.
WANT TO GO GRAB A BITE?
PLINK
Don't.
Read
WcDonald's

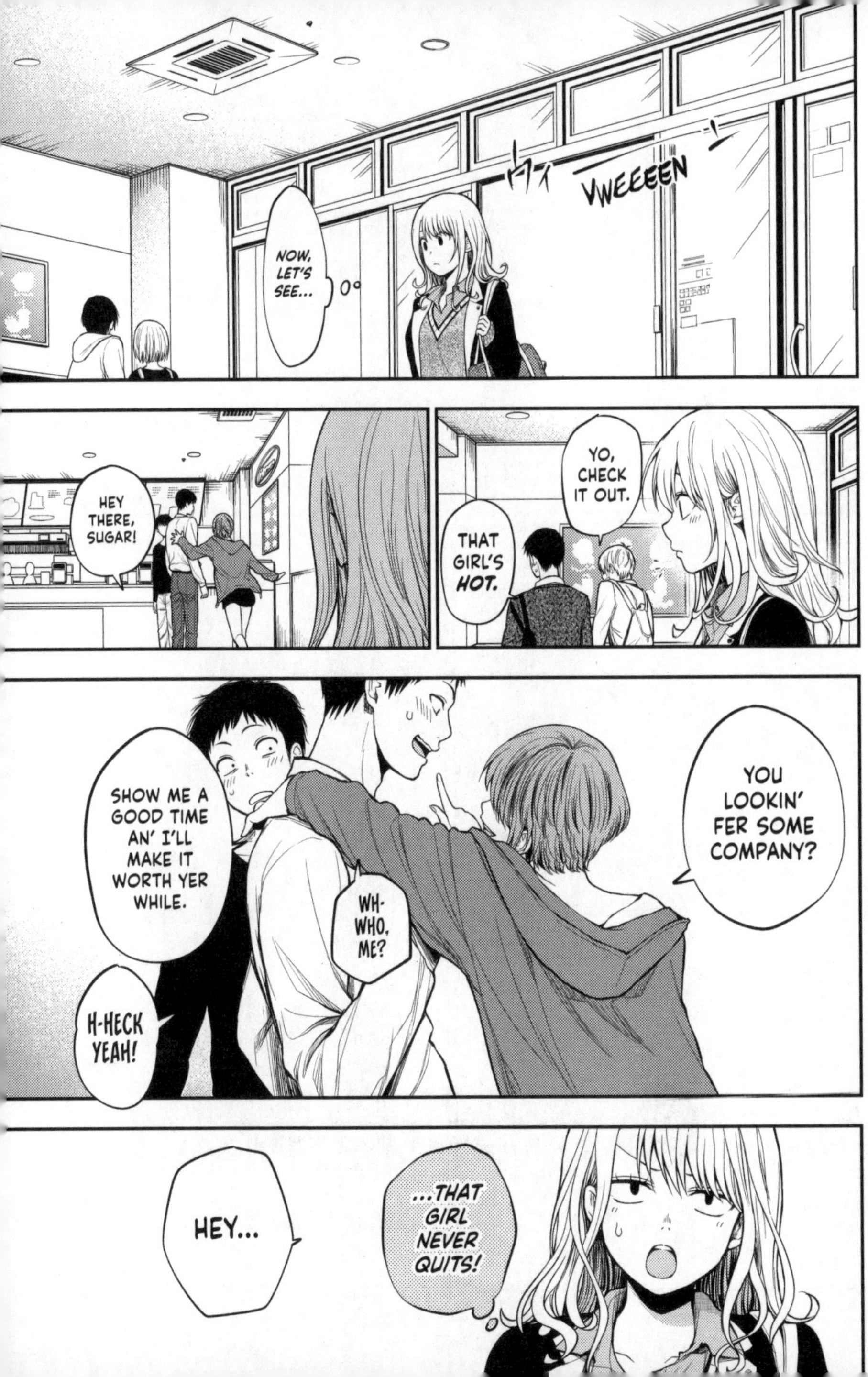
VWEEEEN
NOW, LET'S SEE...
YO, CHECK IT OUT.
THAT GIRL'S HOT.
HEY THERE, SUGAR!
YOU LOOKIN' FER SOME COMPANY?
WH-WHO, ME?
SHOW ME A GOOD TIME AN' I'LL MAKE IT WORTH YER WHILE.
H-HECK YEAH!
...THAT GIRL NEVER QUITS!
HEY...

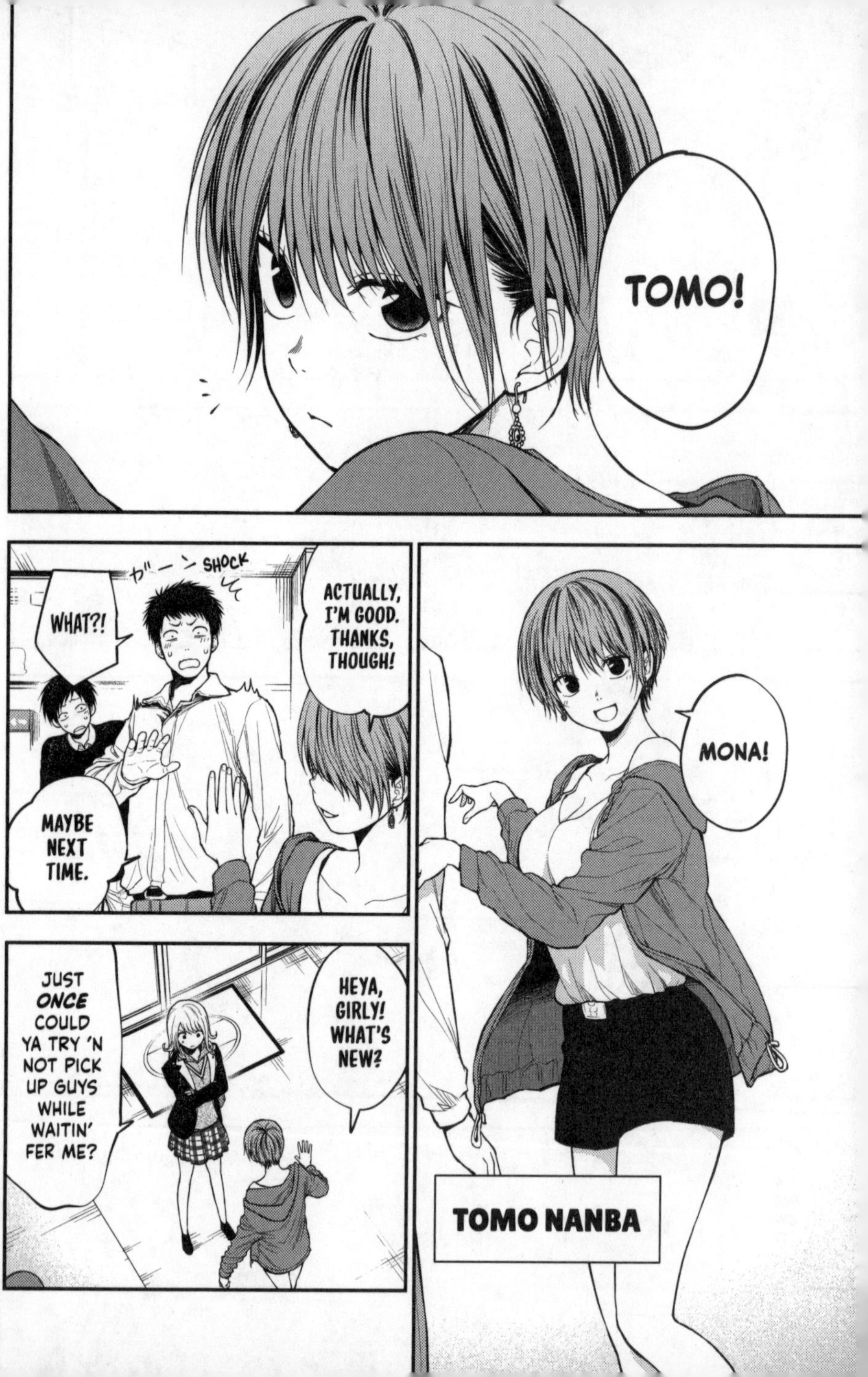
TOMO!
MONA!
TOMO NANBA
ACTUALLY, I'M GOOD. THANKS, THOUGH!
ガーン SHOCK
WHAT?!
MAYBE NEXT TIME.
HEYA, GIRLY! WHAT'S NEW?
JUST ONCE COULD YA TRY 'N NOT PICK UP GUYS WHILE WAITIN' FER ME?

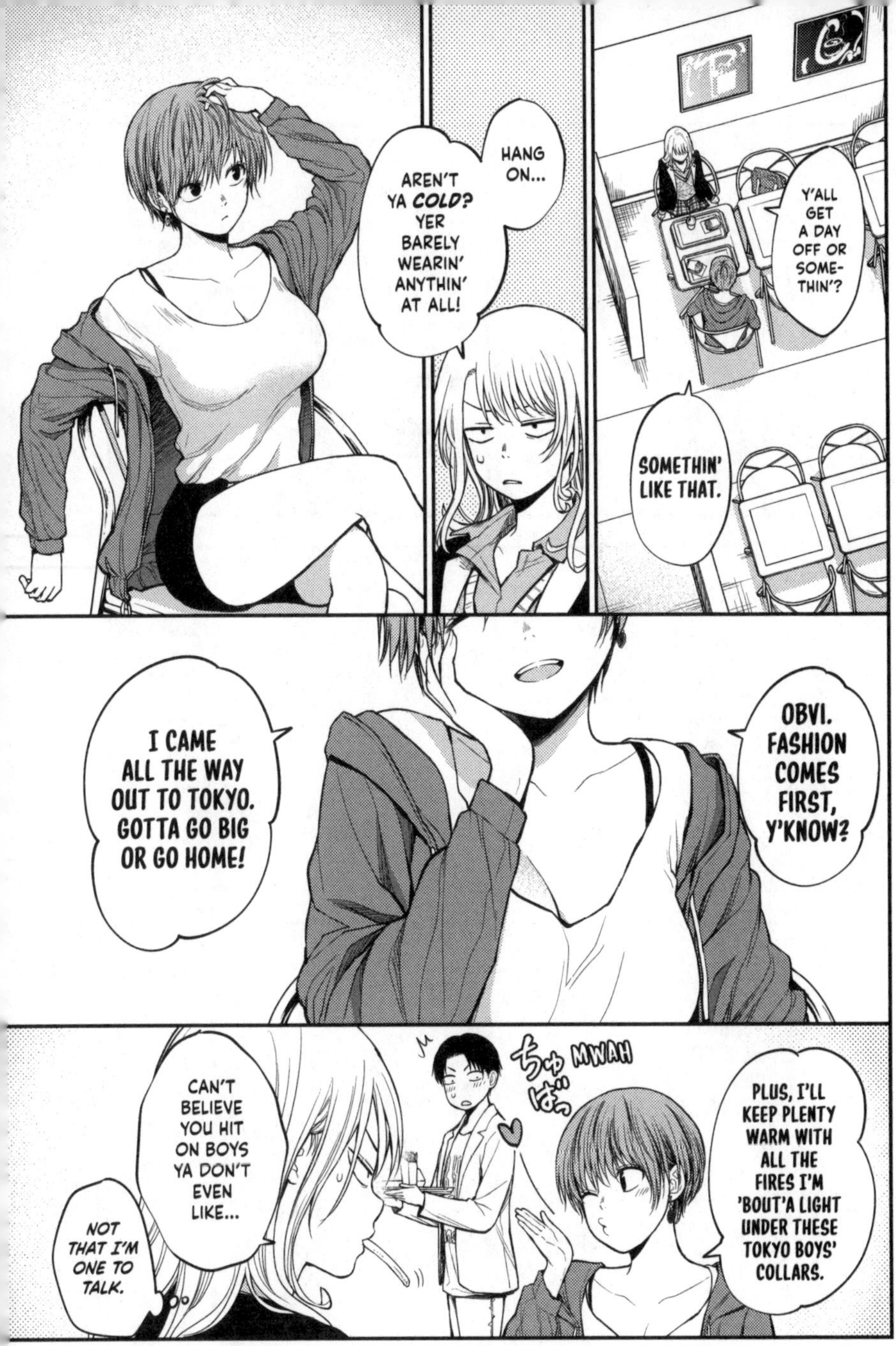
Y'ALL GET A DAY OFF OR SOME- THIN'?
SOMETHIN' LIKE THAT.
HANG ON...
AREN'T YA *COLD?* YER BARELY WEARIN' ANYTHIN' AT ALL!
OBVI. FASHION COMES FIRST, Y'KNOW?
I CAME ALL THE WAY OUT TO TOKYO. GOTTA GO BIG OR GO HOME!
PLUS, I'LL KEEP PLENTY WARM WITH ALL THE FIRES I'M 'BOUT'A LIGHT UNDER THESE TOKYO BOYS' COLLARS.
ちゅぱっ MWAH
CAN'T BELIEVE YOU HIT ON BOYS YA DON'T EVEN LIKE...
NOT THAT I'M ONE TO TALK.

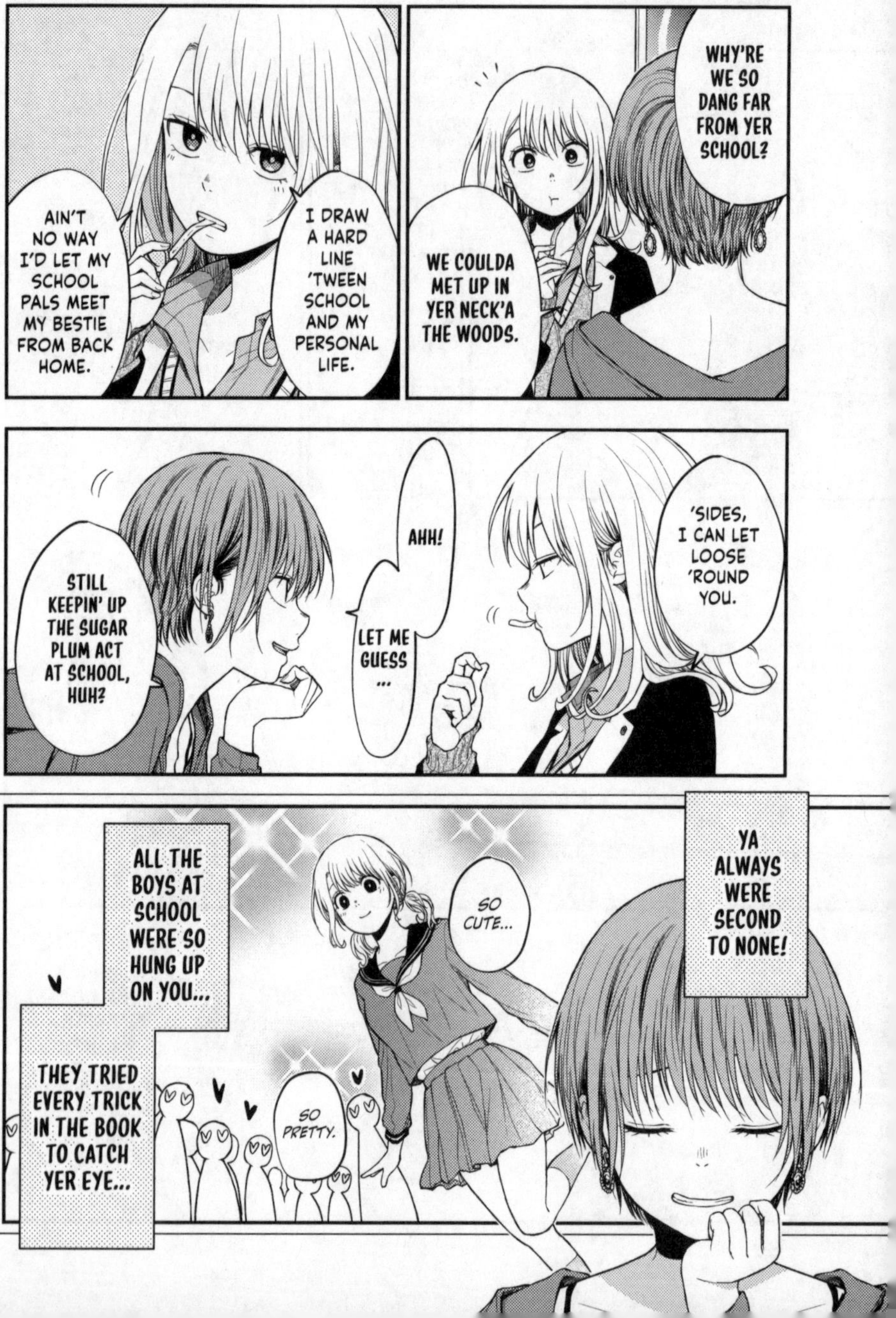
WHY'RE WE SO DANG FAR FROM YER SCHOOL?
WE COULDA MET UP IN YER NECK'A THE WOODS.
I DRAW A HARD LINE 'TWEEN SCHOOL AND MY PERSONAL LIFE.
AIN'T NO WAY I'D LET MY SCHOOL PALS MEET MY BESTIE FROM BACK HOME.
'SIDES, I CAN LET LOOSE 'ROUND YOU.
AHH!
LET ME GUESS...
STILL KEEPIN' UP THE SUGAR PLUM ACT AT SCHOOL, HUH?
YA ALWAYS WERE SECOND TO NONE!
SO CUTE...
ALL THE BOYS AT SCHOOL WERE SO HUNG UP ON YOU...
SO PRETTY.
THEY TRIED EVERY TRICK IN THE BOOK TO CATCH YER EYE...

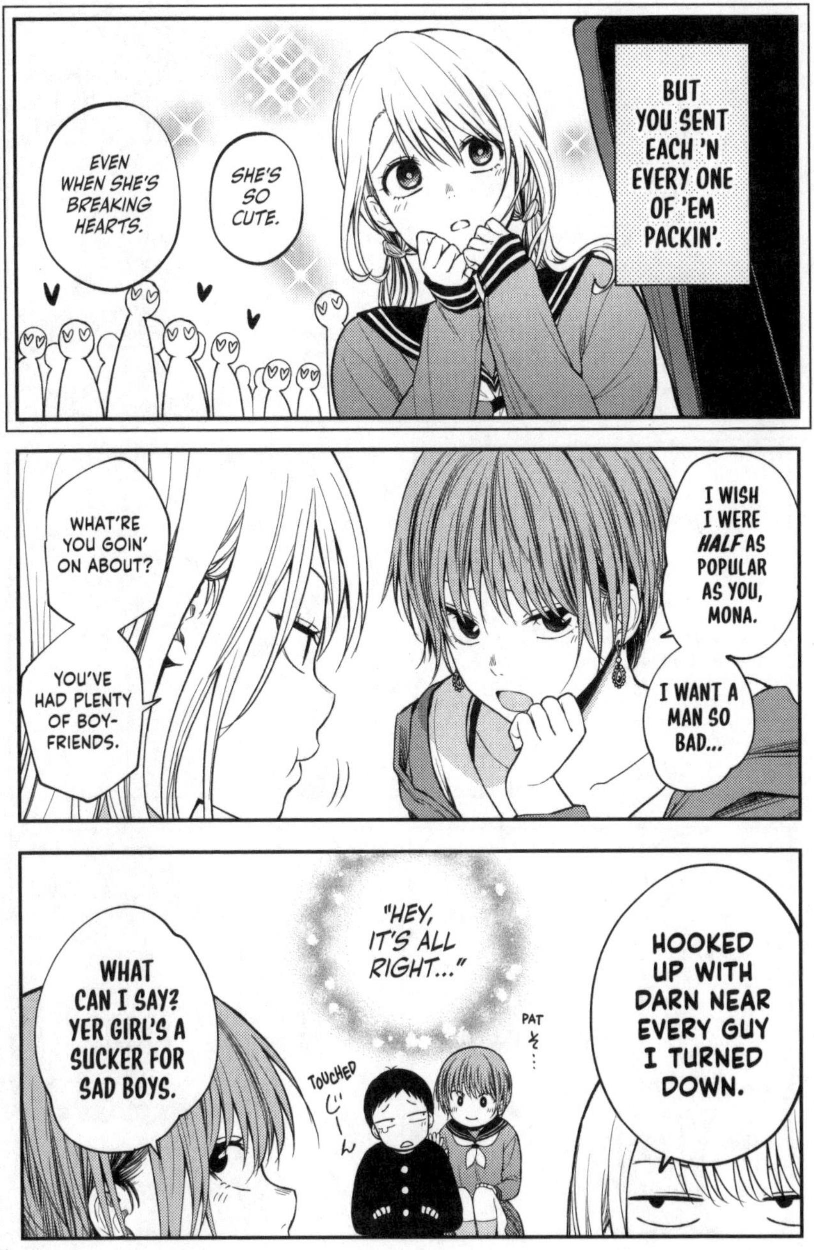
BUT YOU SENT EACH 'N EVERY ONE OF 'EM PACKIN'.
SHE'S SO CUTE.
EVEN WHEN SHE'S BREAKING HEARTS.
I WISH I WERE *HALF* AS POPULAR AS YOU, MONA.
I WANT A MAN SO BAD...
WHAT'RE YOU GOIN' ON ABOUT?
YOU'VE HAD PLENTY OF BOY-FRIENDS.
HOOKED UP WITH DARN NEAR EVERY GUY I TURNED DOWN.
PAT
"HEY, IT'S ALL RIGHT..."
TOUCHED
じーん
WHAT CAN I SAY? YER GIRL'S A SUCKER FOR SAD BOYS.

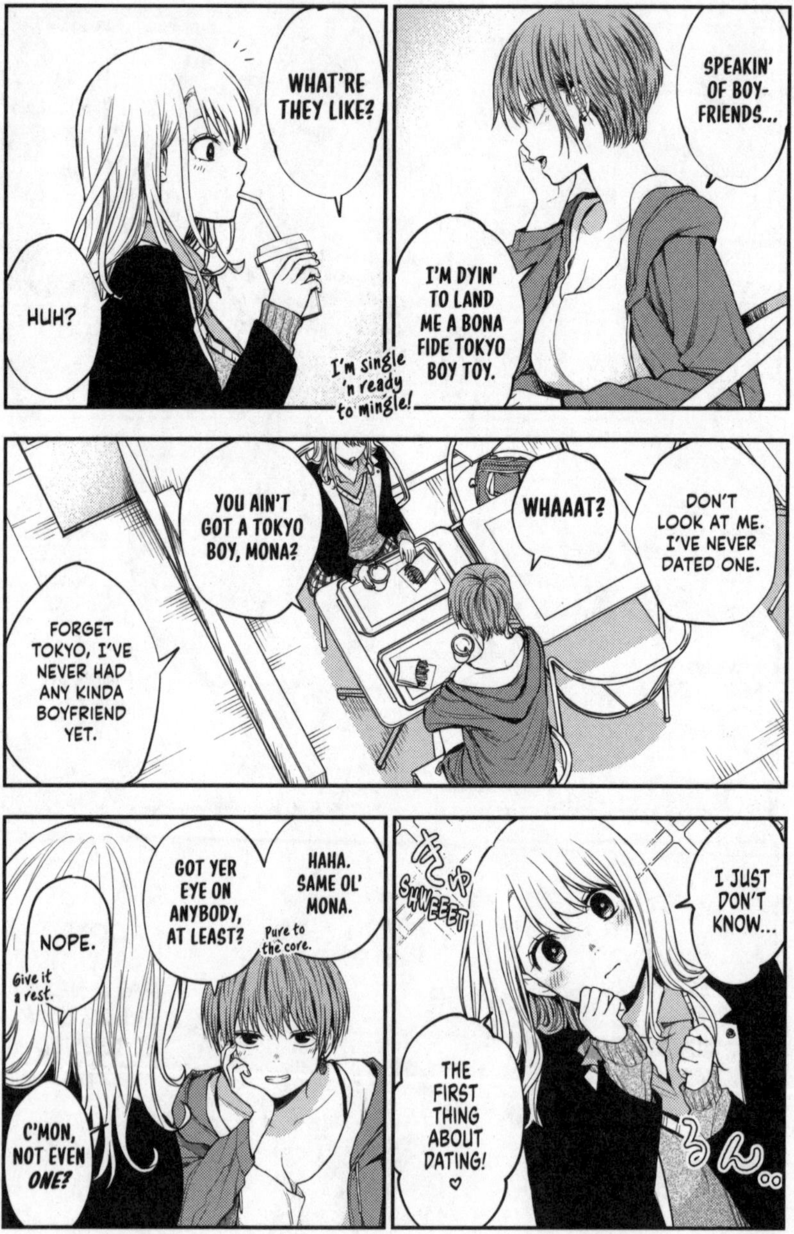
SPEAKIN' OF BOY-FRIENDS...
I'M DYIN' TO LAND ME A BONA FIDE TOKYO BOY TOY.
I'm single 'n ready to mingle!
WHAT'RE THEY LIKE?
HUH?
DON'T LOOK AT ME. I'VE NEVER DATED ONE.
WHAAAT?
YOU AIN'T GOT A TOKYO BOY, MONA?
FORGET TOKYO, I'VE NEVER HAD ANY KINDA BOYFRIEND YET.
きゅ
SHWEEET
I JUST DON'T KNOW...
THE FIRST THING ABOUT DATING! ♡
るん
HAHA. SAME OL' MONA.
Pure to the core.
GOT YER EYE ON ANYBODY, AT LEAST?
NOPE.
Give it a rest.
C'MON, NOT EVEN *ONE?*

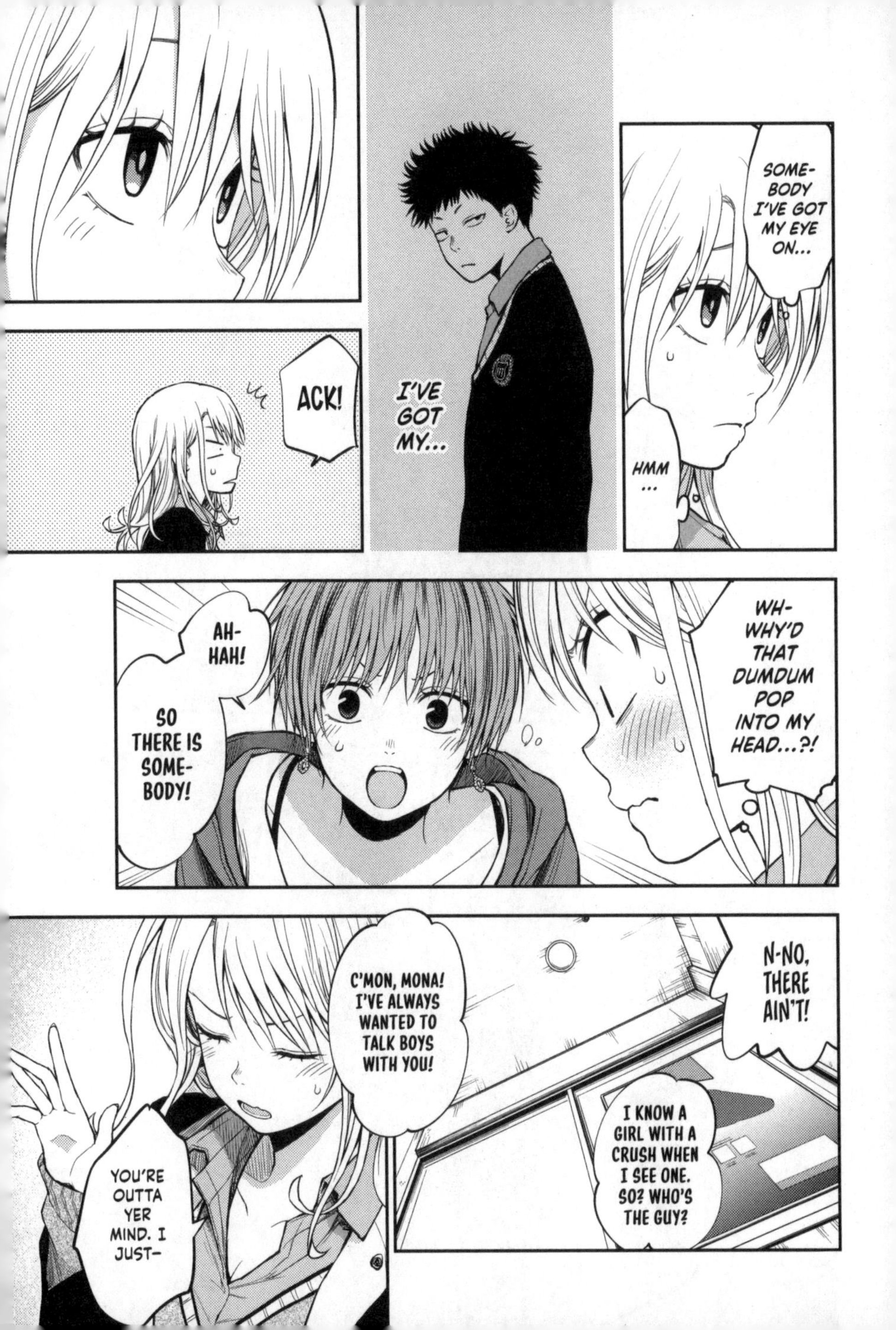
SOME-BODY I'VE GOT MY EYE ON...
HMM ...
I'VE GOT MY...
ACK!
WH-WHY'D THAT DUMDUM POP INTO MY HEAD...?!
AH-HAH!
SO THERE IS SOMEBODY!
N-NO, THERE AIN'T!
I KNOW A GIRL WITH A CRUSH WHEN I SEE ONE. SO? WHO'S THE GUY?
C'MON, MONA! I'VE ALWAYS WANTED TO TALK BOYS WITH YOU!
YOU'RE OUTTA YER MIND. I JUST-

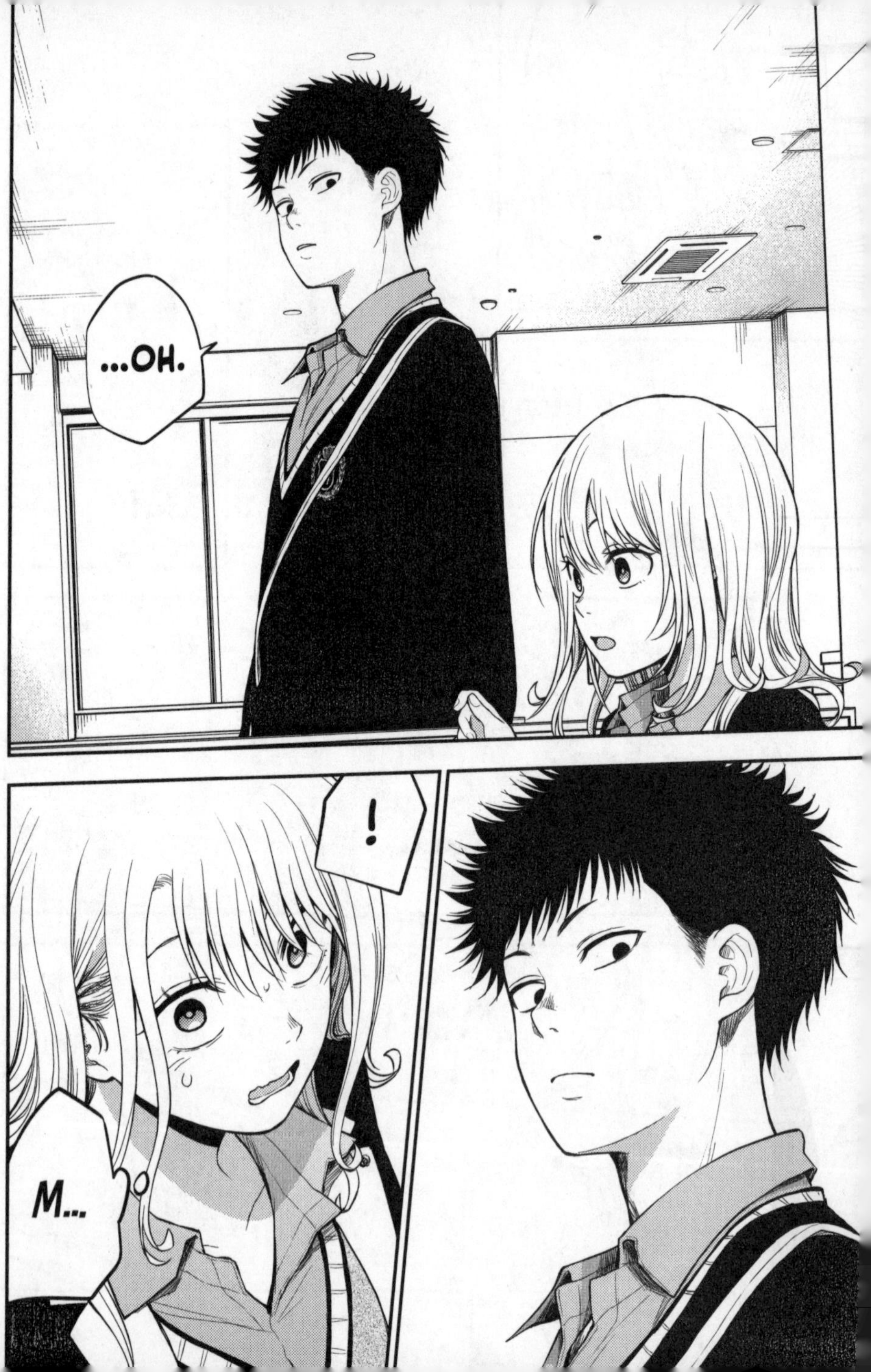
...OH.
!
M...

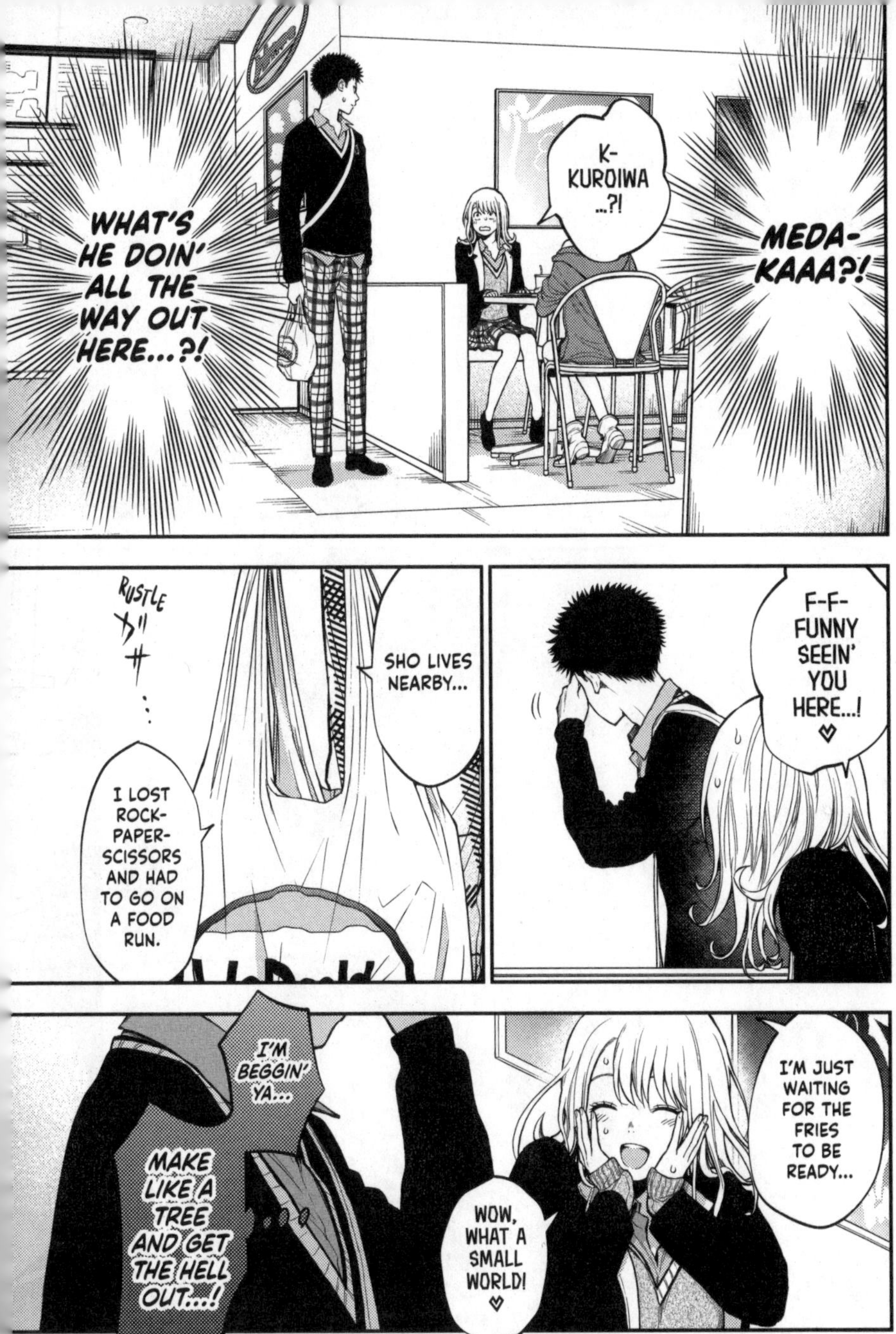
MEDA-KAAA?!
K-KUROIWA ...?!
WHAT'S HE DOIN' ALL THE WAY OUT HERE...?!
F-F-FUNNY SEEIN' YOU HERE...! ♡
SHO LIVES NEARBY...
RUSTLE
I LOST ROCK-PAPER-SCISSORS AND HAD TO GO ON A FOOD RUN.
I'M JUST WAITING FOR THE FRIES TO BE READY...
WOW, WHAT A SMALL WORLD! ♡
I'M BEGGIN' YA...
MAKE LIKE A TREE AND GET THE HELL OUT...!

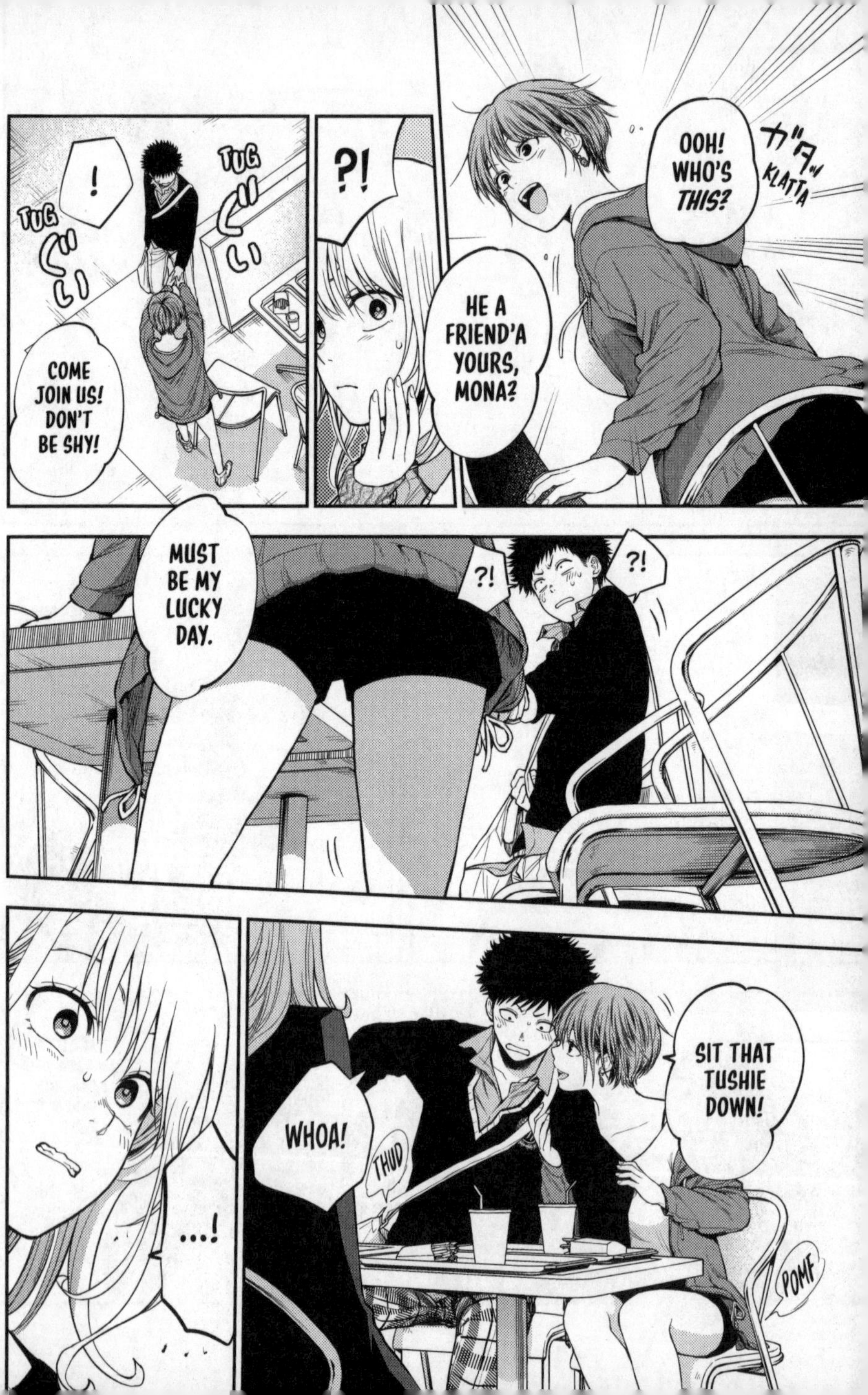
OOH! WHO'S THIS?
ガタッ KLATTA
HE A FRIEND'A YOURS, MONA?
?!
!
TUG ぐい
TUG ぐい
COME JOIN US! DON'T BE SHY!
?!
?!
MUST BE MY LUCKY DAY.
SIT THAT TUSHIE DOWN!
POMF
WHOA!
THUD
...!

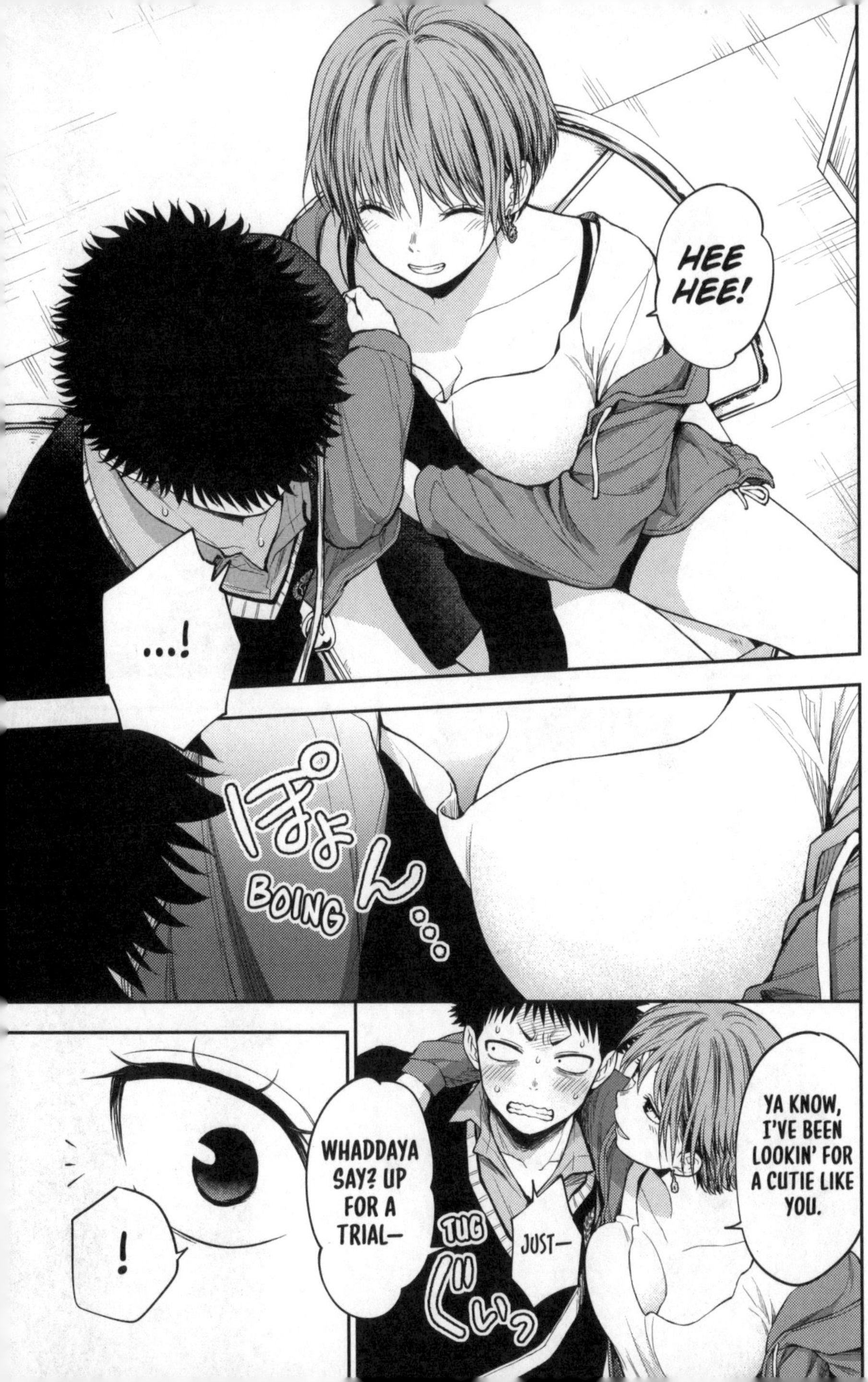
HEE HEE!
...!
ぽよん...
BOING
YA KNOW, I'VE BEEN LOOKIN' FOR A CUTIE LIKE YOU.
JUST—
TUG
ぐいっ
WHADDAYA SAY? UP FOR A TRIAL—
!

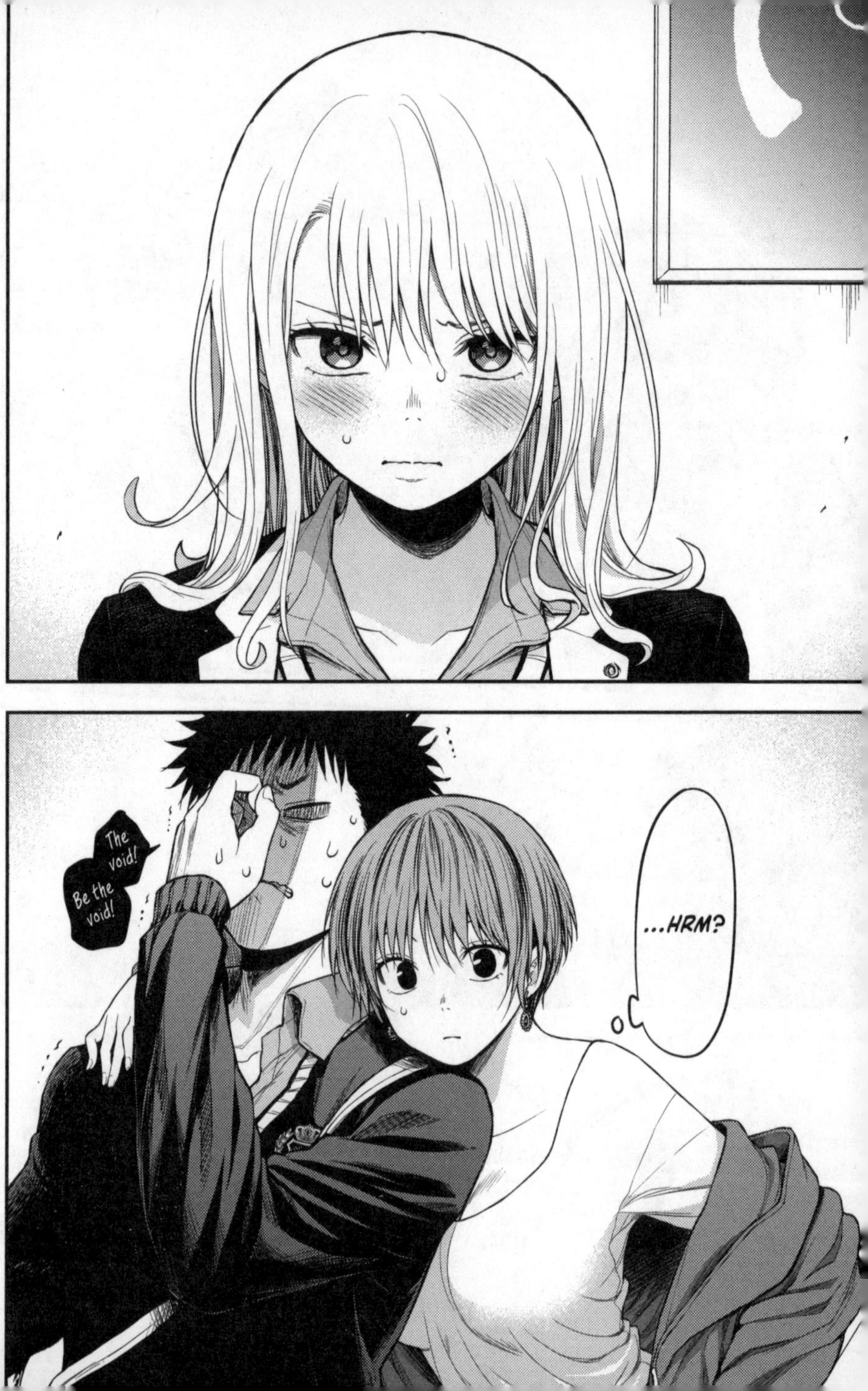
...HRM?
The void! Be the void!

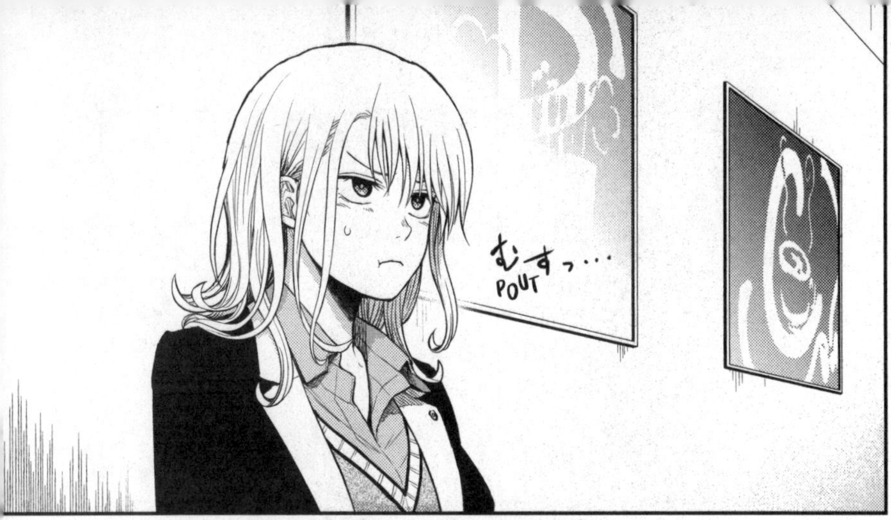
むすっ…
POUT

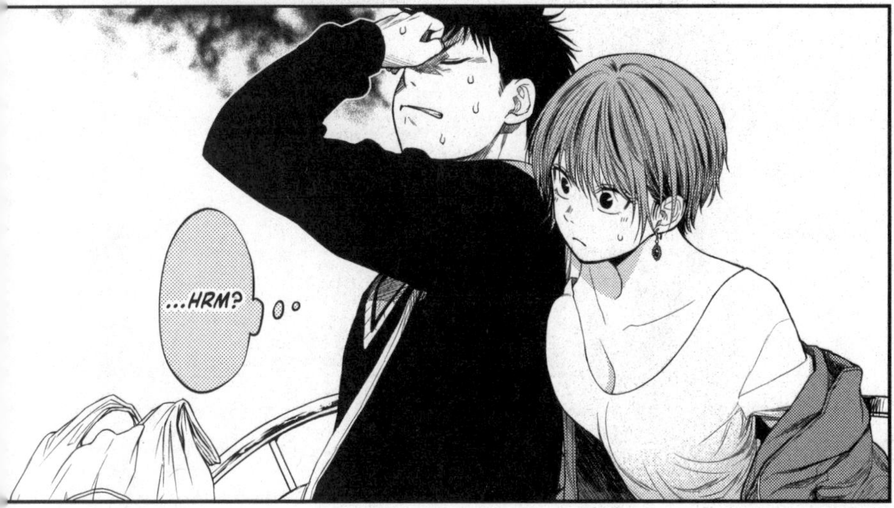
...HRM?

Chapter 32 ★ Teasing That Jerk

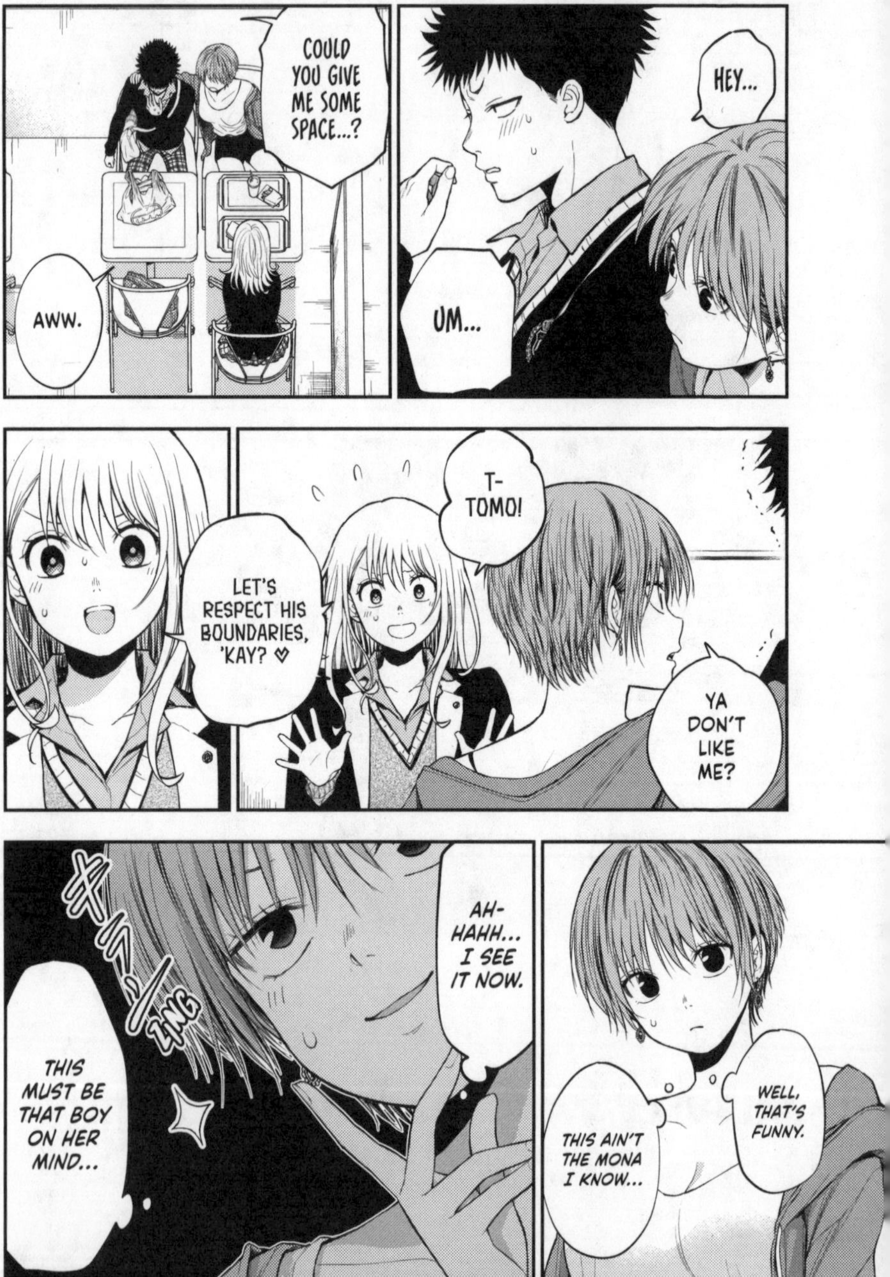
HEY...
UM...
COULD YOU GIVE ME SOME SPACE...?
AWW.
YA DON'T LIKE ME?
T- TOMO!
LET'S RESPECT HIS BOUNDARIES, 'KAY? ♡
WELL, THAT'S FUNNY.
THIS AIN'T THE MONA I KNOW...
AH- HAHH... I SEE IT NOW.
ZING
THIS MUST BE THAT BOY ON HER MIND...

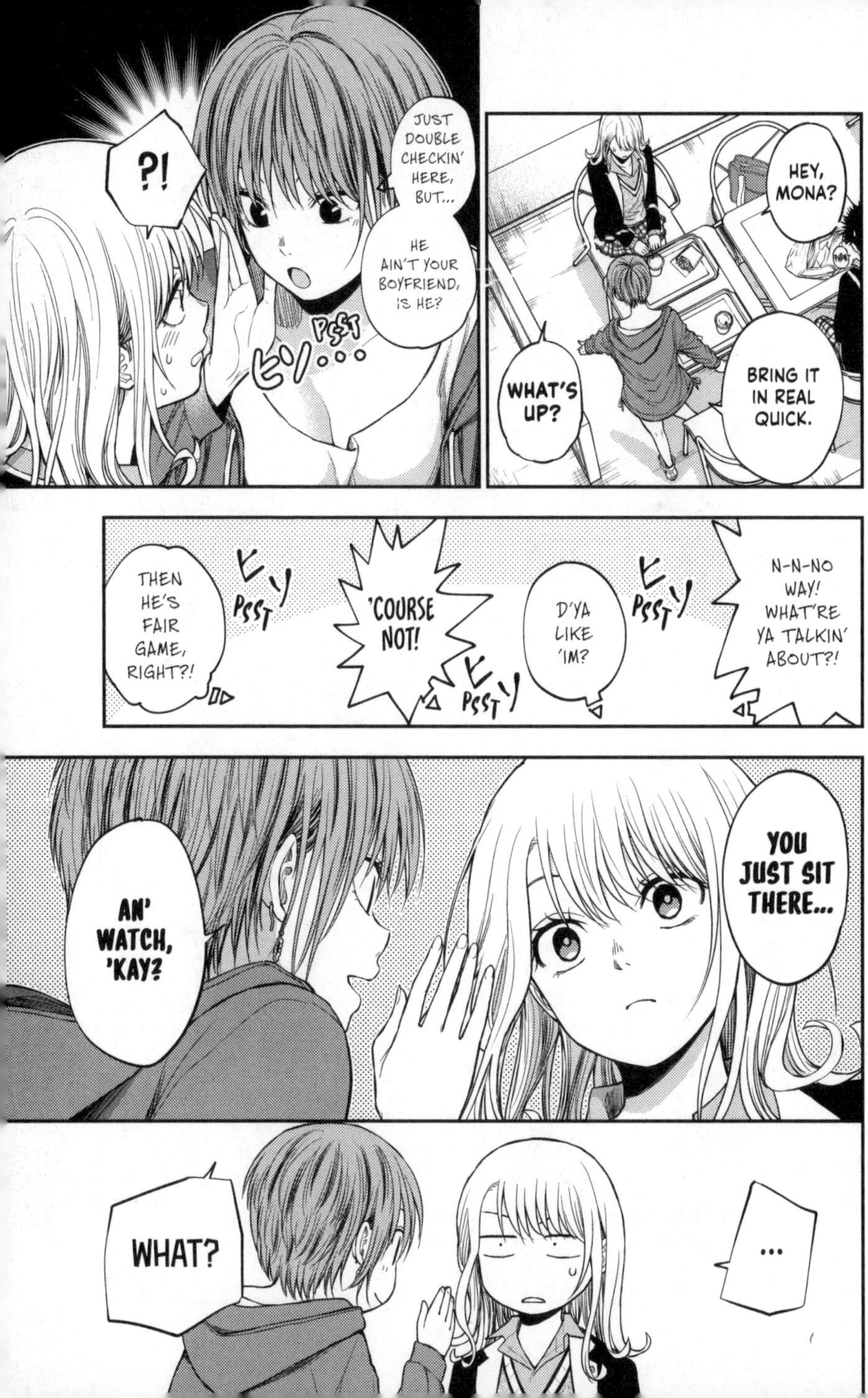
HEY, MONA?
BRING IT IN REAL QUICK.
WHAT'S UP?
JUST DOUBLE CHECKIN' HERE, BUT...
HE AIN'T YOUR BOYFRIEND, IS HE?
?!
PSST
ヒソ…
N-N-NO WAY! WHAT'RE YA TALKIN' ABOUT?!
PSST
ヒソ
D'YA LIKE 'IM?
PSST
ヒソ
'COURSE NOT!
PSST
ヒソ
THEN HE'S FAIR GAME, RIGHT?!
YOU JUST SIT THERE...
AN' WATCH, 'KAY?
...
WHAT?

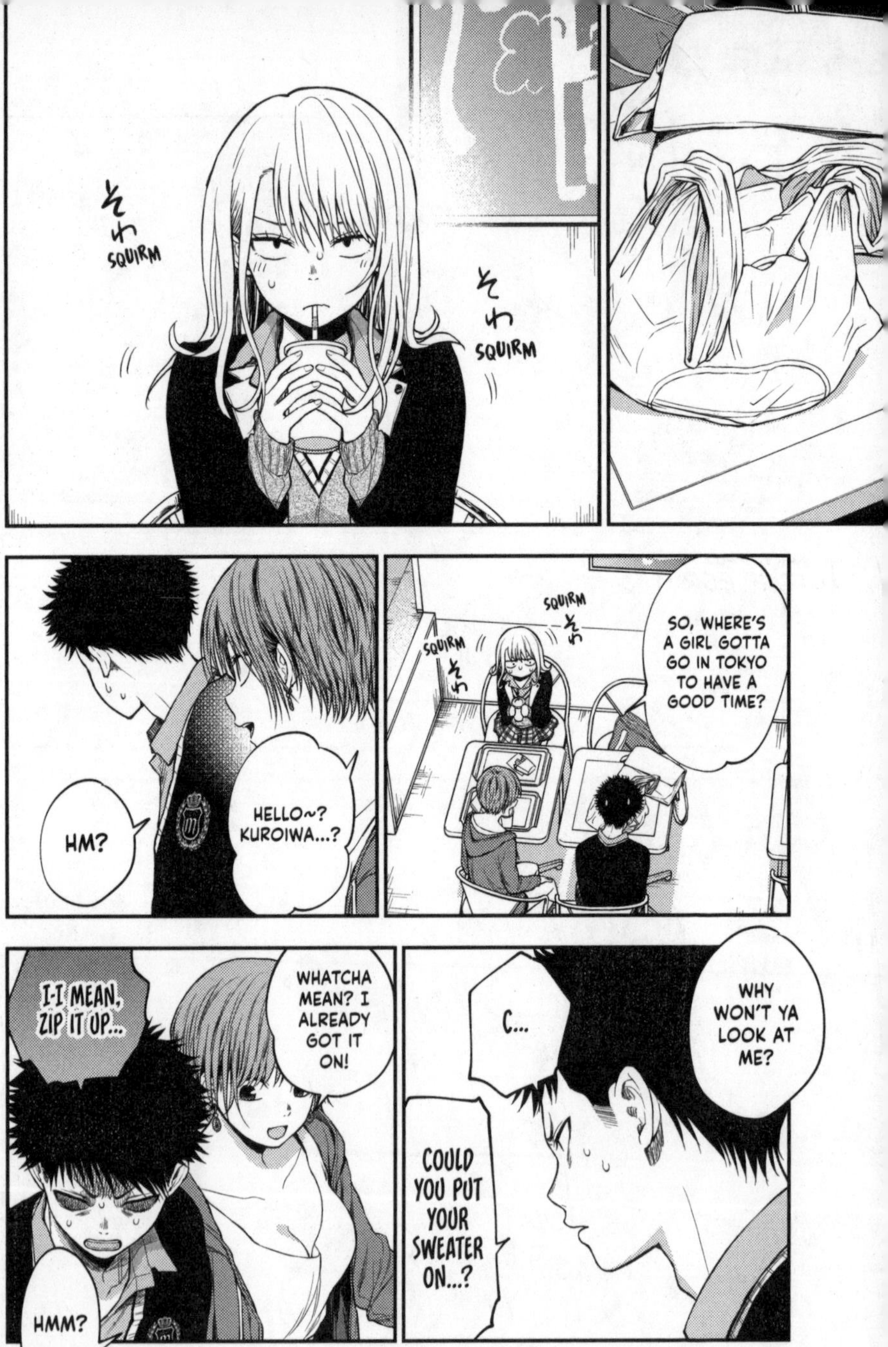
そわ
SQUIRM
そわ
SQUIRM
SQUIRM
そわ
SQUIRM
そわ
SO, WHERE'S A GIRL GOTTA GO IN TOKYO TO HAVE A GOOD TIME?
HELLO~? KUROIWA...?
HM?
WHY WON'T YA LOOK AT ME?
C...
COULD YOU PUT YOUR SWEATER ON...?
WHATCHA MEAN? I ALREADY GOT IT ON!
I-I MEAN, ZIP IT UP...
HMM?

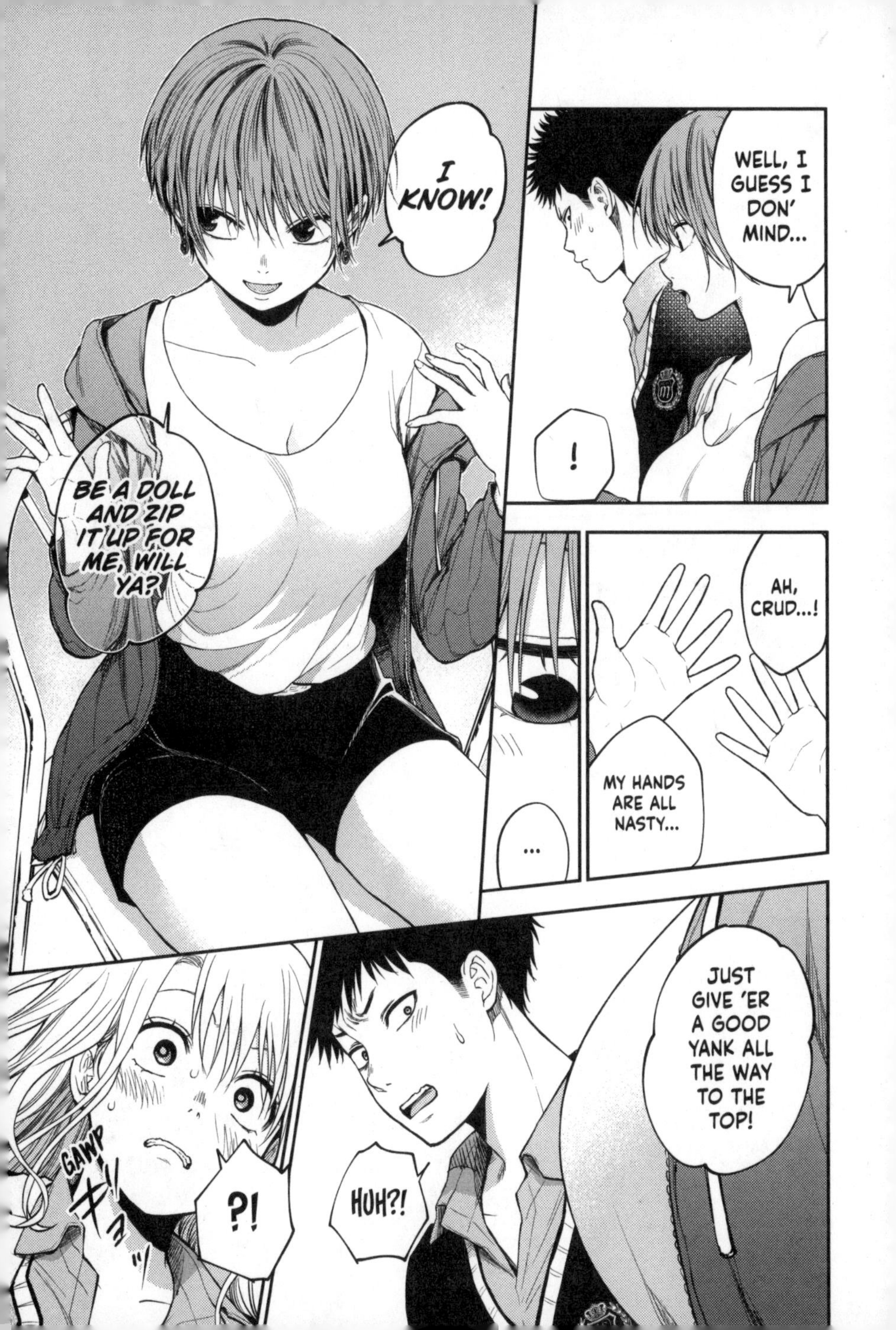
WELL, I GUESS I DON' MIND...
!
AH, CRUD...!
MY HANDS ARE ALL NASTY...
...
I KNOW!
BE A DOLL AND ZIP IT UP FOR ME, WILL YA?
JUST GIVE 'ER A GOOD YANK ALL THE WAY TO THE TOP!
HUH?!
?!
GAWP

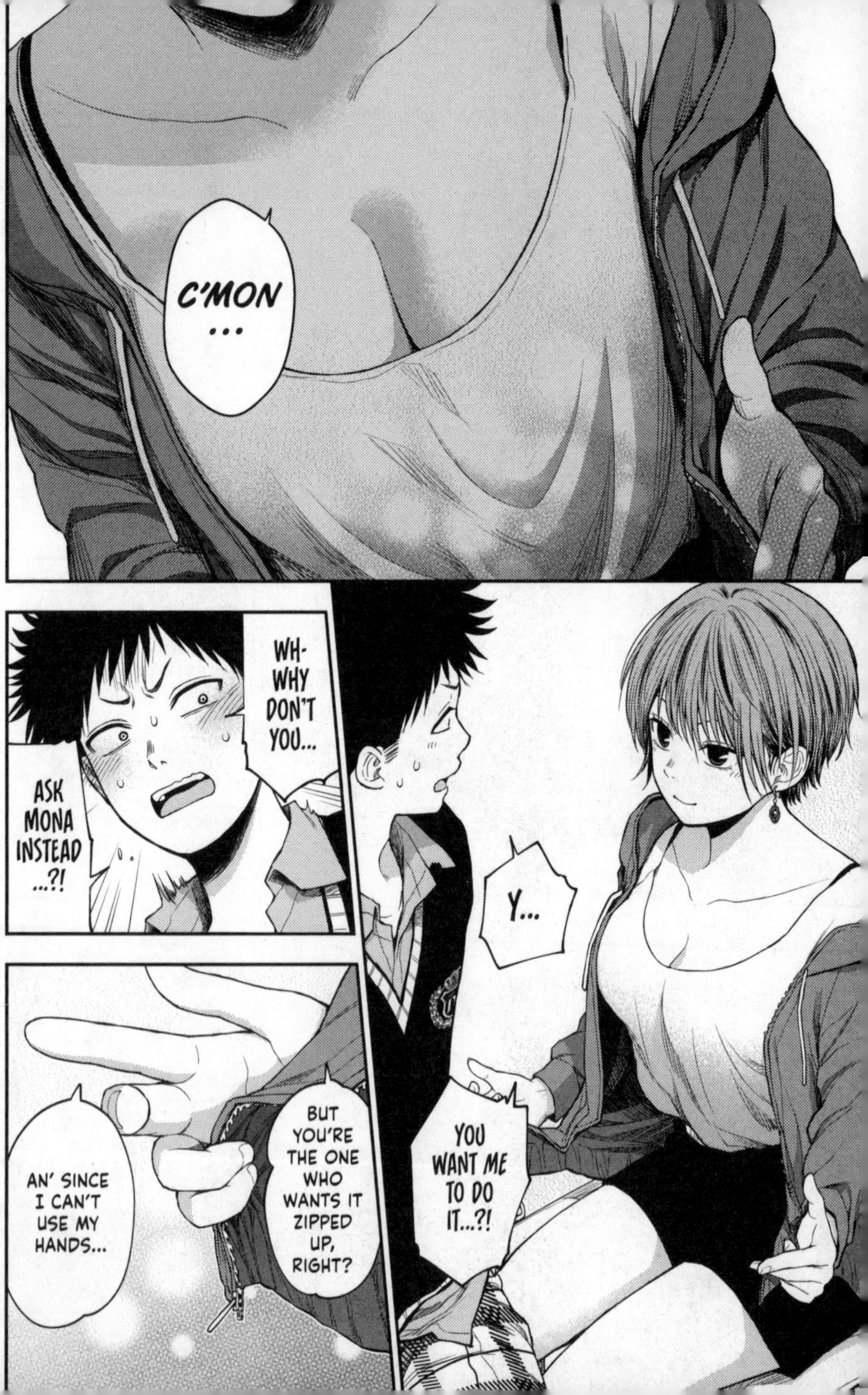
C'MON ...
Y...
YOU WANT ME TO DO IT...?!
WH- WHY DON'T YOU...
ASK MONA INSTEAD ...?!
BUT YOU'RE THE ONE WHO WANTS IT ZIPPED UP, RIGHT?
AN' SINCE I CAN'T USE MY HANDS...

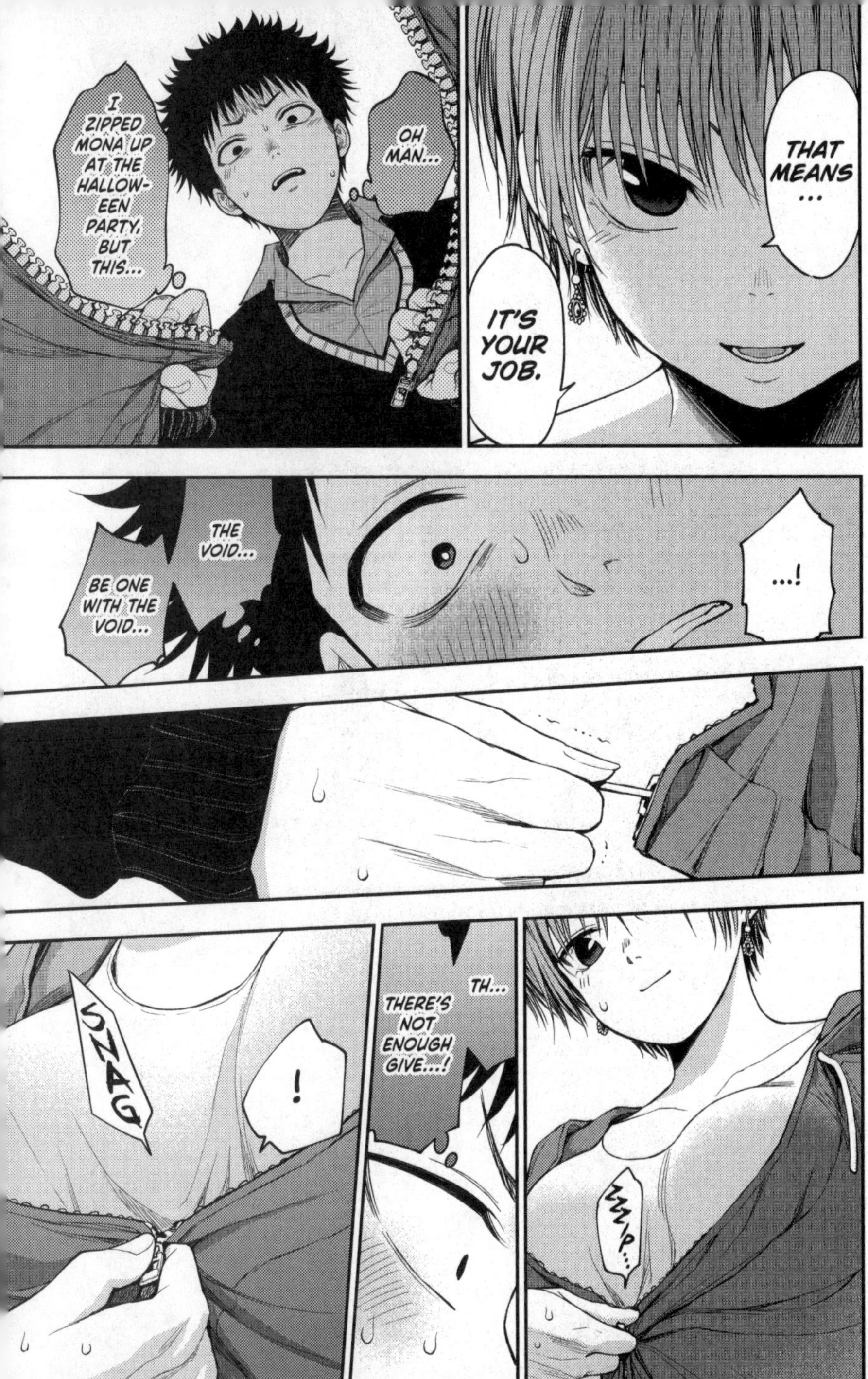
THAT MEANS ...
IT'S YOUR JOB.
OH MAN...
I ZIPPED MONA UP AT THE HALLOWEEN PARTY, BUT THIS...
...!
THE VOID...
BE ONE WITH THE VOID...
ZZZIP...
TH...
THERE'S NOT ENOUGH GIVE...!
!
SNAG

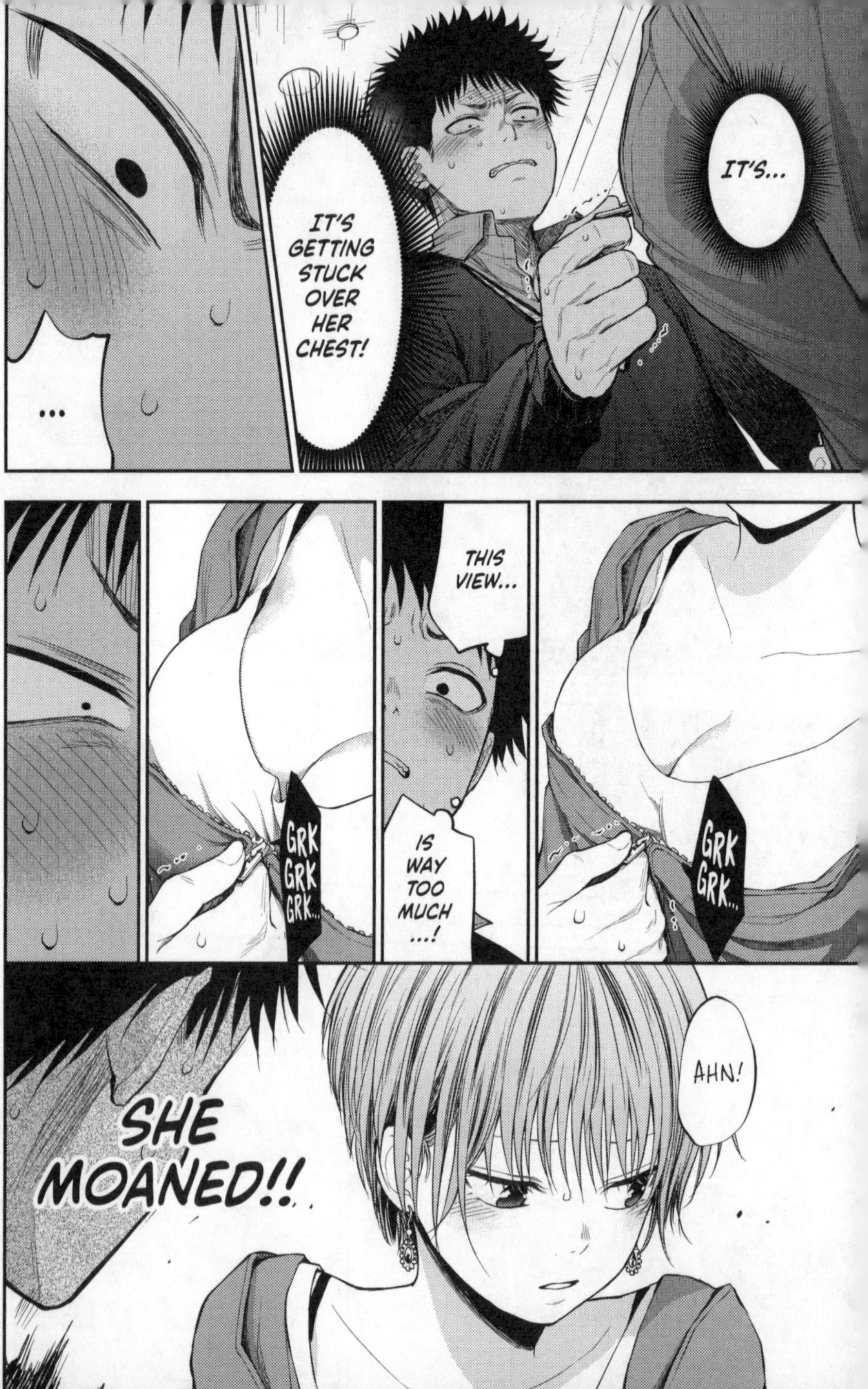
IT'S...
IT'S GETTING STUCK OVER HER CHEST!
...
GRK GRK...
THIS VIEW...
IS WAY TOO MUCH ...!
GRK GRK GRK...
AHN!
SHE MOANED!!

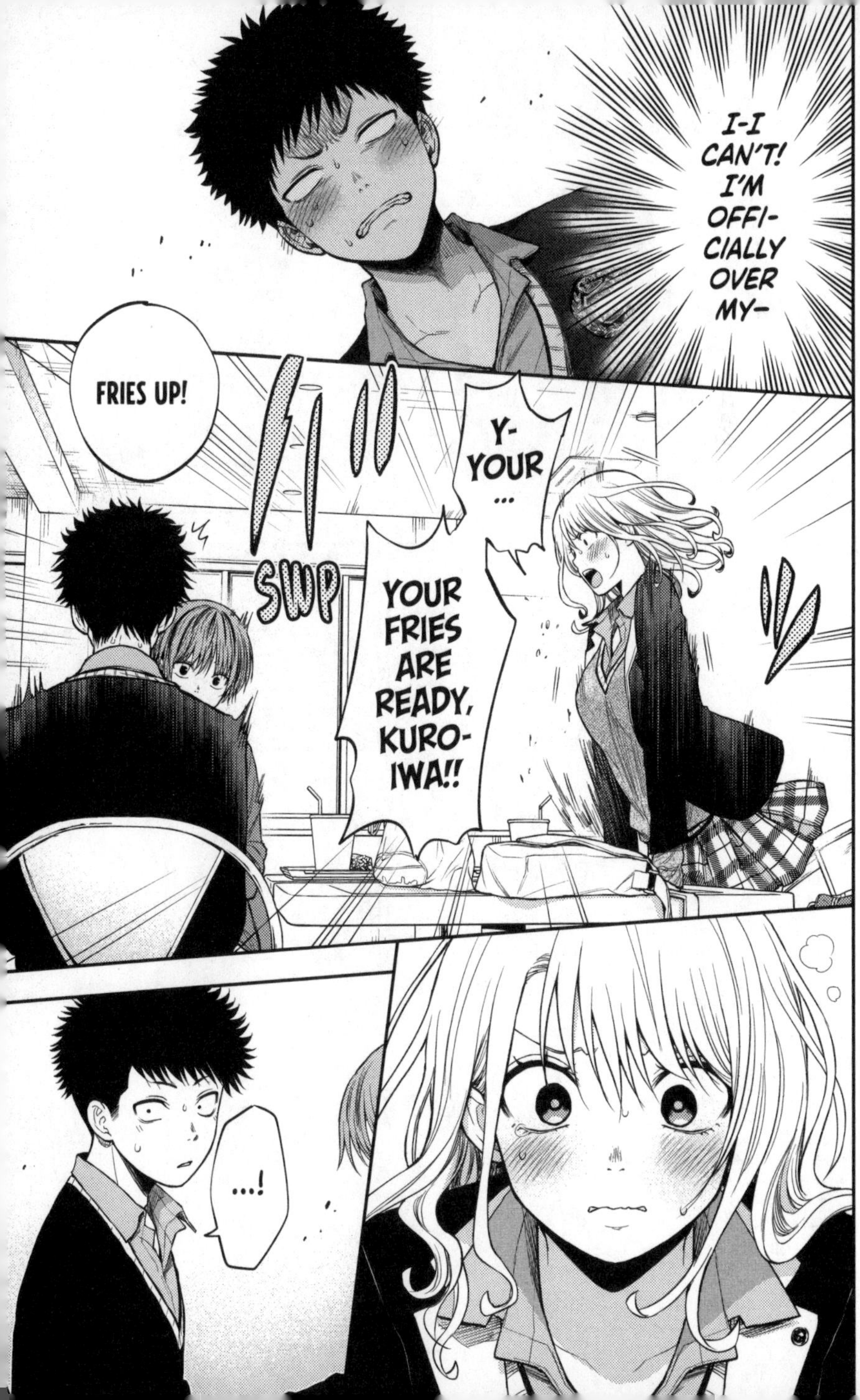
I-I CAN'T! I'M OFFI-CIALLY OVER MY–
Y-YOUR...
FRIES UP!
YOUR FRIES ARE READY, KURO-IWA!!
SWP
...!

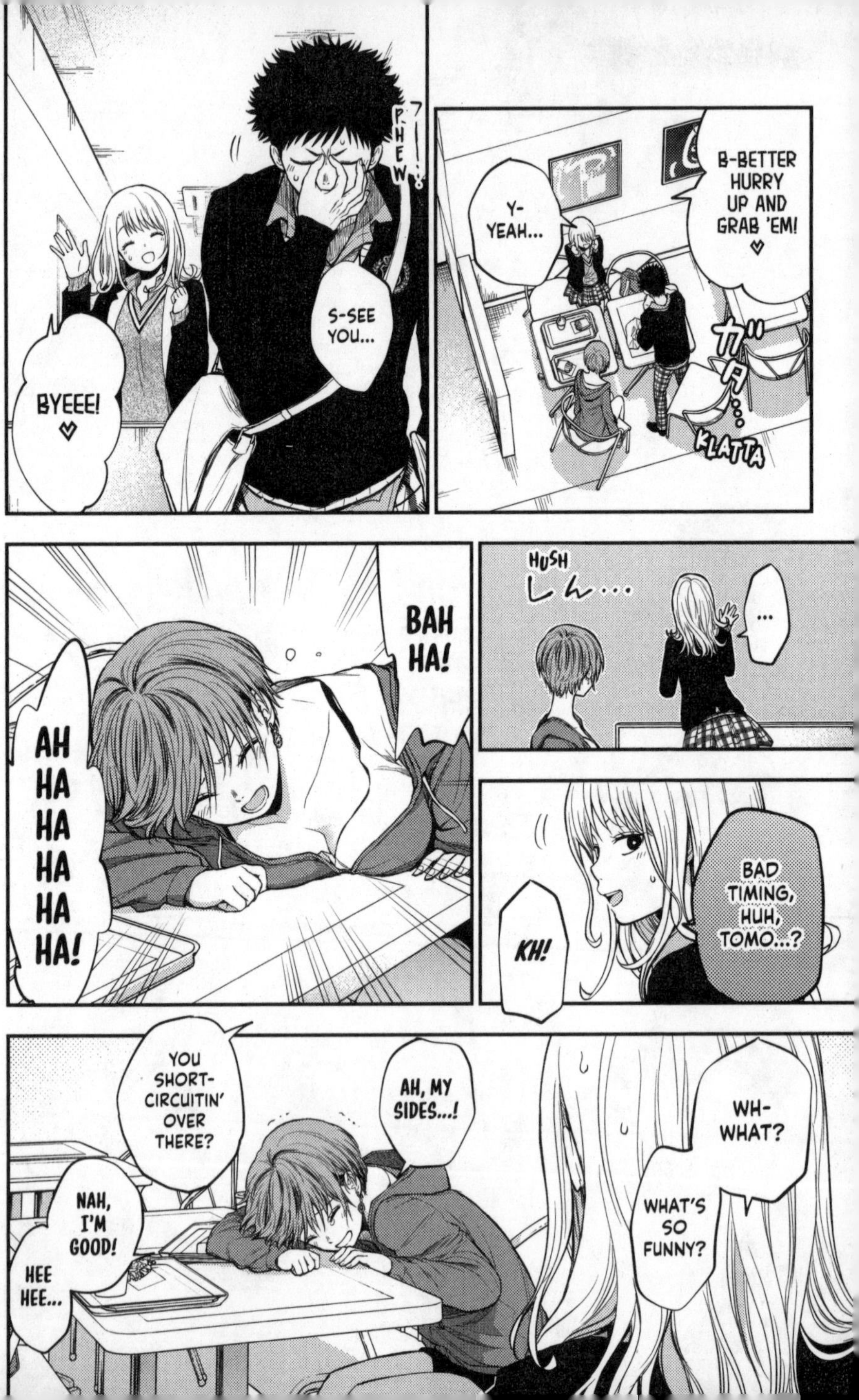
B-BETTER HURRY UP AND GRAB 'EM! ♡
Y-YEAH...
ガタ...
KLATTA
フー
PHEW
S-SEE YOU...
BYEEE! ♡
HUSH
しん...
...
BAD TIMING, HUH, TOMO...?
KH!
BAH HA!
AH HA HA HA HA HA!
WH-WHAT?
WHAT'S SO FUNNY?
AH, MY SIDES...!
YOU SHORT-CIRCUITIN' OVER THERE?
NAH, I'M GOOD!
HEE HEE...

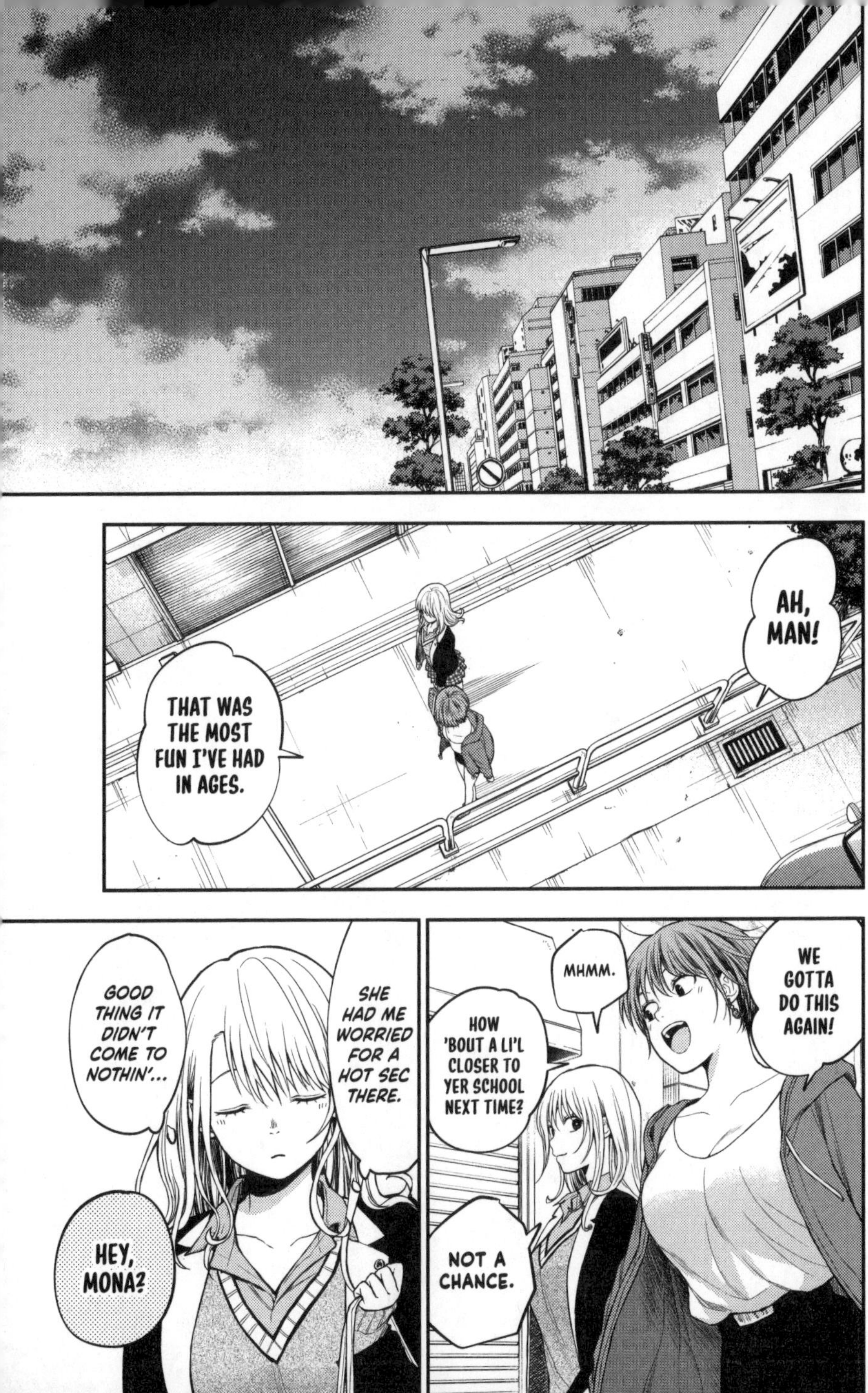
AH, MAN!
THAT WAS THE MOST FUN I'VE HAD IN AGES.
WE GOTTA DO THIS AGAIN!
MHMM.
HOW 'BOUT A LI'L CLOSER TO YER SCHOOL NEXT TIME?
NOT A CHANCE.
SHE HAD ME WORRIED FOR A HOT SEC THERE.
GOOD THING IT DIDN'T COME TO NOTHIN'...
HEY, MONA?

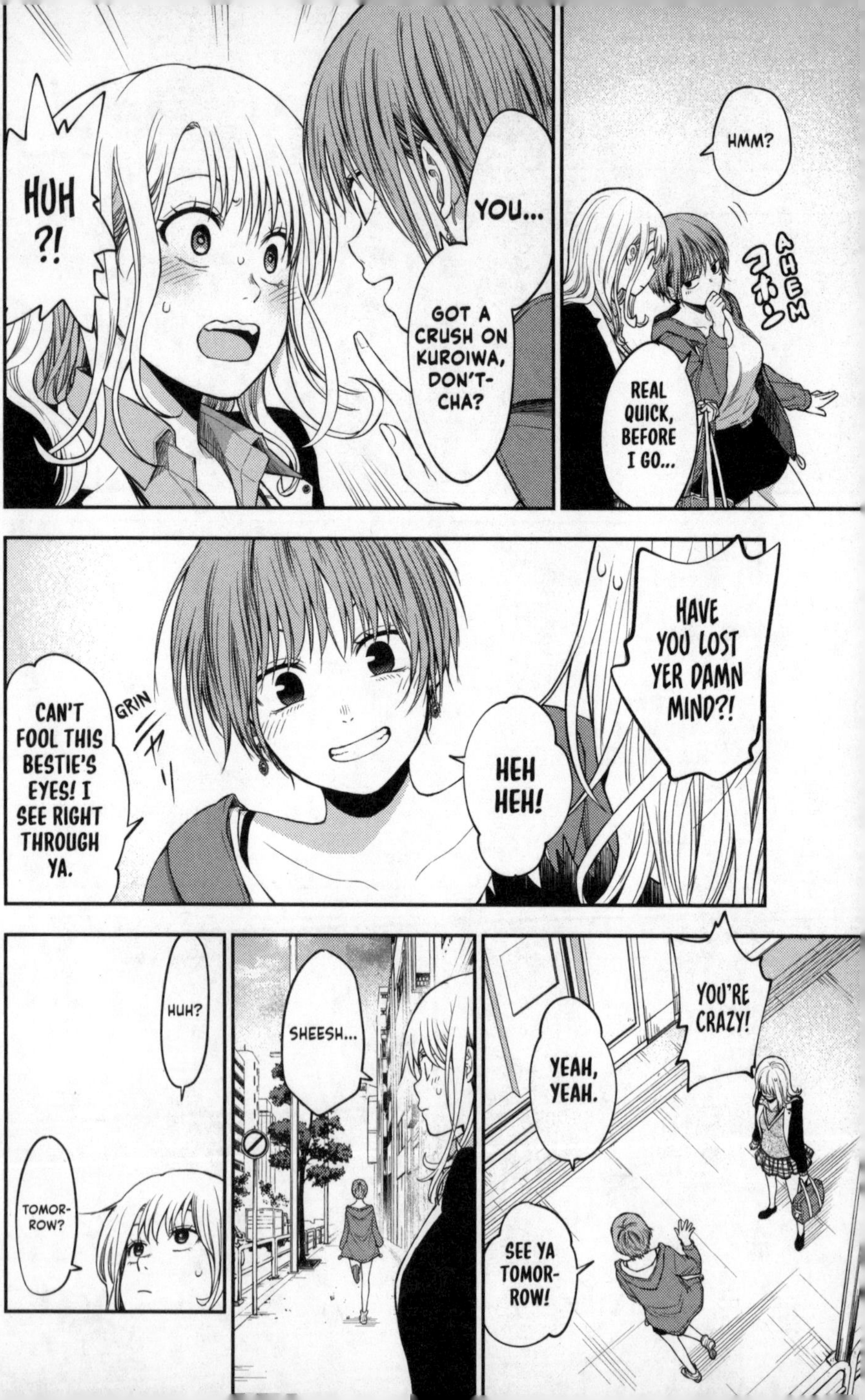
HMM?
AHEM
REAL QUICK, BEFORE I GO...
YOU...
GOT A CRUSH ON KUROIWA, DON'T-CHA?
HUH ?!
HAVE YOU LOST YER DAMN MIND?!
HEH HEH!
GRIN
CAN'T FOOL THIS BESTIE'S EYES! I SEE RIGHT THROUGH YA.
YOU'RE CRAZY!
YEAH, YEAH.
SEE YA TOMOR-ROW!
SHEESH...
HUH?
TOMOR-ROW?

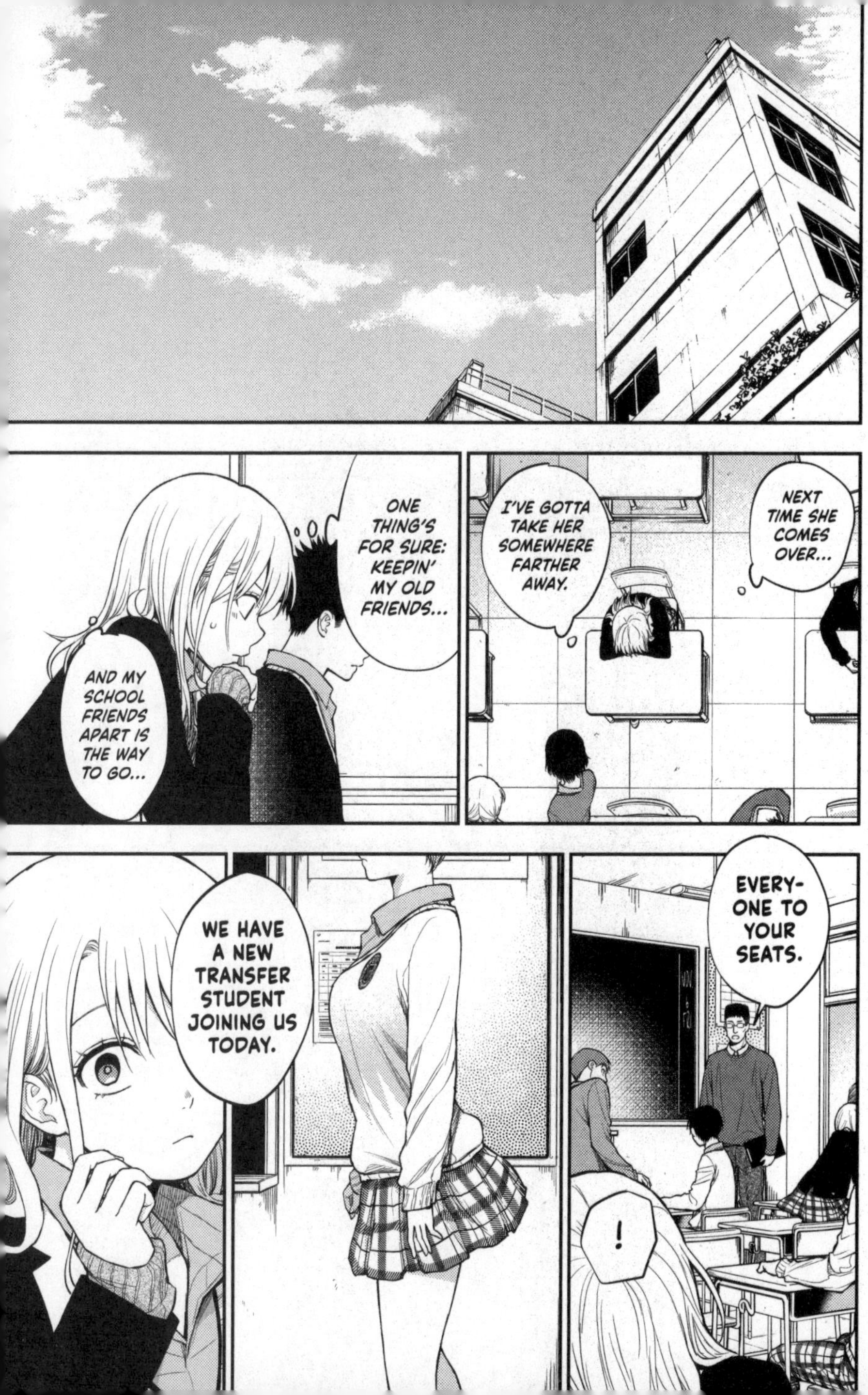
NEXT TIME SHE COMES OVER...
I'VE GOTTA TAKE HER SOMEWHERE FARTHER AWAY.
ONE THING'S FOR SURE: KEEPIN' MY OLD FRIENDS...
AND MY SCHOOL FRIENDS APART IS THE WAY TO GO...
EVERY-ONE TO YOUR SEATS.
!
WE HAVE A NEW TRANSFER STUDENT JOINING US TODAY.

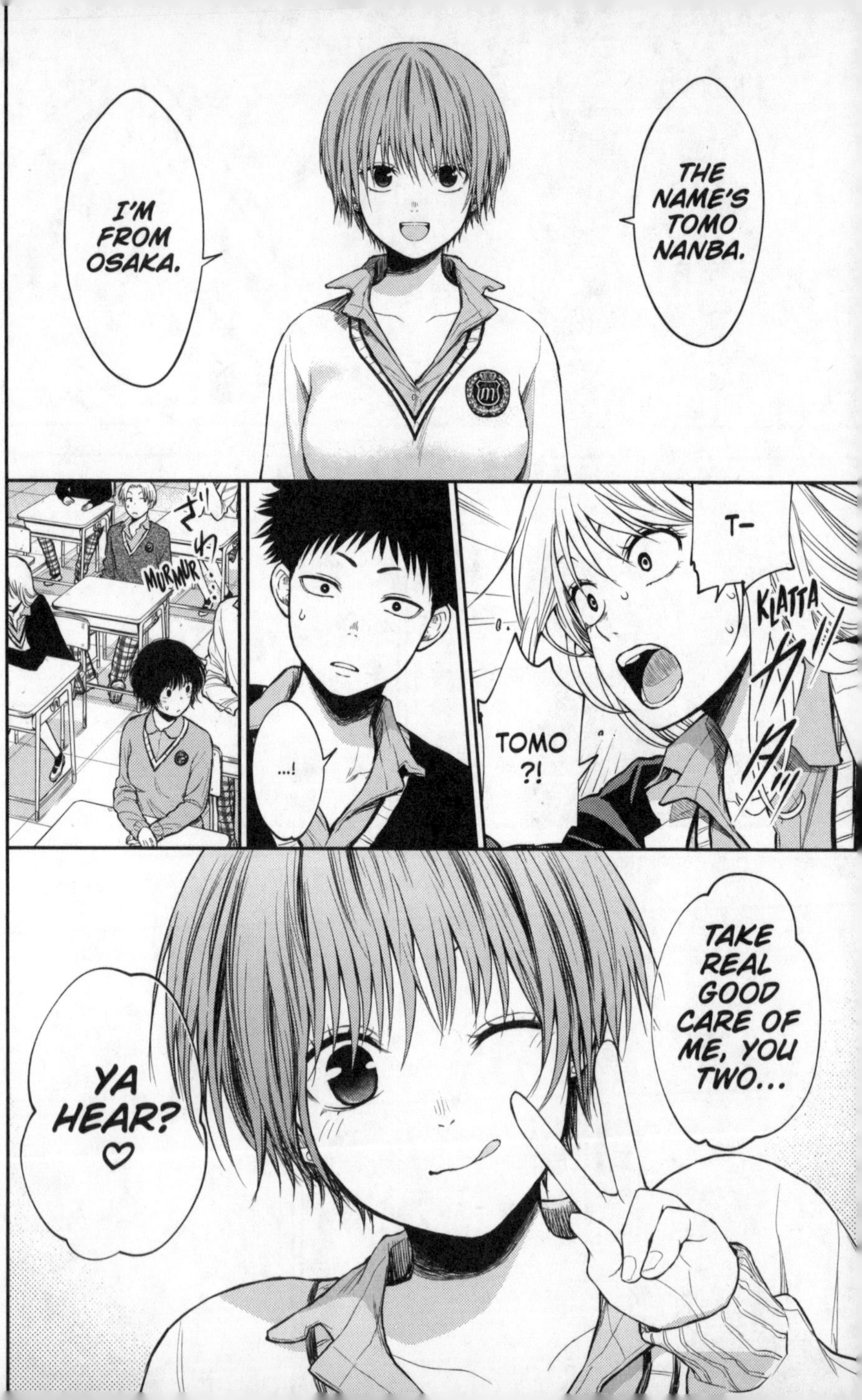
THE NAME'S TOMO NANBA.
I'M FROM OSAKA.
T–
KLATTA
TOMO ?!
...!
MURMUR
TAKE REAL GOOD CARE OF ME, YOU TWO...
YA HEAR? ♡

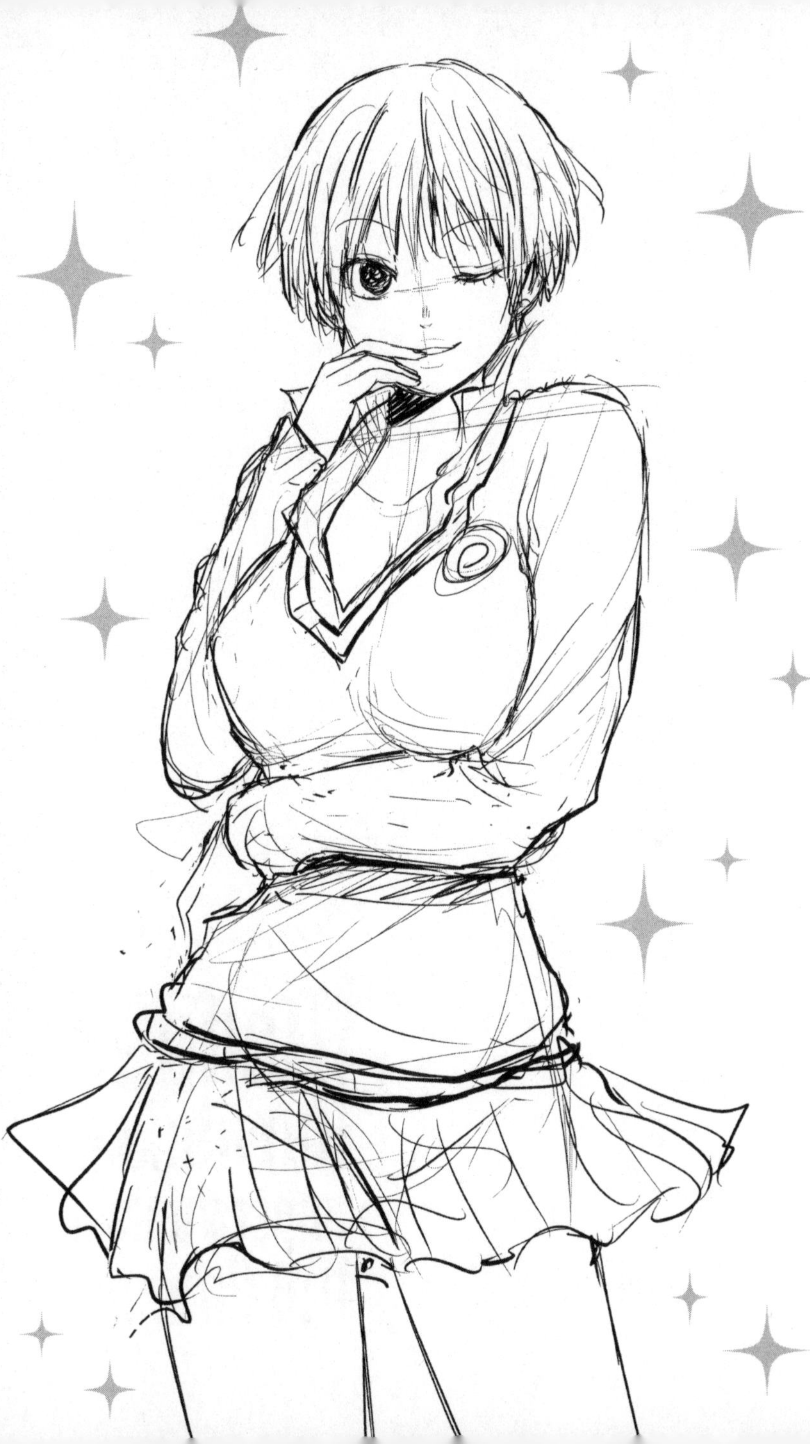

Medaka Kuroiwa is Impervious to My Charms

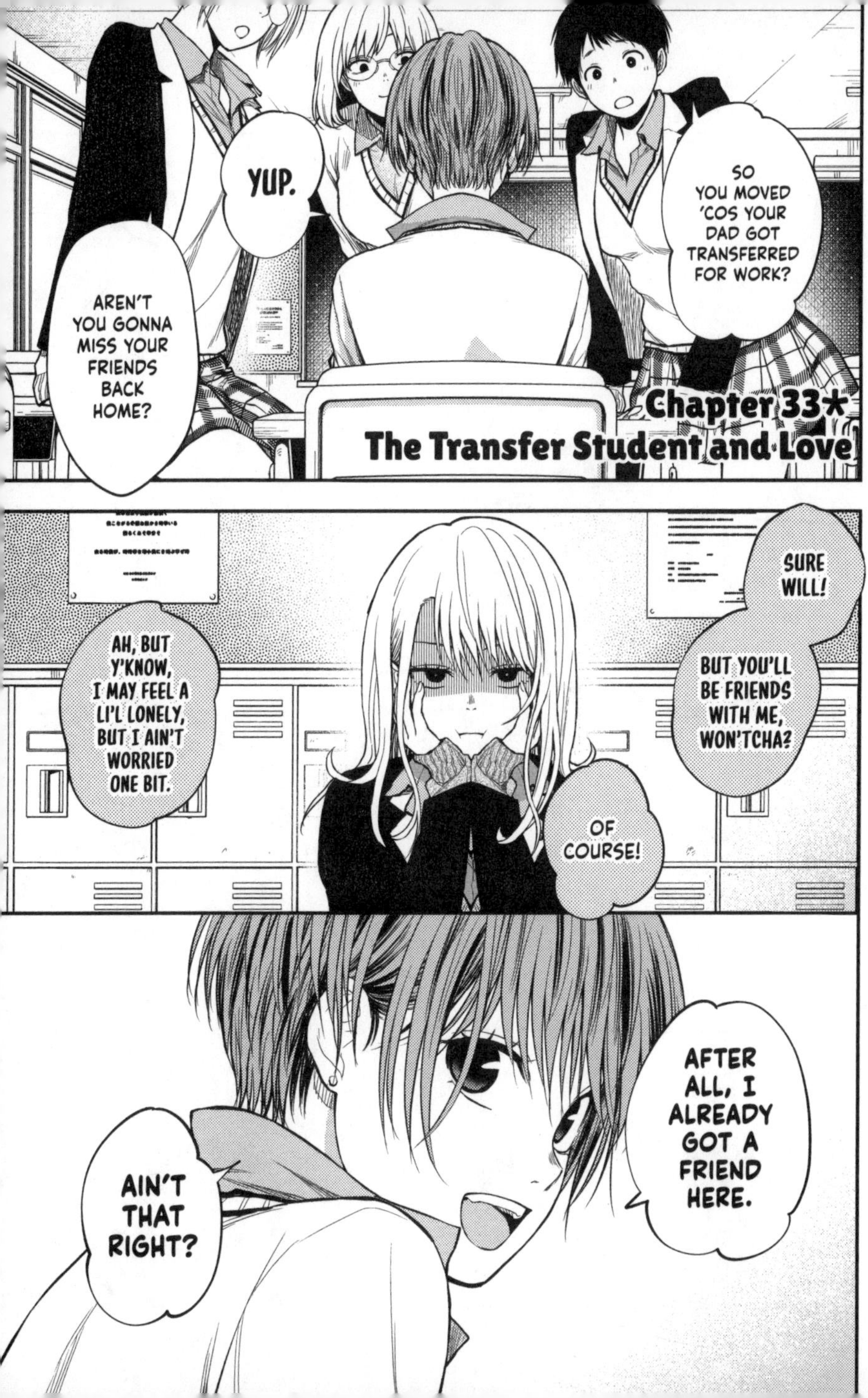
SO YOU MOVED 'COS YOUR DAD GOT TRANSFERRED FOR WORK?
YUP.
AREN'T YOU GONNA MISS YOUR FRIENDS BACK HOME?
Chapter 33★ The Transfer Student and Love
SURE WILL!
BUT YOU'LL BE FRIENDS WITH ME, WON'TCHA?
OF COURSE!
AH, BUT Y'KNOW, I MAY FEEL A LI'L LONELY, BUT I AIN'T WORRIED ONE BIT.
AFTER ALL, I ALREADY GOT A FRIEND HERE.
AIN'T THAT RIGHT?

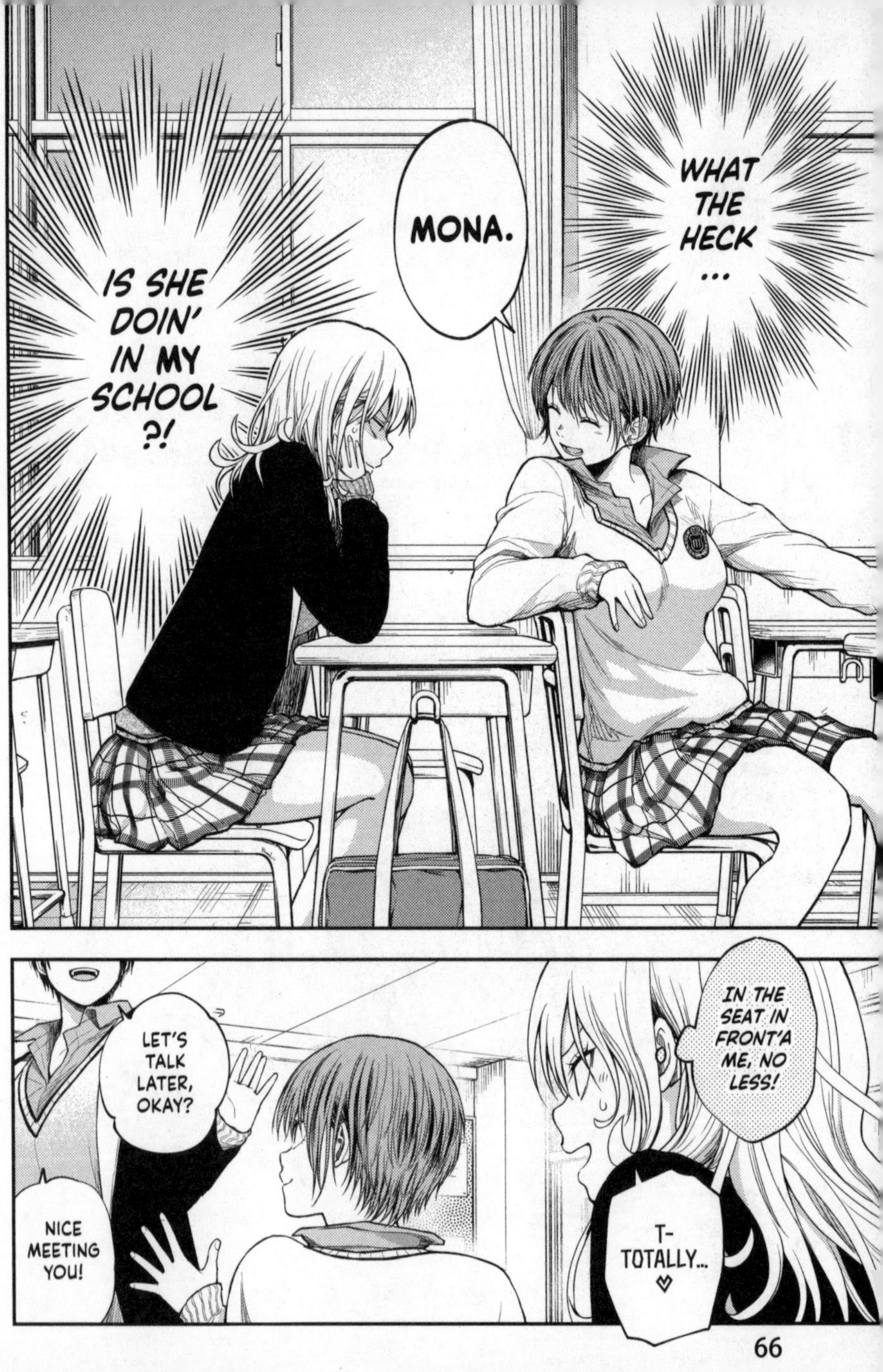
WHAT THE HECK ...
MONA.
IS SHE DOIN' IN MY SCHOOL ?!
IN THE SEAT IN FRONT'A ME, NO LESS!
LET'S TALK LATER, OKAY?
NICE MEETING YOU!
T-TOTALLY... ♡

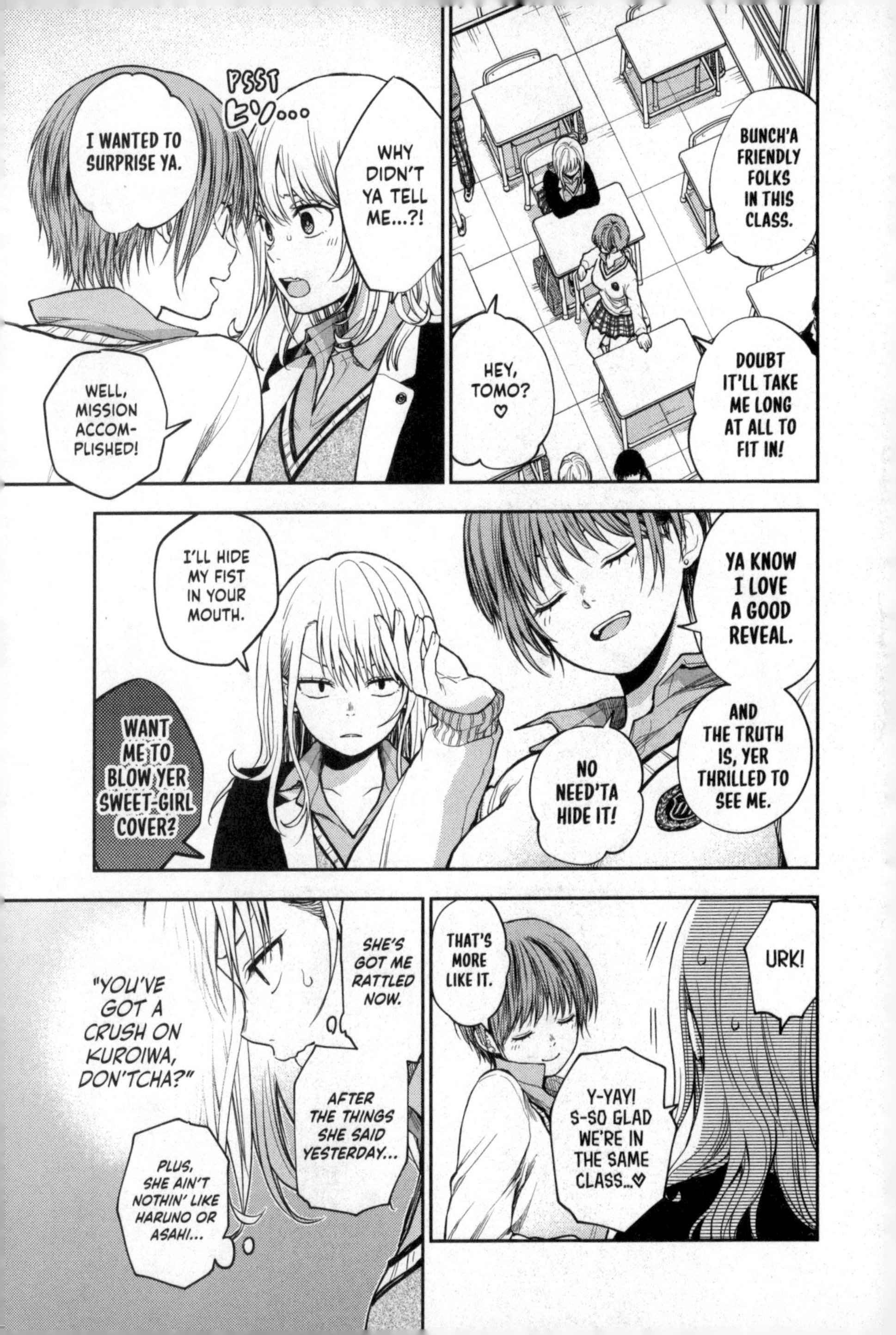
BUNCH'A FRIENDLY FOLKS IN THIS CLASS.
DOUBT IT'LL TAKE ME LONG AT ALL TO FIT IN!
HEY, TOMO? ♡
PSST
WHY DIDN'T YA TELL ME...?!
I WANTED TO SURPRISE YA.
WELL, MISSION ACCOMPLISHED!
YA KNOW I LOVE A GOOD REVEAL.
AND THE TRUTH IS, YER THRILLED TO SEE ME.
NO NEED'TA HIDE IT!
I'LL HIDE MY FIST IN YOUR MOUTH.
WANT ME TO BLOW YER SWEET-GIRL COVER?
URK!
THAT'S MORE LIKE IT.
Y-YAY! S-SO GLAD WE'RE IN THE SAME CLASS...♡
SHE'S GOT ME RATTLED NOW.
"YOU'VE GOT A CRUSH ON KUROIWA, DON'TCHA?"
AFTER THE THINGS SHE SAID YESTERDAY...
PLUS, SHE AIN'T NOTHIN' LIKE HARUNO OR ASAHI...

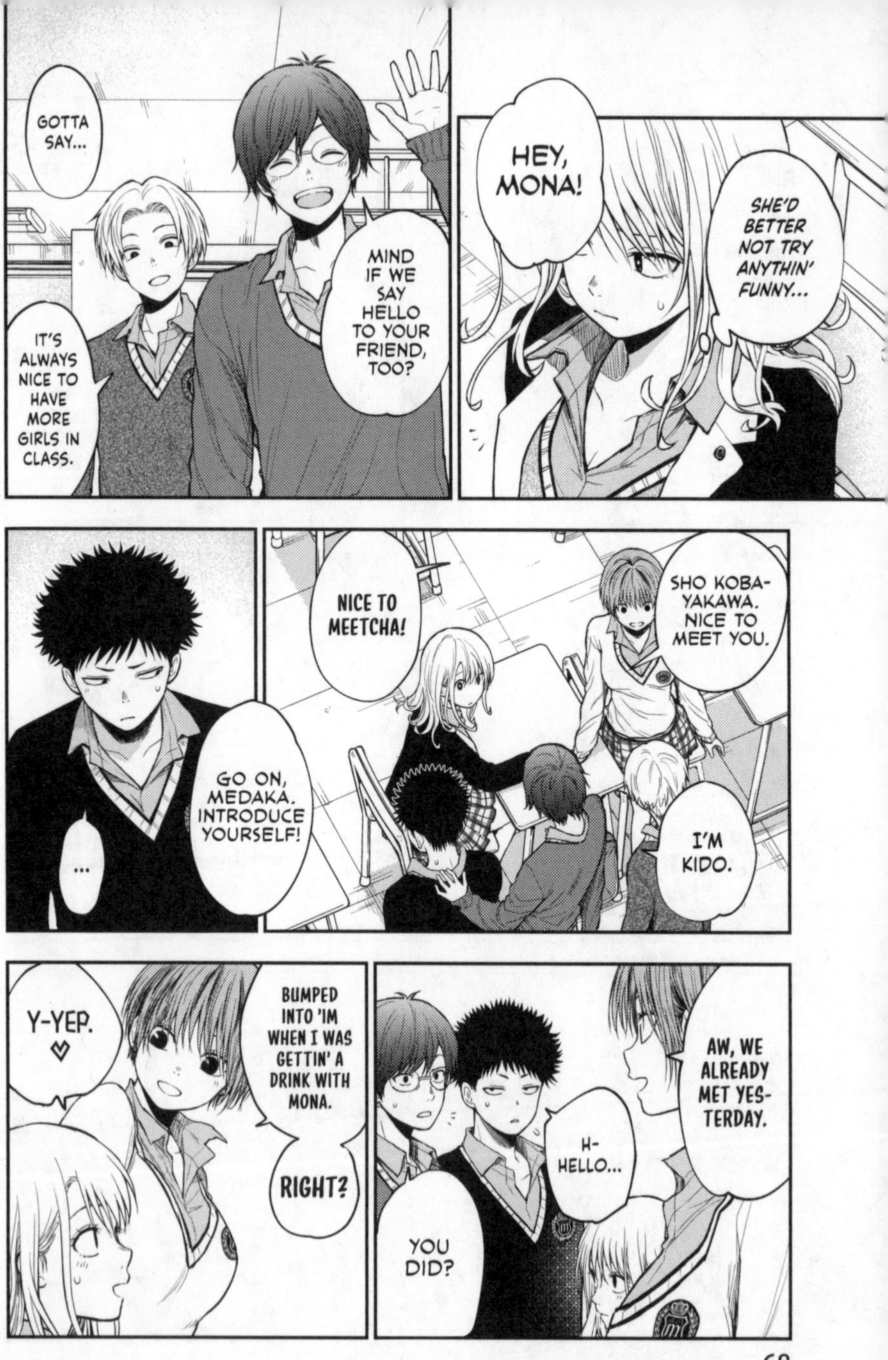
HEY, MONA!
SHE'D BETTER NOT TRY ANYTHIN' FUNNY...
MIND IF WE SAY HELLO TO YOUR FRIEND, TOO?
GOTTA SAY...
IT'S ALWAYS NICE TO HAVE MORE GIRLS IN CLASS.
SHO KOBA-YAKAWA. NICE TO MEET YOU.
NICE TO MEETCHA!
I'M KIDO.
GO ON, MEDAKA. INTRODUCE YOURSELF!
...
AW, WE ALREADY MET YES-TERDAY.
H-HELLO...
YOU DID?
BUMPED INTO 'IM WHEN I WAS GETTIN' A DRINK WITH MONA.
RIGHT?
Y-YEP. ♡

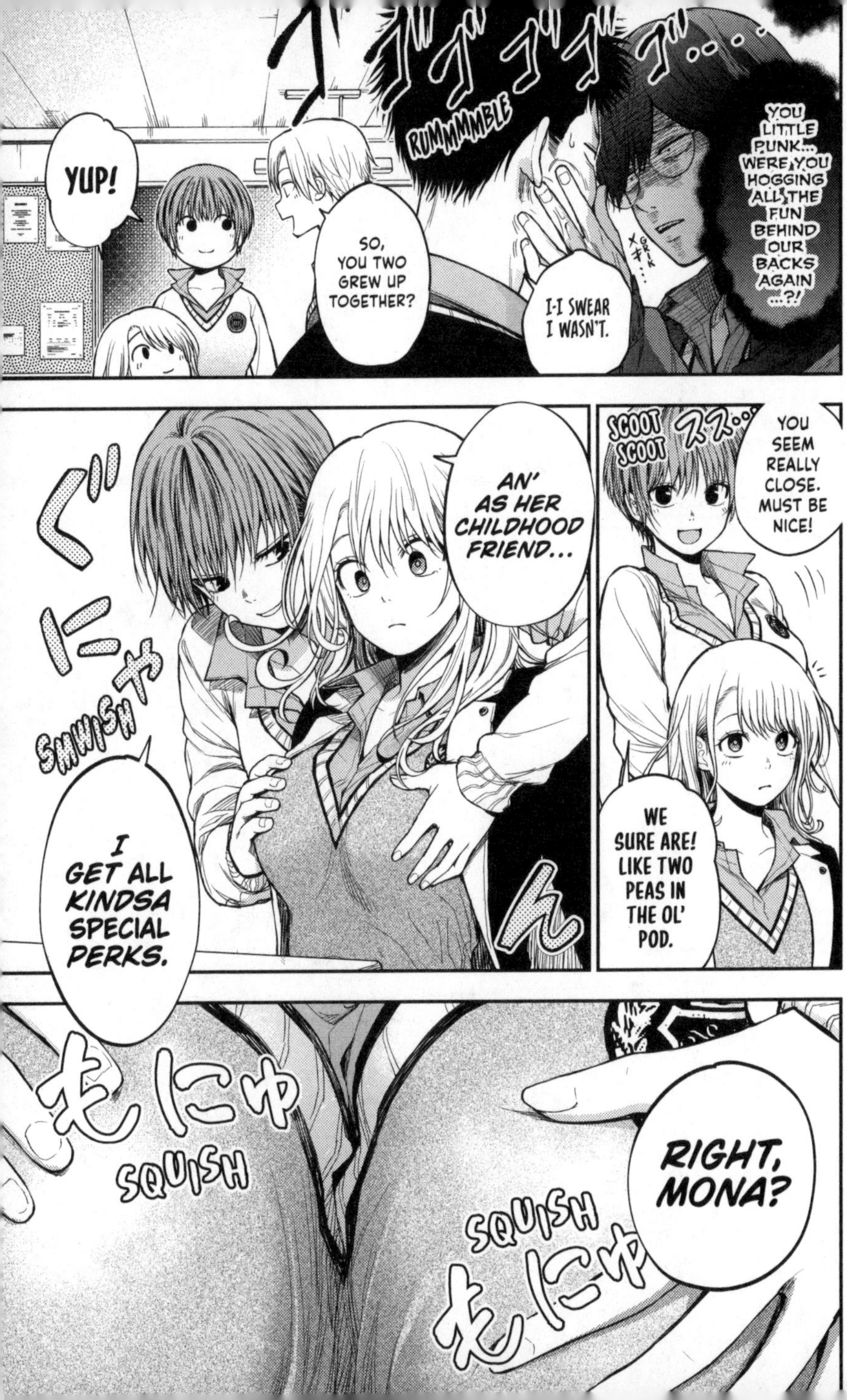
RUMMMMBLE
YOU LITTLE PUNK... WERE YOU HOGGING ALL THE FUN BEHIND OUR BACKS AGAIN...?!
GRIK
I-I SWEAR I WASN'T.
SO, YOU TWO GREW UP TOGETHER?
YUP!
SCOOT SCOOT
スス…
YOU SEEM REALLY CLOSE. MUST BE NICE!
WE SURE ARE! LIKE TWO PEAS IN THE OL' POD.
AN' AS HER CHILDHOOD FRIEND...
SMWISH
I GET ALL KINDSA SPECIAL PERKS.
RIGHT, MONA?
もにゅ
SQUISH
もにゅ
SQUISH

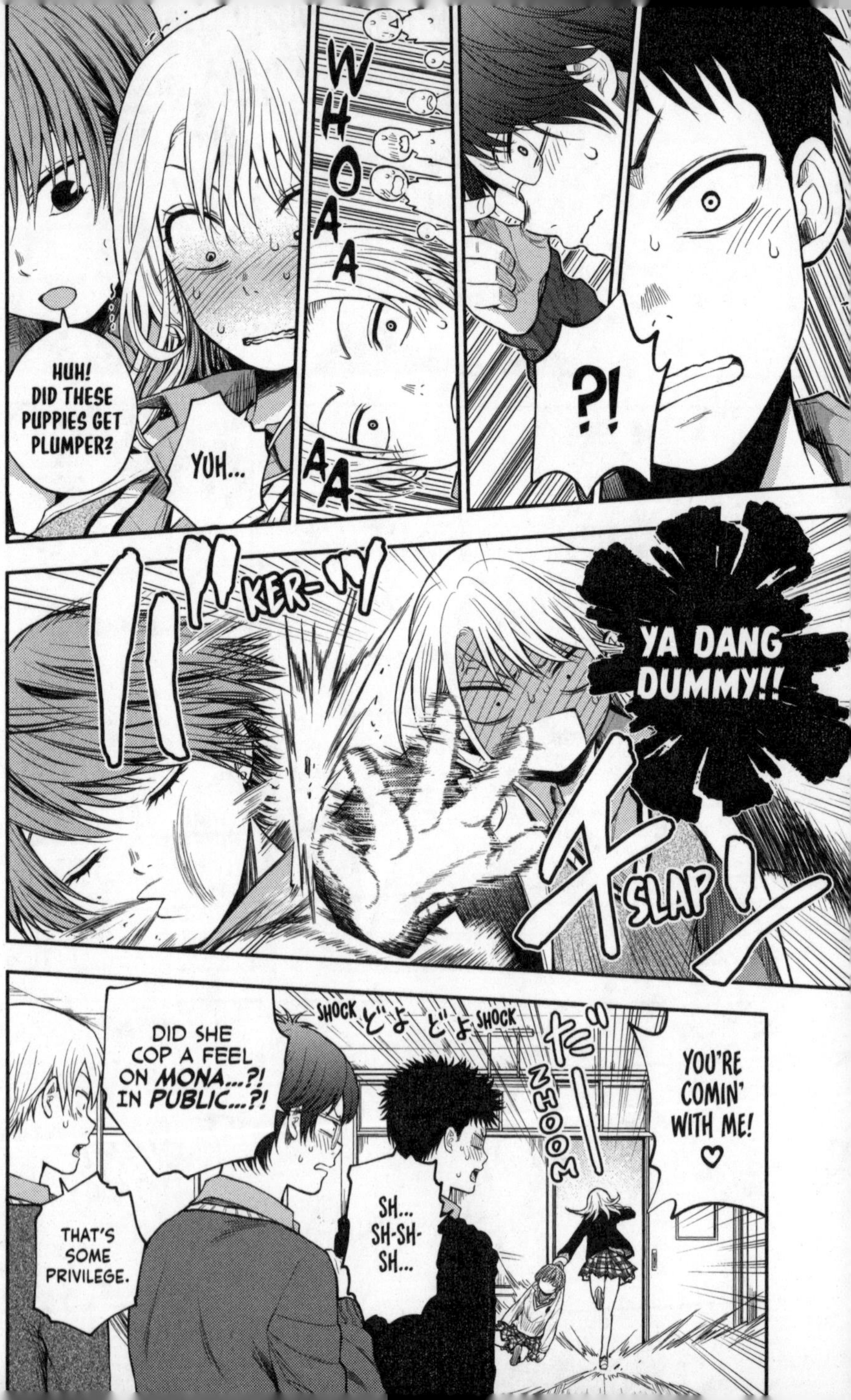
?!
WHOA
AA
HUH! DID THESE PUPPIES GET PLUMPER?
YUH...
YA DANG DUMMY!!
KER-
SLAP
YOU'RE COMIN' WITH ME! ♡
SHOCK どよ どよ SHOCK
だー
ZHOOM
SH... SH-SH-SH...
DID SHE COP A FEEL ON *MONA*...?! IN *PUBLIC*...?!
THAT'S SOME PRIVILEGE.

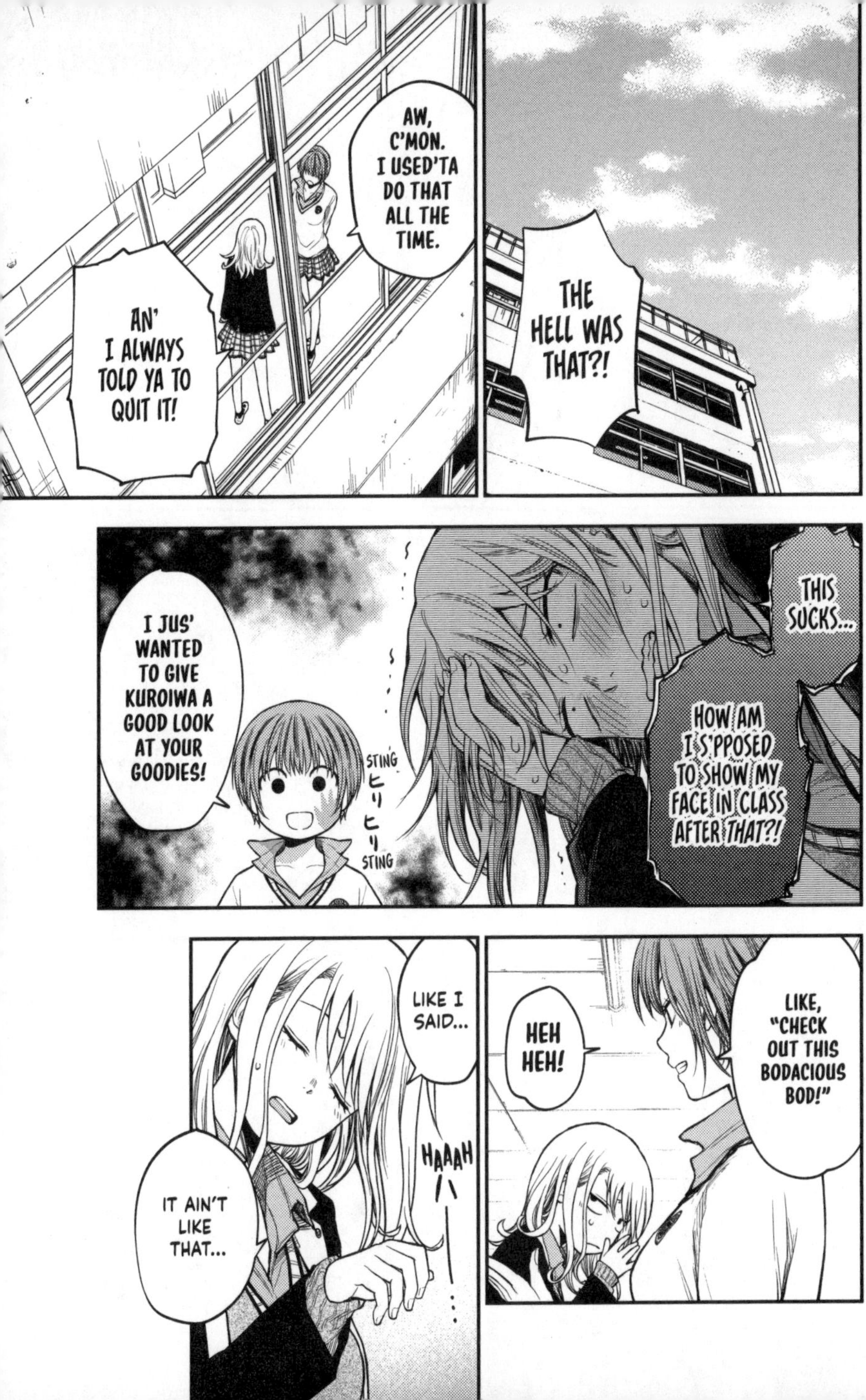
THE HELL WAS THAT?!
AW, C'MON. I USED'TA DO THAT ALL THE TIME.
AN' I ALWAYS TOLD YA TO QUIT IT!
THIS SUCKS...
HOW AM I S'PPOSED TO SHOW MY FACE IN CLASS AFTER THAT?!
STING ヒリ
ヒリ STING
I JUS' WANTED TO GIVE KUROIWA A GOOD LOOK AT YOUR GOODIES!
LIKE, "CHECK OUT THIS BODACIOUS BOD!"
HEH HEH!
LIKE I SAID...
HAAAH ハ
IT AIN'T LIKE THAT...

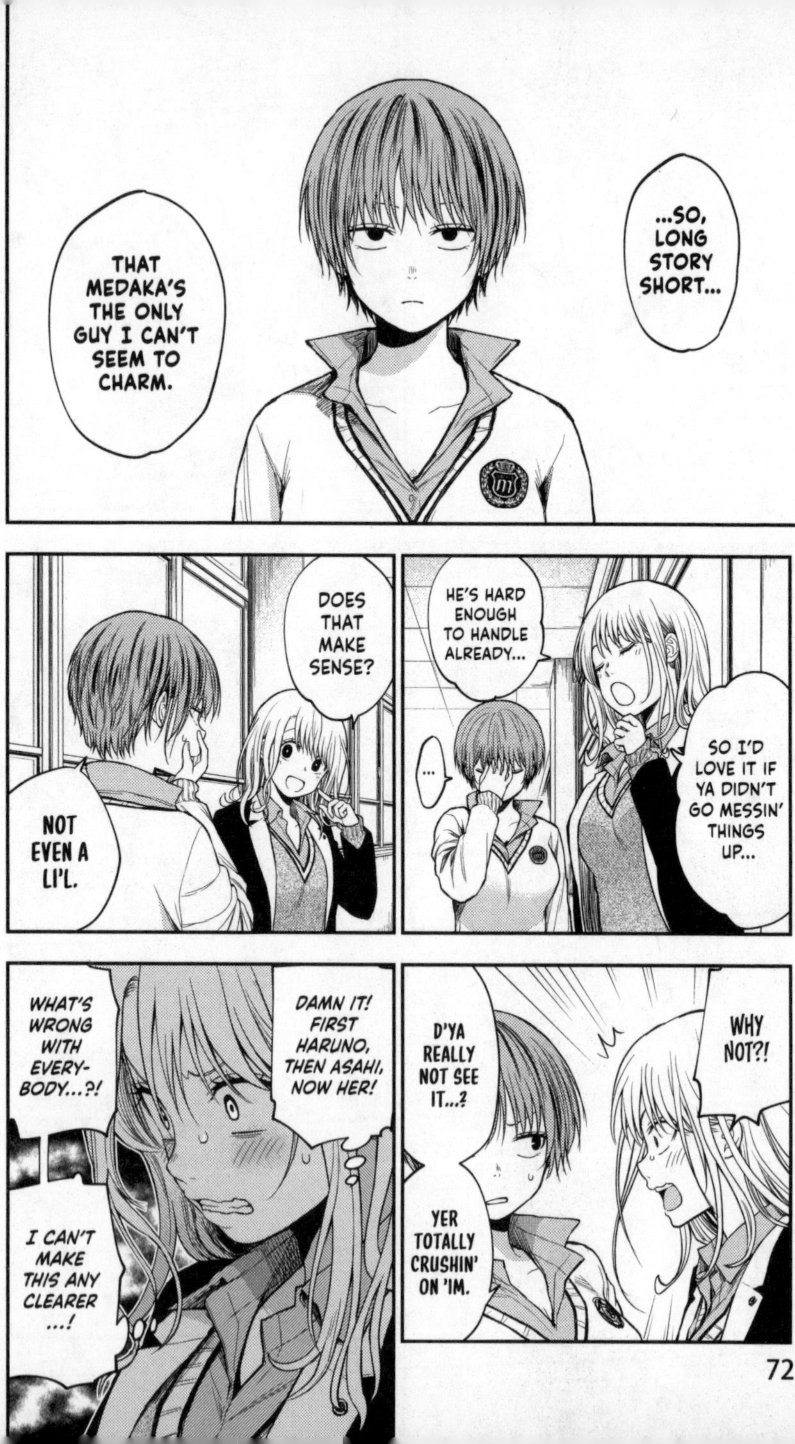

...SO, LONG STORY SHORT...
THAT MEDAKA'S THE ONLY GUY I CAN'T SEEM TO CHARM.
HE'S HARD ENOUGH TO HANDLE ALREADY...
...
SO I'D LOVE IT IF YA DIDN'T GO MESSIN' THINGS UP...
DOES THAT MAKE SENSE?
NOT EVEN A LI'L.
WHY NOT?!
D'YA REALLY NOT SEE IT...?
YER TOTALLY CRUSHIN' ON 'IM.
DAMN IT! FIRST HARUNO, THEN ASAHI, NOW HER!
WHAT'S WRONG WITH EVERY-BODY...?!
I CAN'T MAKE THIS ANY CLEARER...!

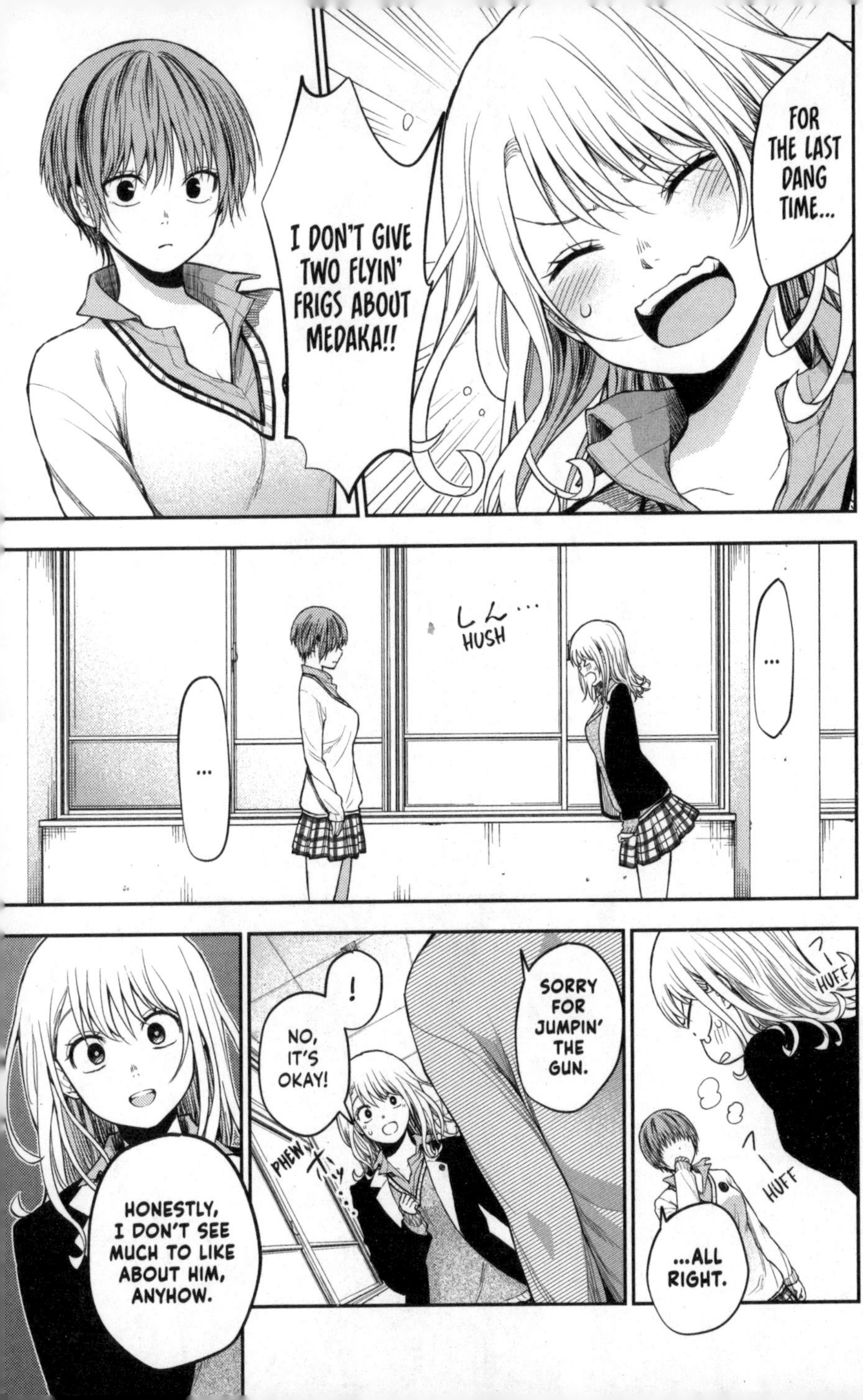
FOR THE LAST DANG TIME...
I DON'T GIVE TWO FLYIN' FRIGS ABOUT MEDAKA!!
...
しん…
HUSH
...
HUFF
HUFF
...ALL RIGHT.
SORRY FOR JUMPIN' THE GUN.
!
NO, IT'S OKAY!
PHEW
HONESTLY, I DON'T SEE MUCH TO LIKE ABOUT HIM, ANYHOW.

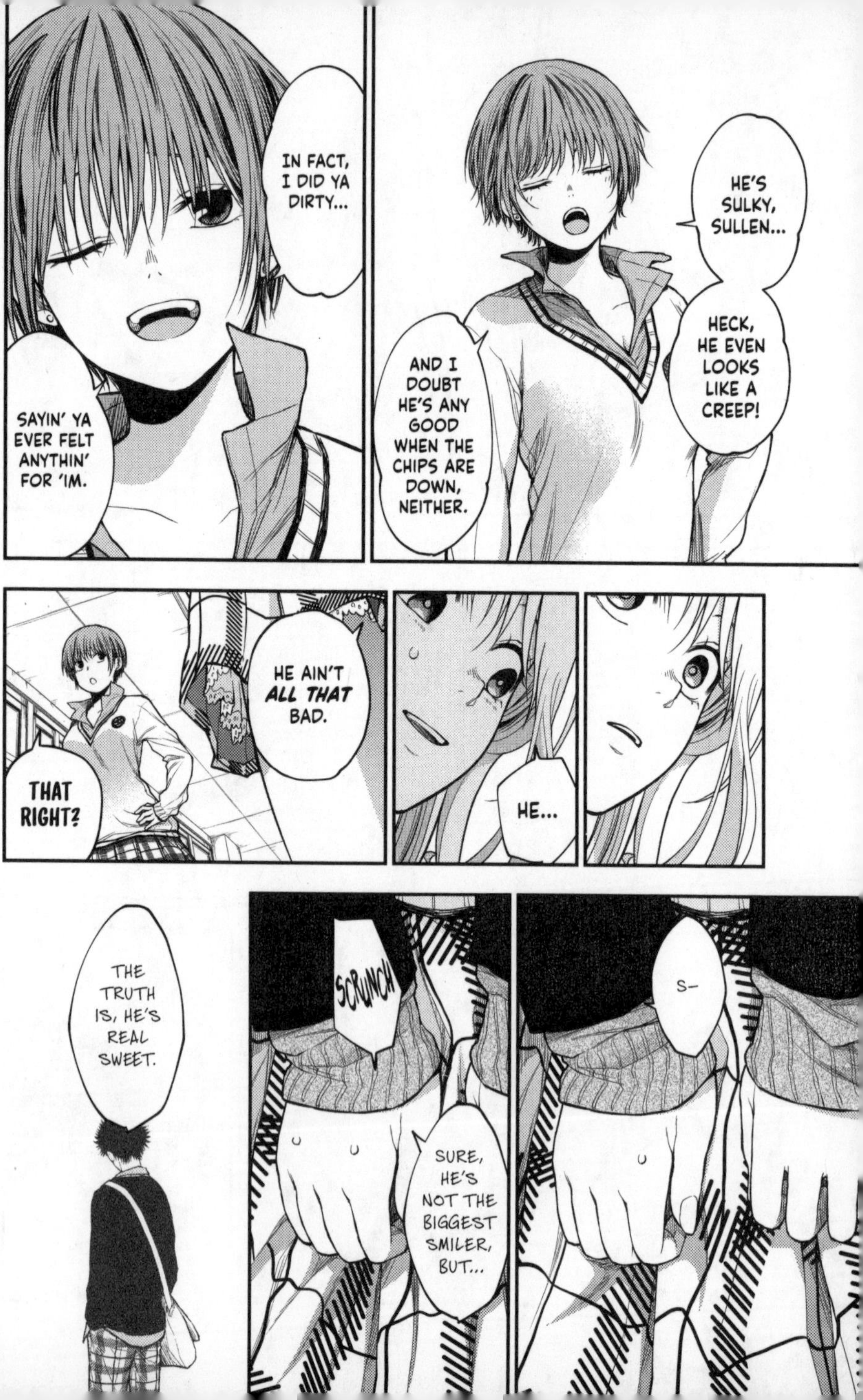
HE'S SULKY, SULLEN...
HECK, HE EVEN LOOKS LIKE A CREEP!
AND I DOUBT HE'S ANY GOOD WHEN THE CHIPS ARE DOWN, NEITHER.
IN FACT, I DID YA DIRTY...
SAYIN' YA EVER FELT ANYTHIN' FOR 'IM.
HE...
HE AIN'T ALL THAT BAD.
THAT RIGHT?
S-
SCRUNCH
SURE, HE'S NOT THE BIGGEST SMILER, BUT...
THE TRUTH IS, HE'S REAL SWEET.

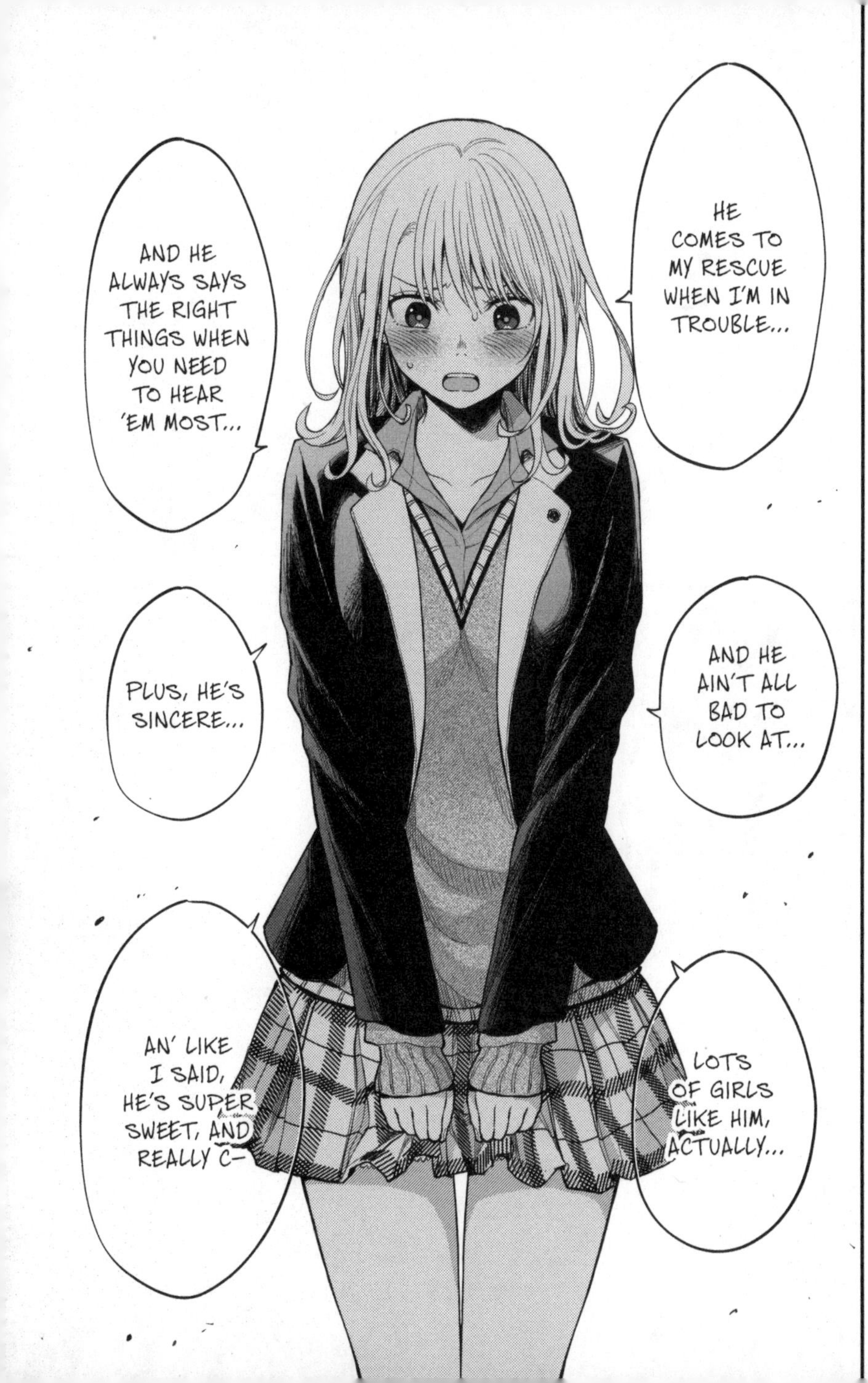
HE COMES TO MY RESCUE WHEN I'M IN TROUBLE...
AND HE ALWAYS SAYS THE RIGHT THINGS WHEN YOU NEED TO HEAR 'EM MOST...
AND HE AIN'T ALL BAD TO LOOK AT...
PLUS, HE'S SINCERE...
LOTS OF GIRLS LIKE HIM, ACTUALLY...
AN' LIKE I SAID, HE'S SUPER SWEET, AND REALLY C-

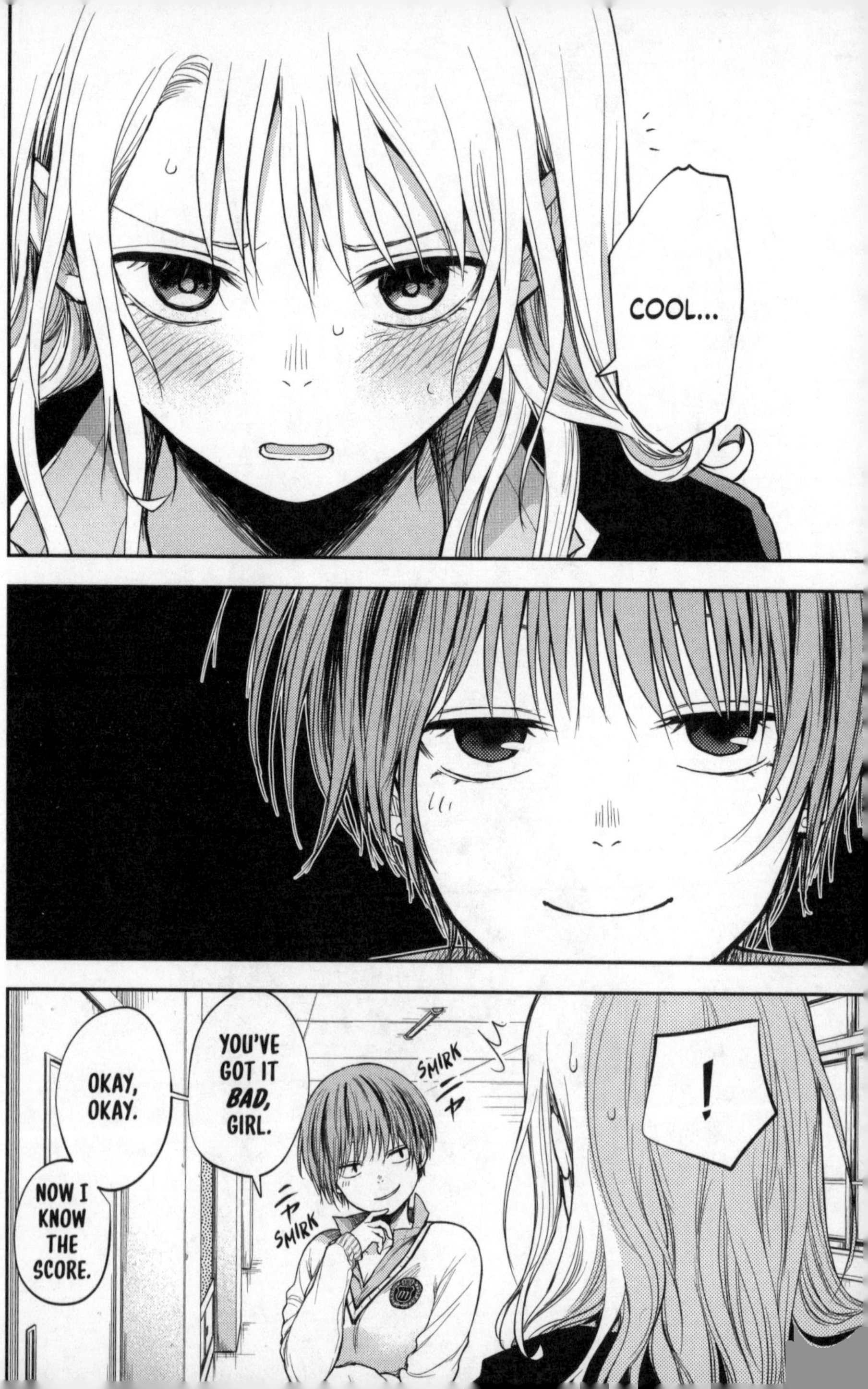
COOL...
!
ニヤ SMIRK
YOU'VE GOT IT *BAD,* GIRL.
OKAY, OKAY.
NOW I KNOW THE SCORE.
ニヤ SMIRK

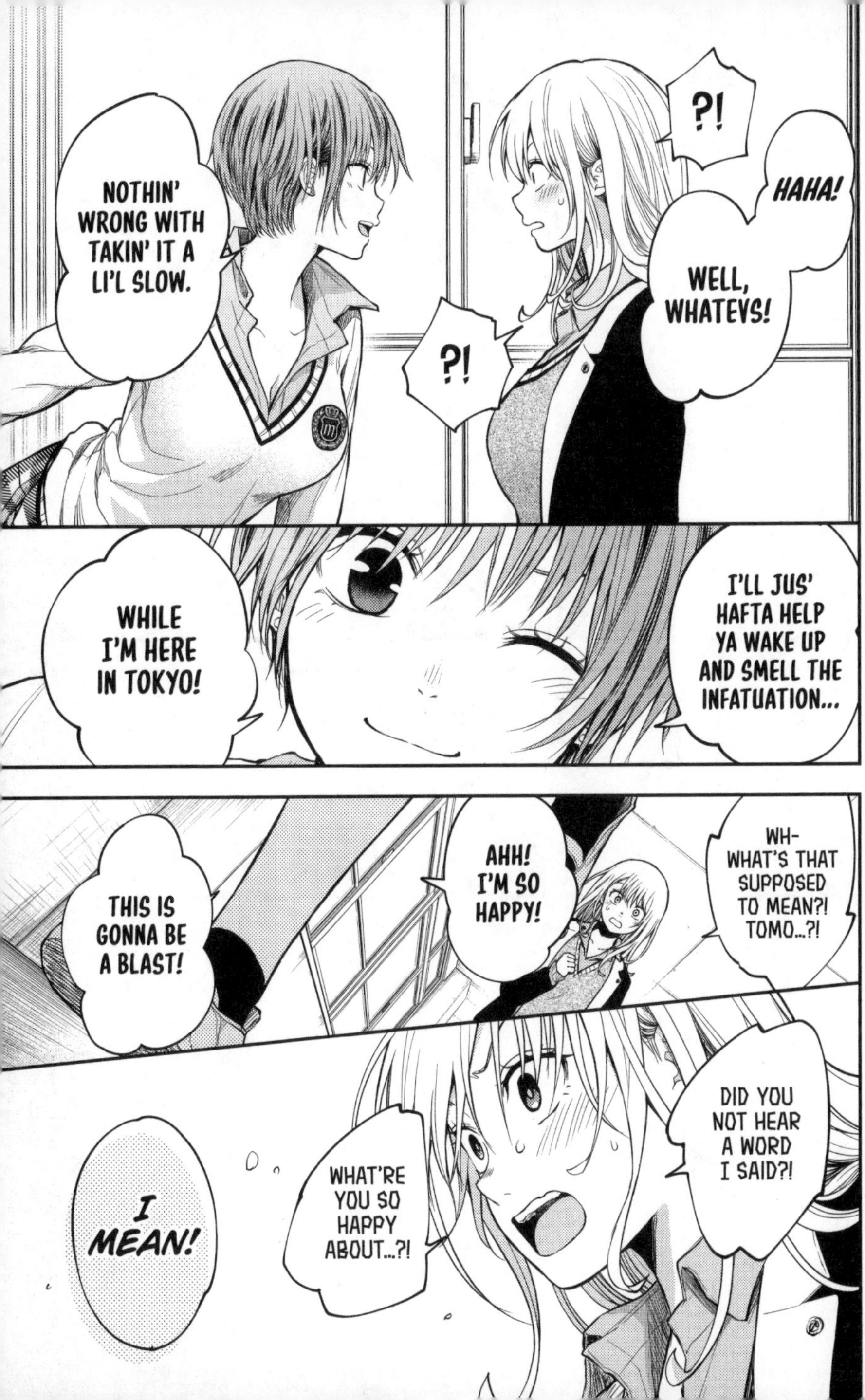
?!
HAHA!
WELL, WHATEVS!
?!
NOTHIN' WRONG WITH TAKIN' IT A LI'L SLOW.
I'LL JUS' HAFTA HELP YA WAKE UP AND SMELL THE INFATUATION...
WHILE I'M HERE IN TOKYO!
WH- WHAT'S THAT SUPPOSED TO MEAN?! TOMO...?!
AHH! I'M SO HAPPY!
THIS IS GONNA BE A BLAST!
DID YOU NOT HEAR A WORD I SAID?!
WHAT'RE YOU SO HAPPY ABOUT...?!
I MEAN!

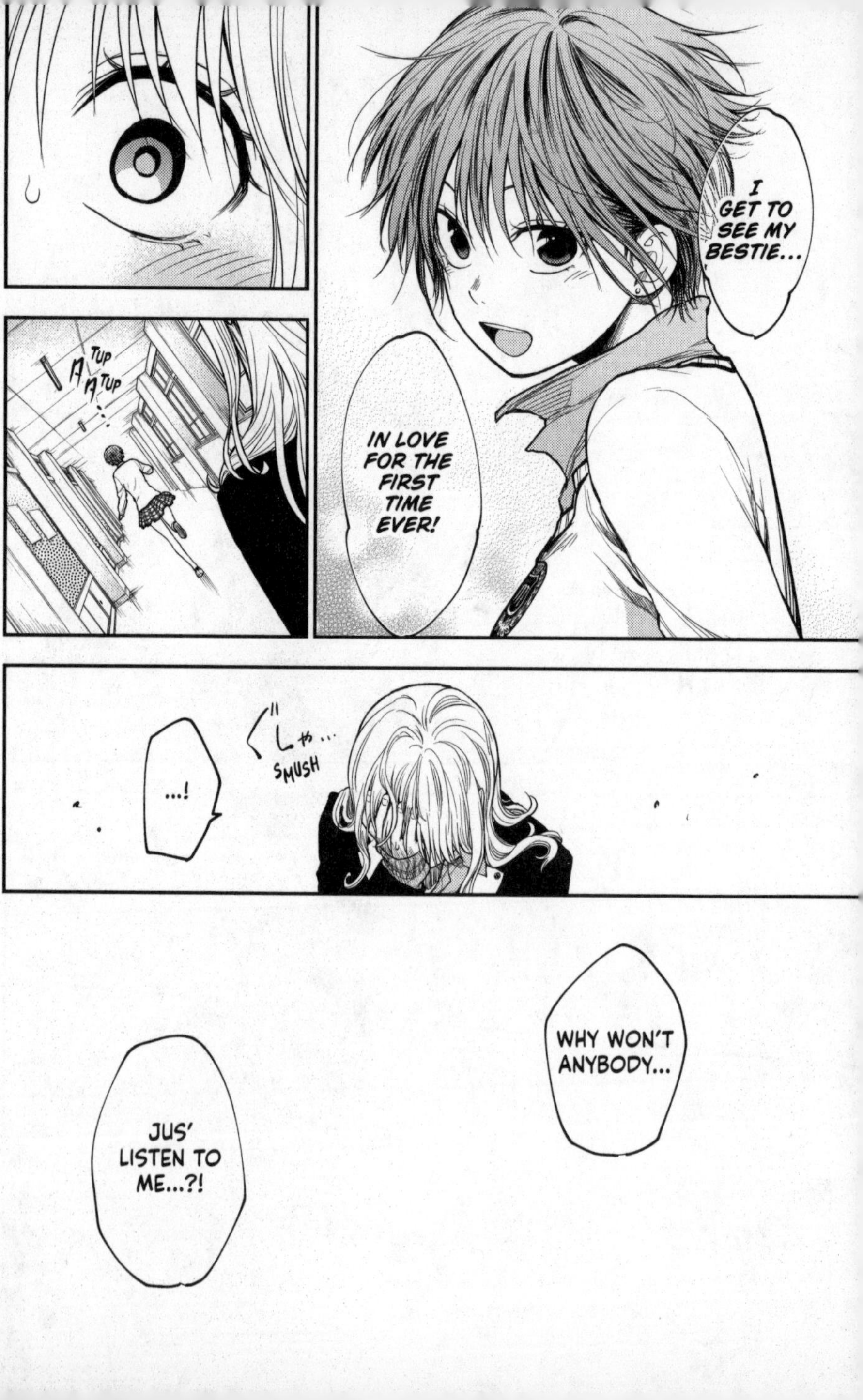
I GET TO SEE MY BESTIE…
IN LOVE FOR THE FIRST TIME EVER!
TUP TUP
ぐしゃ…
SMUSH
…!
WHY WON'T ANYBODY…
JUS' LISTEN TO ME…?!

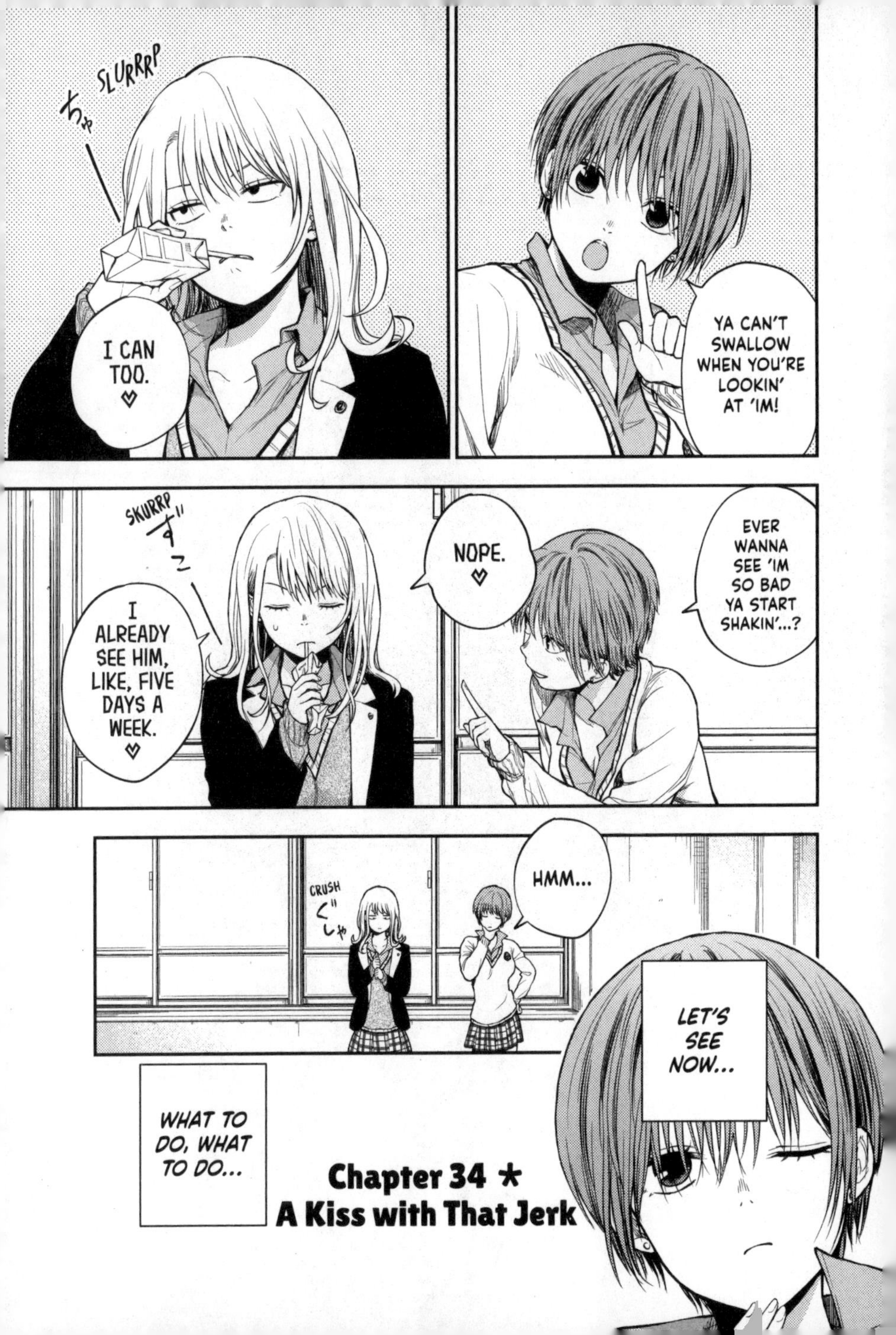
YA CAN'T SWALLOW WHEN YOU'RE LOOKIN' AT 'IM!
SLURRRP
ちゅ
I CAN TOO. ♡
EVER WANNA SEE 'IM SO BAD YA START SHAKIN'...?
NOPE. ♡
SKURRP
ずこ
I ALREADY SEE HIM, LIKE, FIVE DAYS A WEEK. ♡
HMM...
CRUSH
ぐしゃ
LET'S SEE NOW...
WHAT TO DO, WHAT TO DO...

Chapter 34 ★ A Kiss with That Jerk

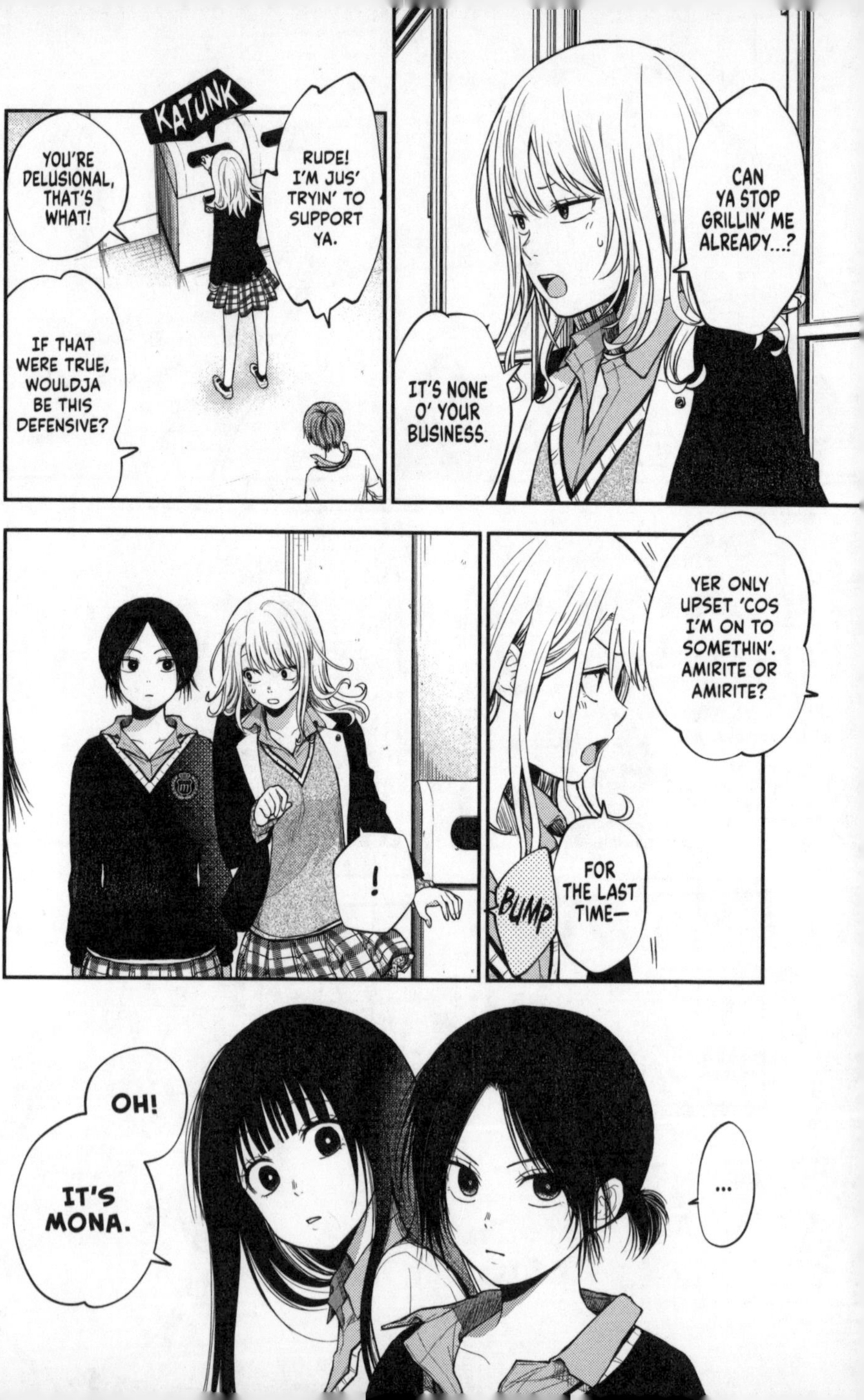
CAN YA STOP GRILLIN' ME ALREADY...?
IT'S NONE O' YOUR BUSINESS.
KATUNK
RUDE! I'M JUS' TRYIN' TO SUPPORT YA.
YOU'RE DELUSIONAL, THAT'S WHAT!
IF THAT WERE TRUE, WOULDJA BE THIS DEFENSIVE?
YER ONLY UPSET 'COS I'M ON TO SOMETHIN'. AMIRITE OR AMIRITE?
FOR THE LAST TIME—
BUMP
!
...
OH!
IT'S MONA.

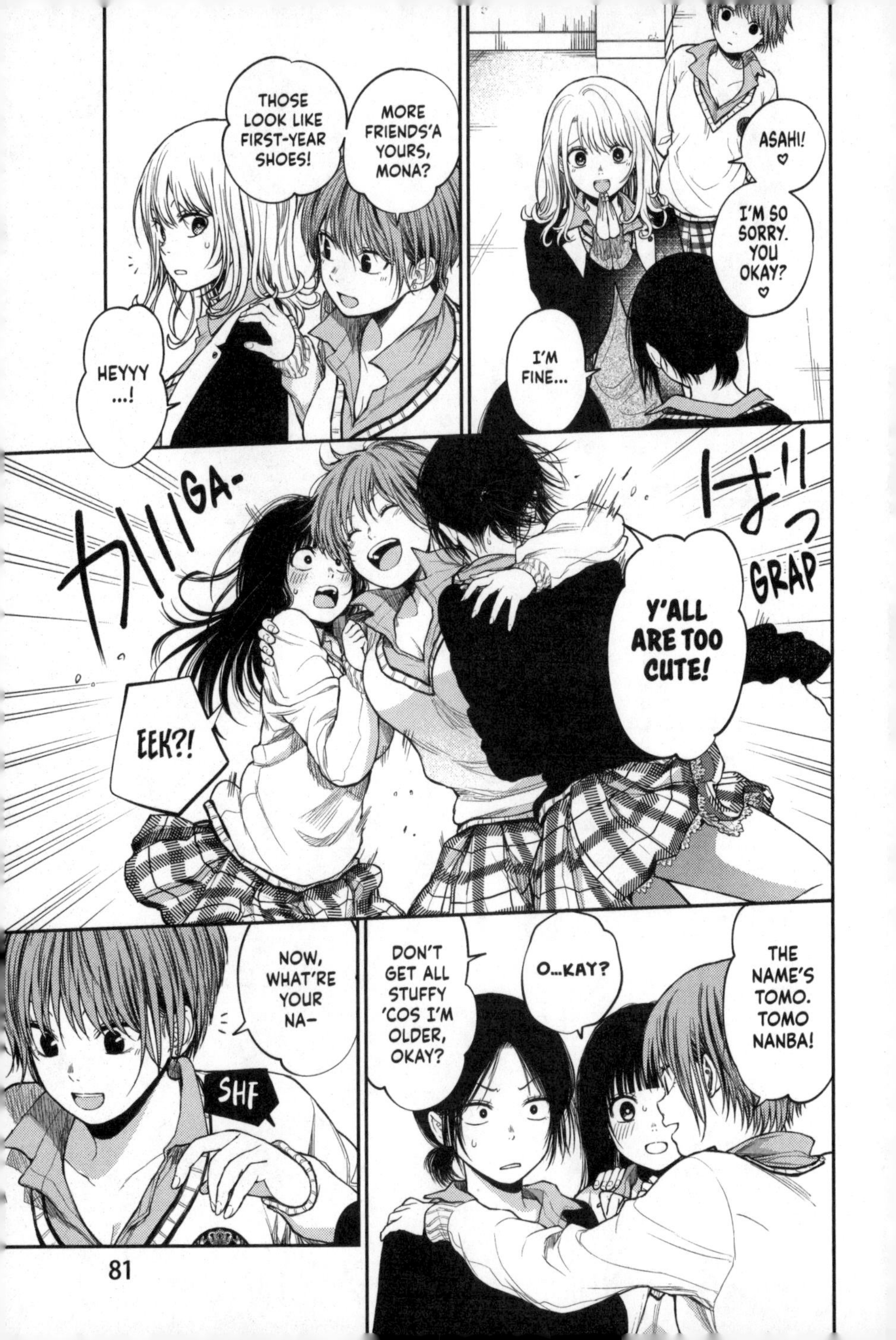
ASAHI! ♡
I'M SO SORRY. YOU OKAY? ♡
I'M FINE...
MORE FRIENDS'A YOURS, MONA?
THOSE LOOK LIKE FIRST-YEAR SHOES!
HEYYY ...!
はっ
GRAP
Y'ALL ARE TOO CUTE!
GA-
EEK?!
THE NAME'S TOMO. TOMO NANBA!
O...KAY?
DON'T GET ALL STUFFY 'COS I'M OLDER, OKAY?
NOW, WHAT'RE YOUR NA-
SHF

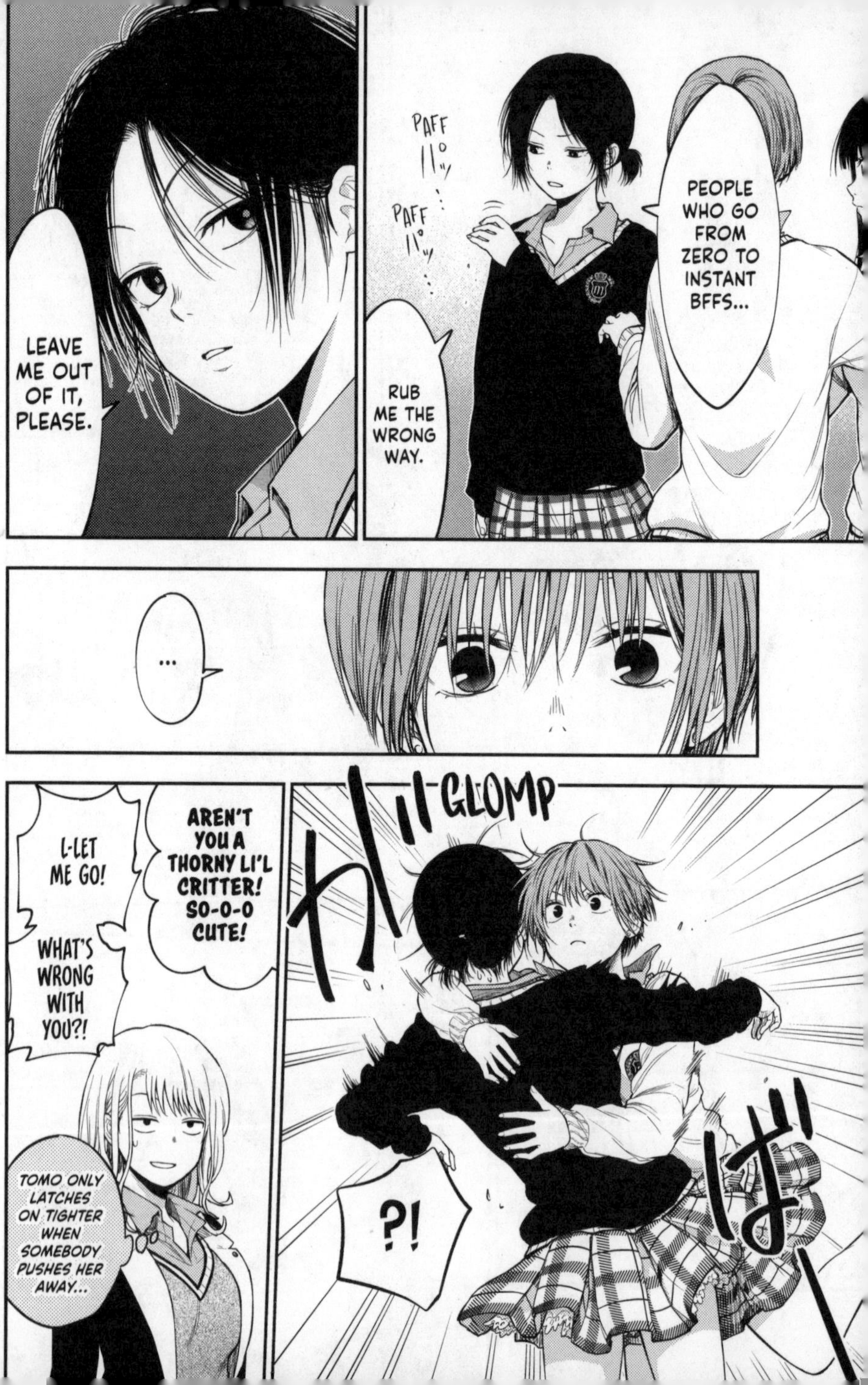
PEOPLE WHO GO FROM ZERO TO INSTANT BFFS...
PAFF
パッ
PAFF
パッ
RUB ME THE WRONG WAY.
LEAVE ME OUT OF IT, PLEASE.
...
GLOMP
?!
AREN'T YOU A THORNY LI'L CRITTER! SO-O-O CUTE!
L-LET ME GO!
WHAT'S WRONG WITH YOU?!
TOMO ONLY LATCHES ON TIGHTER WHEN SOMEBODY PUSHES HER AWAY...

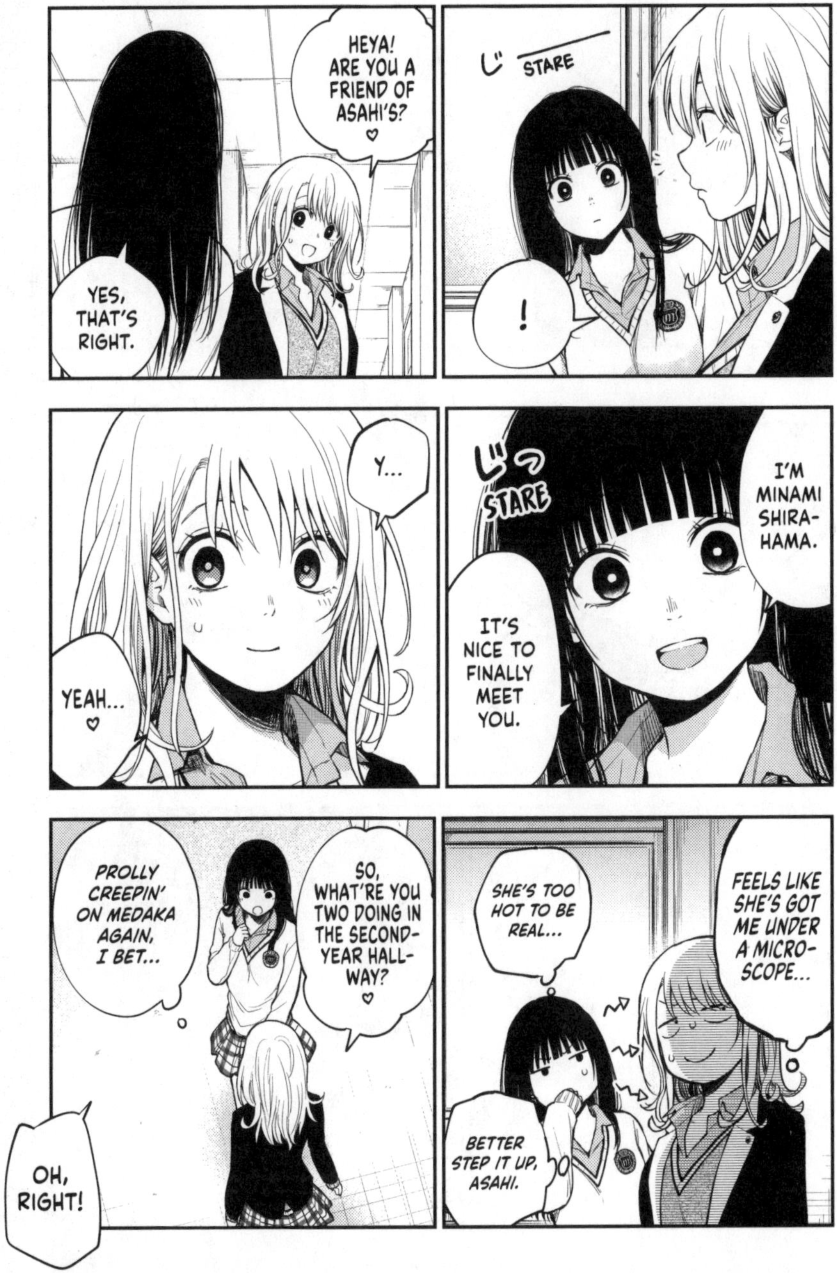

じ STARE
!
HEYA! ARE YOU A FRIEND OF ASAHI'S? ♡
YES, THAT'S RIGHT.
I'M MINAMI SHIRA-HAMA.
じっ STARE
IT'S NICE TO FINALLY MEET YOU.
Y...
YEAH... ♡
FEELS LIKE SHE'S GOT ME UNDER A MICRO-SCOPE...
SHE'S TOO HOT TO BE REAL...
BETTER STEP IT UP, ASAHI.
SO, WHAT'RE YOU TWO DOING IN THE SECOND-YEAR HALL-WAY? ♡
PROLLY CREEPIN' ON MEDAKA AGAIN, I BET...
OH, RIGHT!

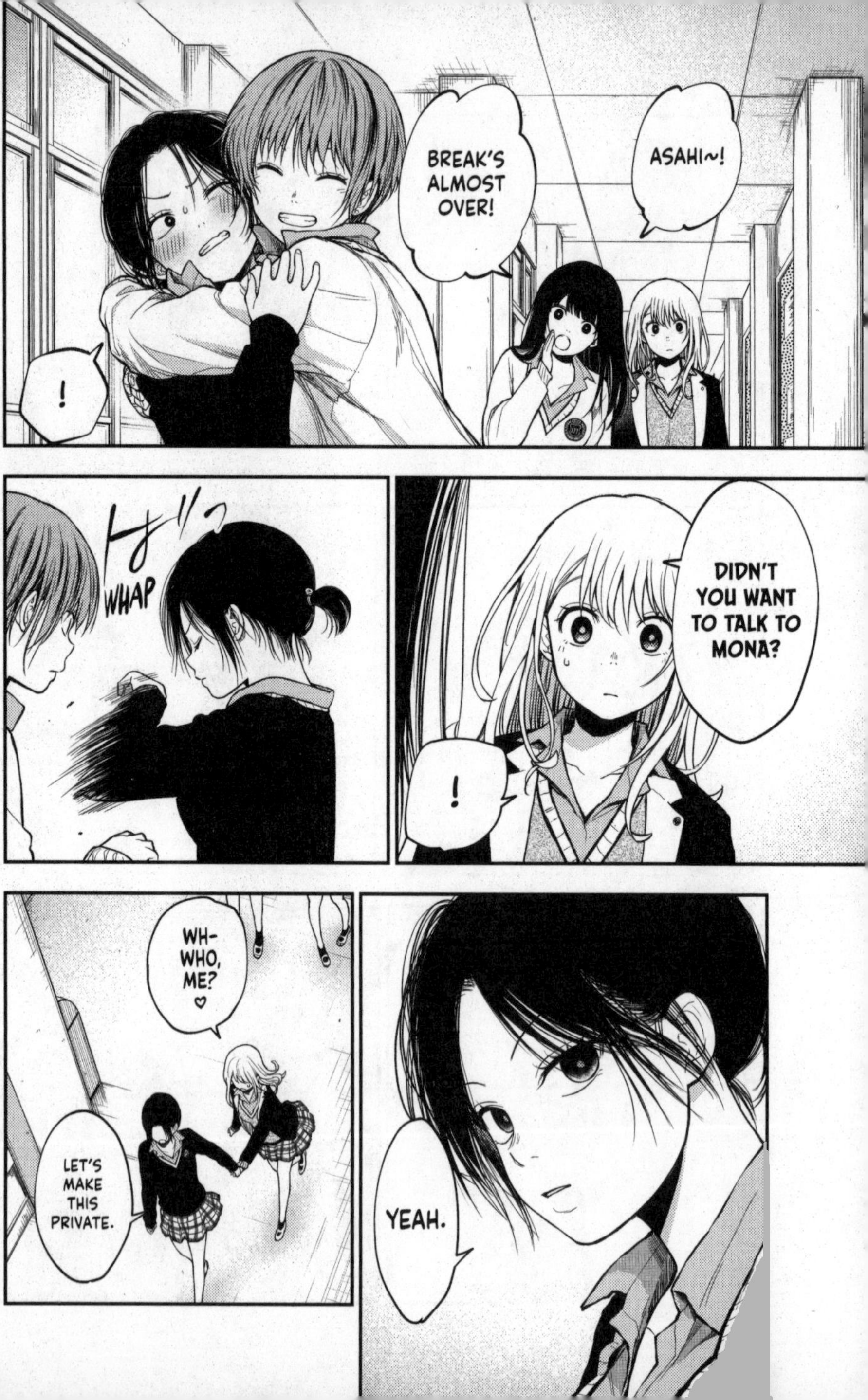
ASAHI~!
BREAK'S ALMOST OVER!
!
DIDN'T YOU WANT TO TALK TO MONA?
!
WHAP
YEAH.
WH- WHO, ME? ♡
LET'S MAKE THIS PRIVATE.

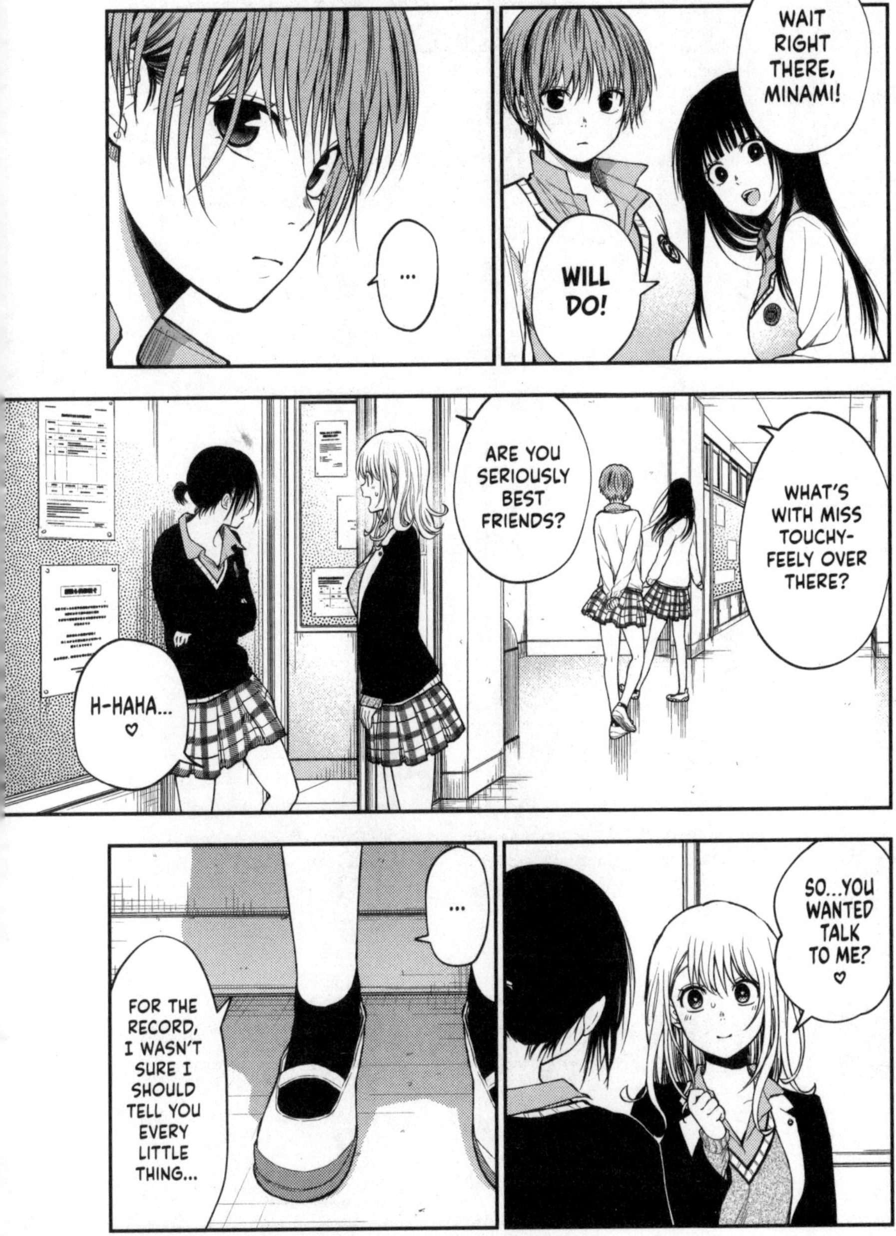
WAIT RIGHT THERE, MINAMI!
WILL DO!
...
WHAT'S WITH MISS TOUCHY-FEELY OVER THERE?
ARE YOU SERIOUSLY BEST FRIENDS?
H-HAHA... ♡
SO...YOU WANTED TALK TO ME? ♡
...
FOR THE RECORD, I WASN'T SURE I SHOULD TELL YOU EVERY LITTLE THING...

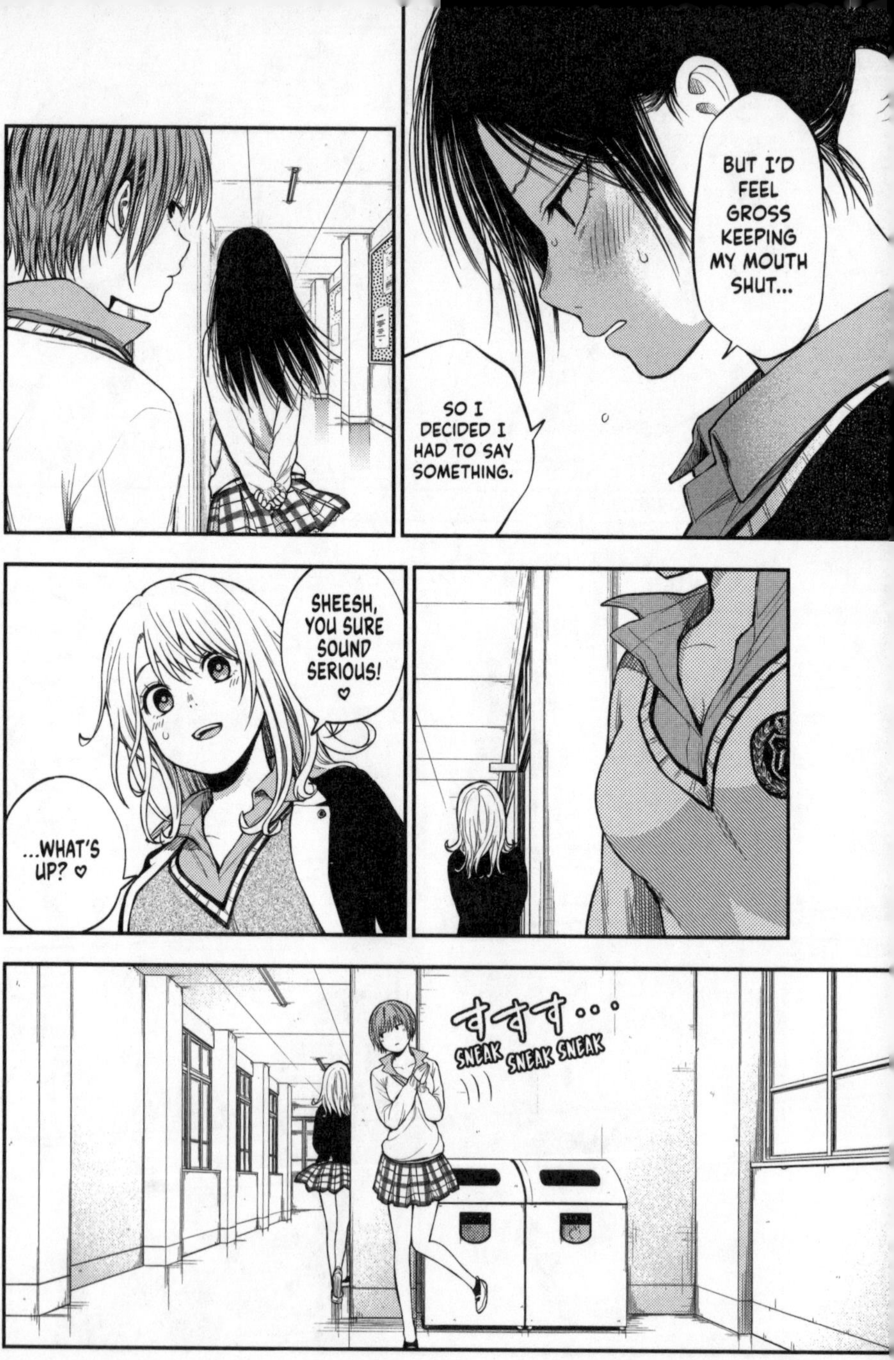
BUT I'D FEEL GROSS KEEPING MY MOUTH SHUT...
SO I DECIDED I HAD TO SAY SOMETHING.
SHEESH, YOU SURE SOUND SERIOUS! ♡
...WHAT'S UP? ♡
すすす…
SNEAK SNEAK SNEAK

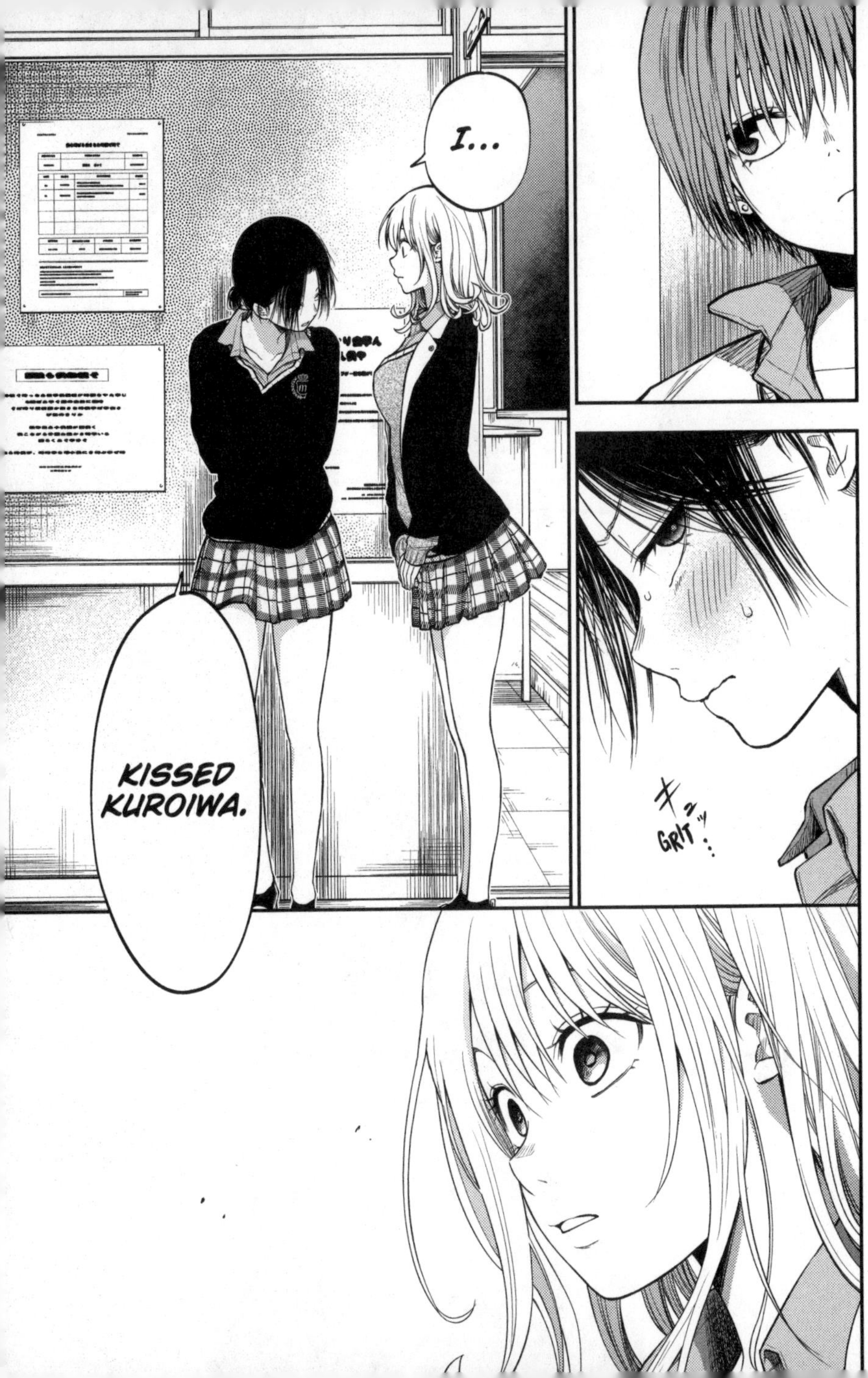
GRIT...
I...
KISSED KUROIWA.

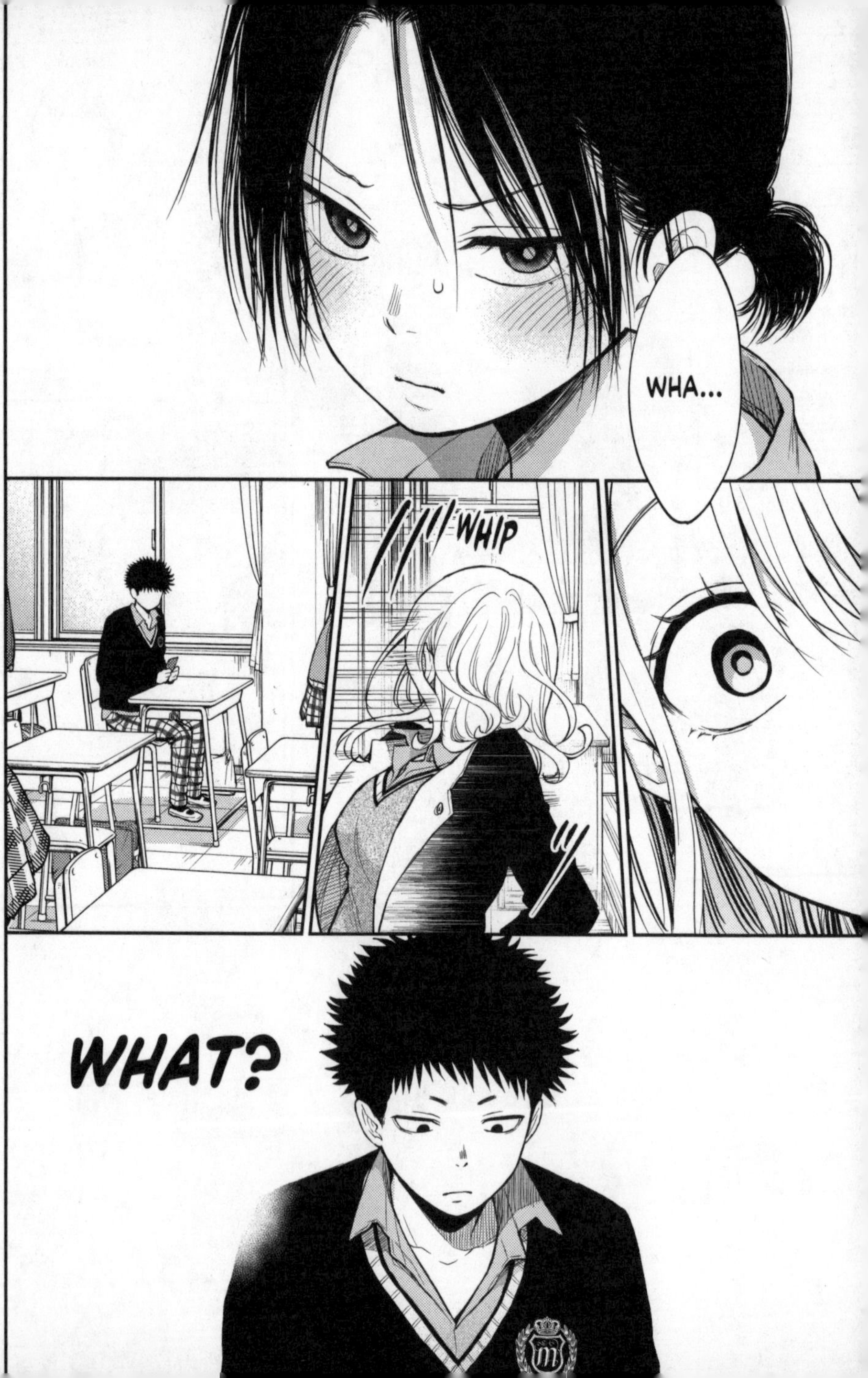
WHA...
WHIP
WHAT?

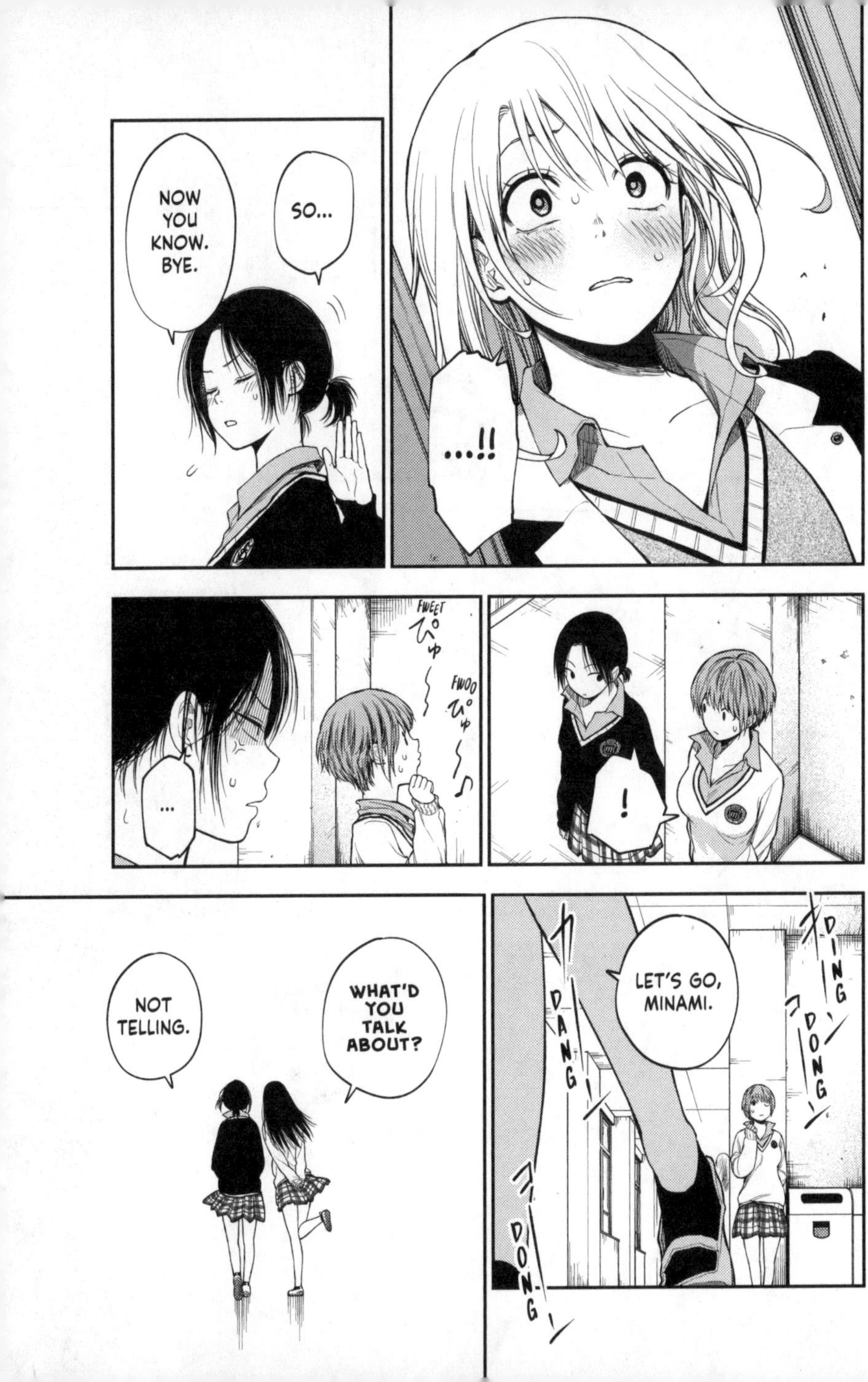
...!!
SO...
NOW YOU KNOW. BYE.
!
FWEET ぴゅ~
FWOO ぴゅ~♪
...
DING DONG
LET'S GO, MINAMI.
DANG
DONG
WHAT'D YOU TALK ABOUT?
NOT TELLING.

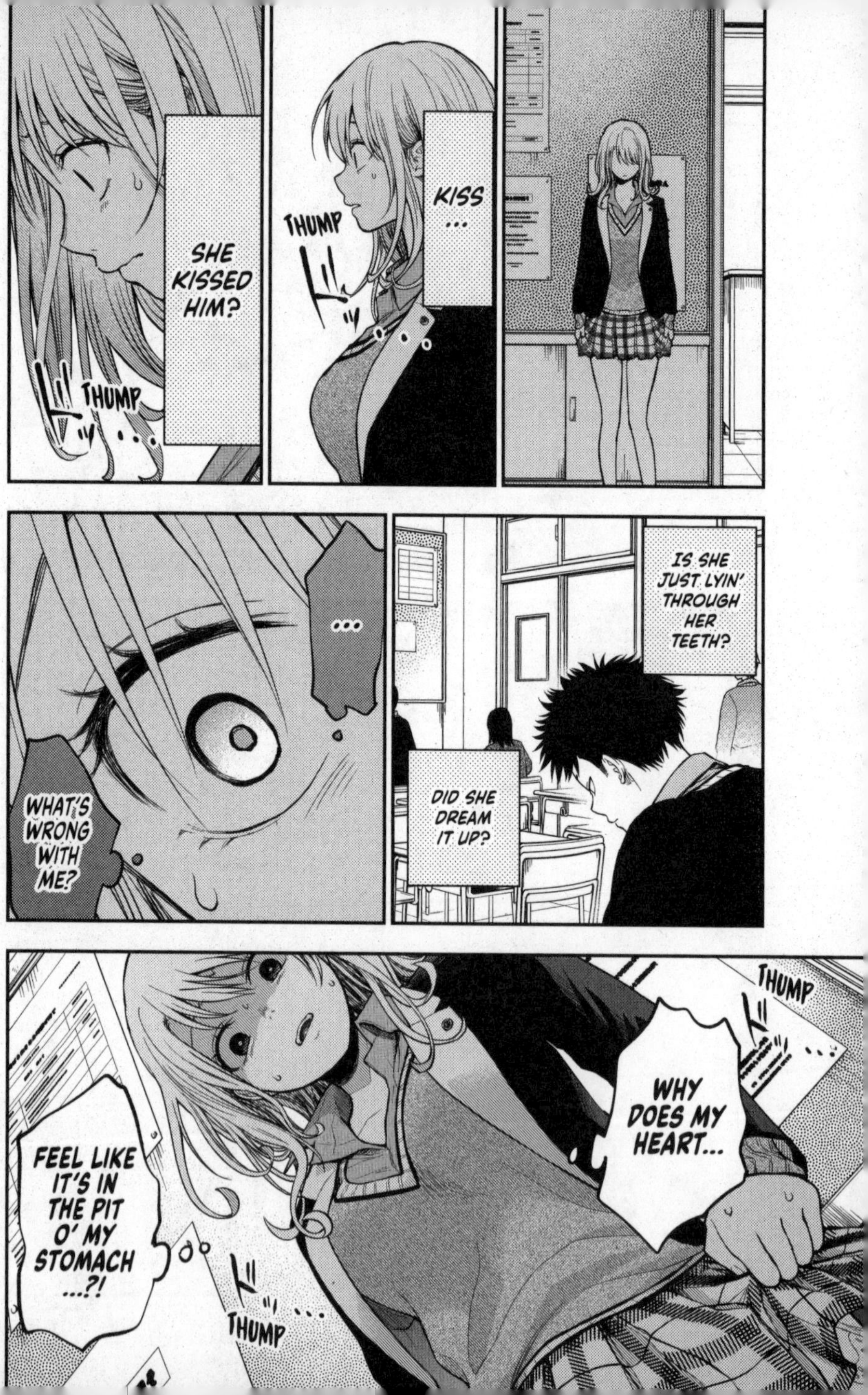
KISS ...
THUMP
SHE KISSED HIM?
THUMP
IS SHE JUST LYIN' THROUGH HER TEETH?
DID SHE DREAM IT UP?
...
WHAT'S WRONG WITH ME?
THUMP
WHY DOES MY HEART...
FEEL LIKE IT'S IN THE PIT O' MY STOMACH ...?!
THUMP

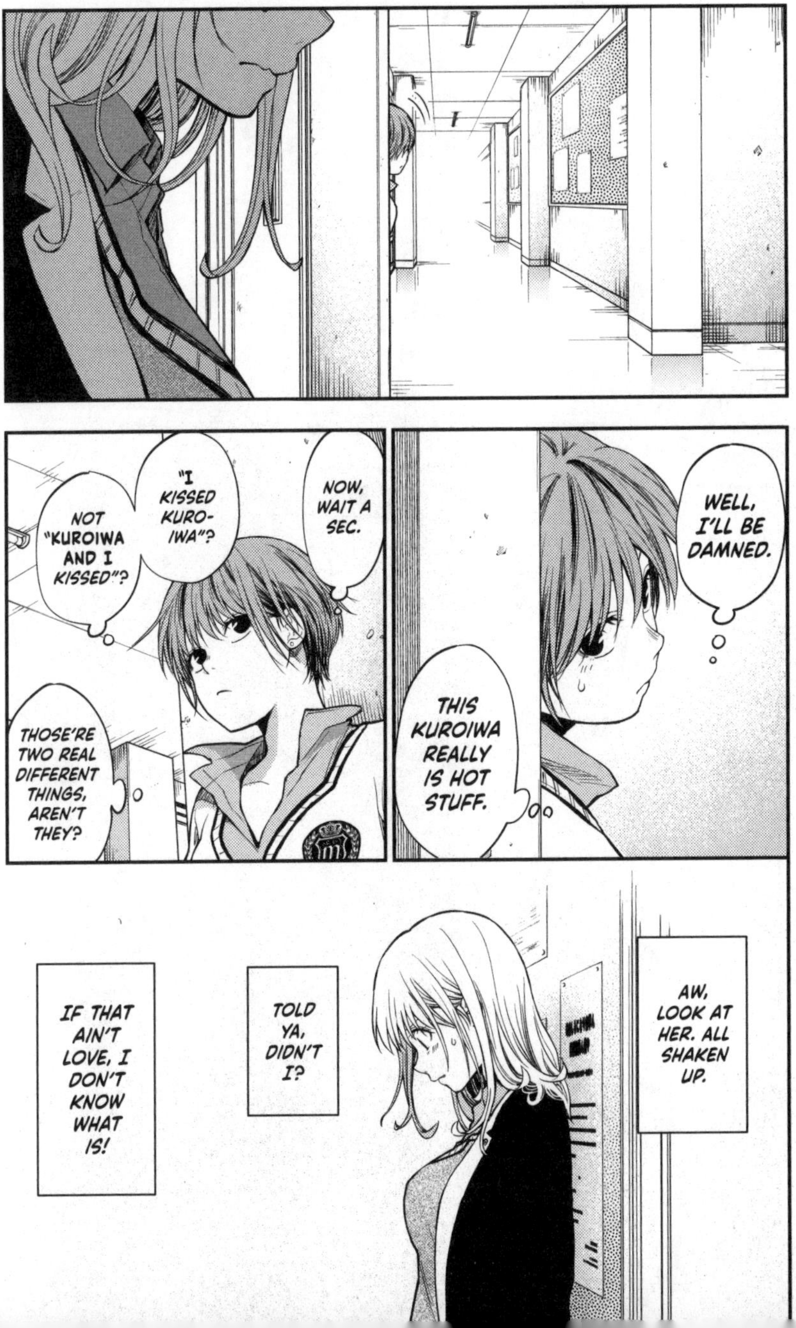
WELL, I'LL BE DAMNED.
THIS KUROIWA REALLY IS HOT STUFF.
NOW, WAIT A SEC.
"I KISSED KURO-IWA"?
NOT "KUROIWA AND I KISSED"?
THOSE'RE TWO REAL DIFFERENT THINGS, AREN'T THEY?
AW, LOOK AT HER. ALL SHAKEN UP.
TOLD YA, DIDN'T I?
IF THAT AIN'T LOVE, I DON'T KNOW WHAT IS!

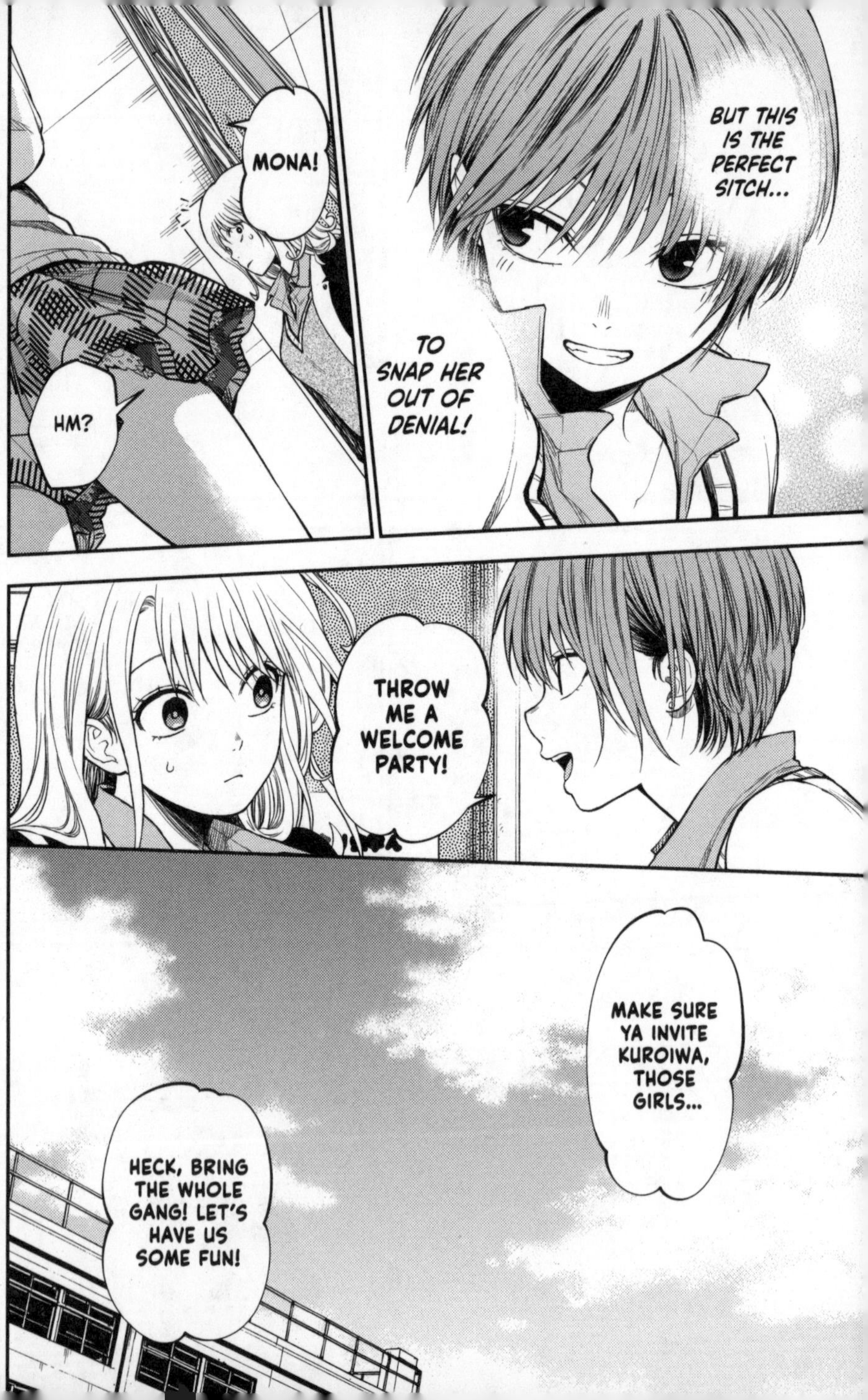
BUT THIS IS THE PERFECT SITCH...
TO SNAP HER OUT OF DENIAL!
MONA!
HM?
THROW ME A WELCOME PARTY!
MAKE SURE YA INVITE KUROIWA, THOSE GIRLS...
HECK, BRING THE WHOLE GANG! LET'S HAVE US SOME FUN!

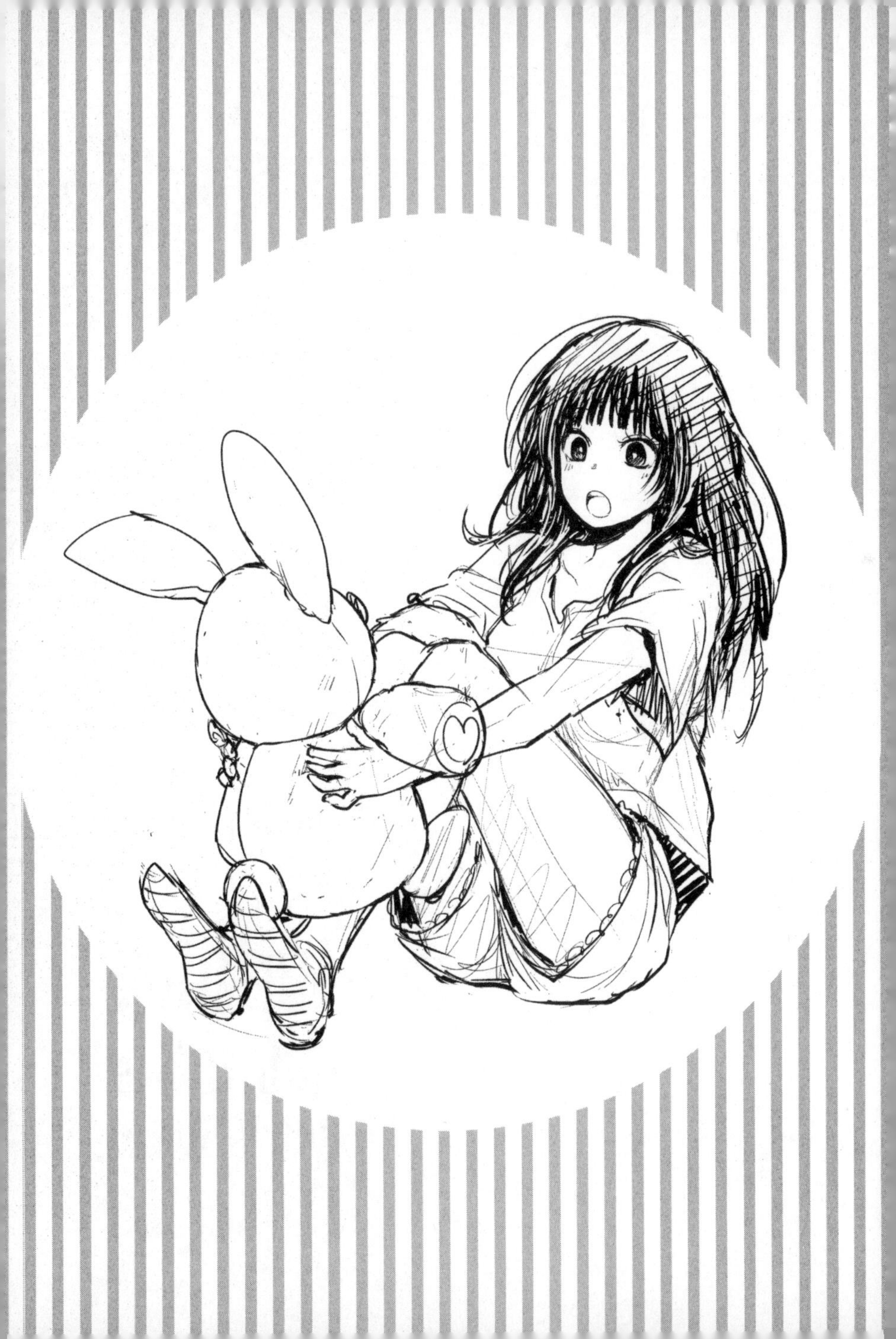

Medaka Kuroiwa is Impervious to My Charms

Chapter 35 ★ The Welcome Party and That Jerk

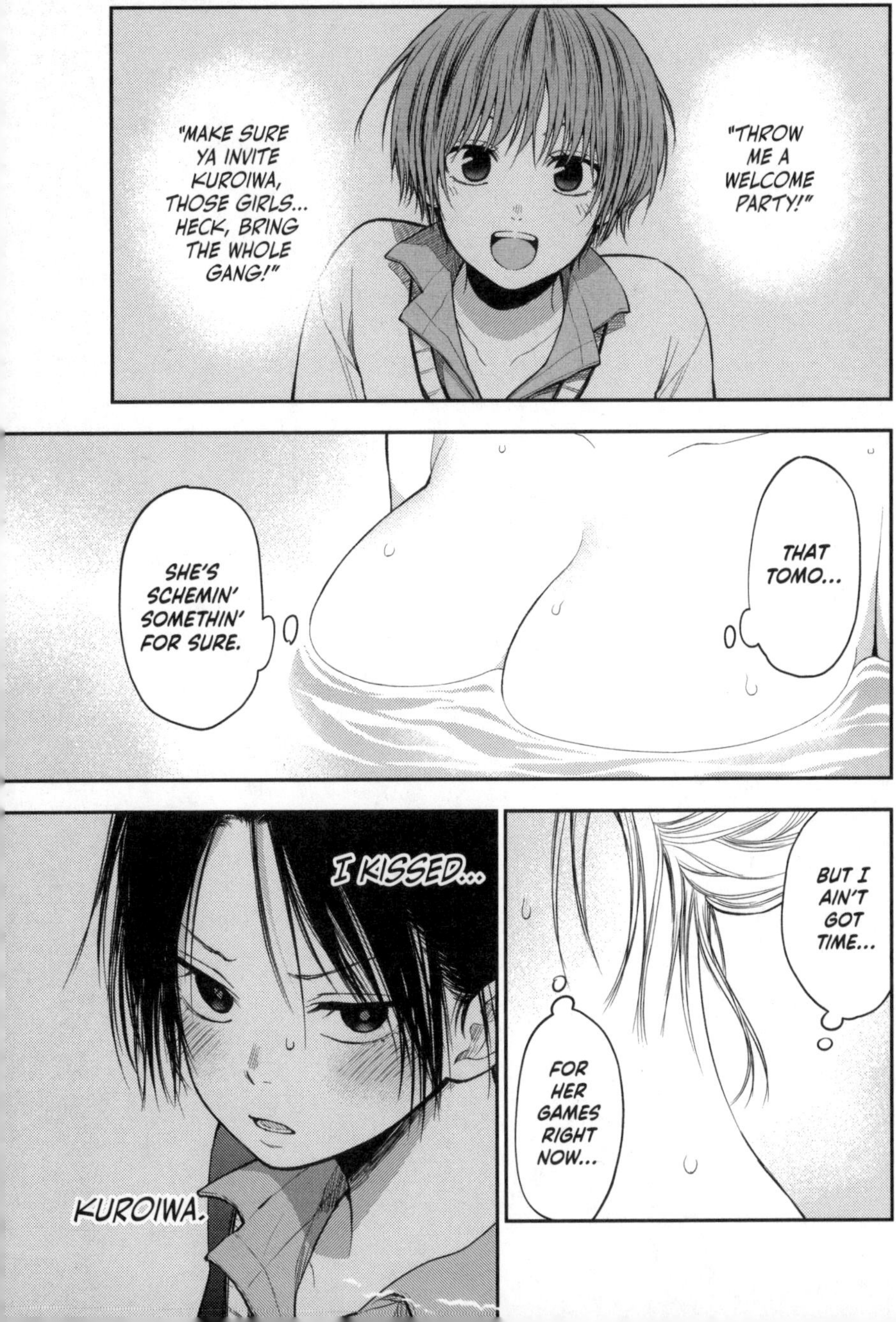
"THROW ME A WELCOME PARTY!"
"MAKE SURE YA INVITE KUROIWA, THOSE GIRLS... HECK, BRING THE WHOLE GANG!"
THAT TOMO...
SHE'S SCHEMIN' SOMETHIN' FOR SURE.
BUT I AIN'T GOT TIME...
FOR HER GAMES RIGHT NOW...
I KISSED...
KUROIWA.

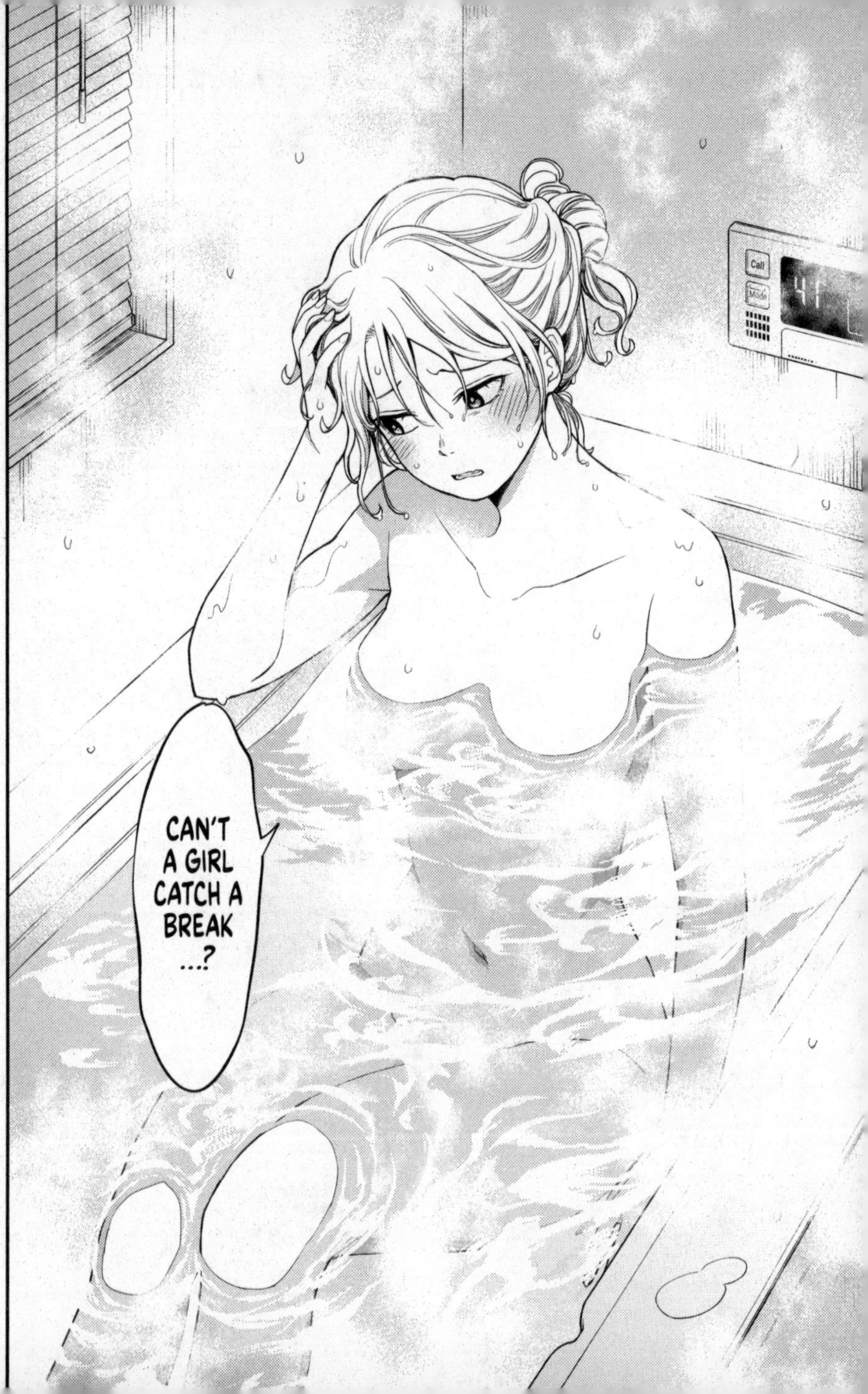
Call
Mode
CAN'T A GIRL CATCH A BREAK ...?

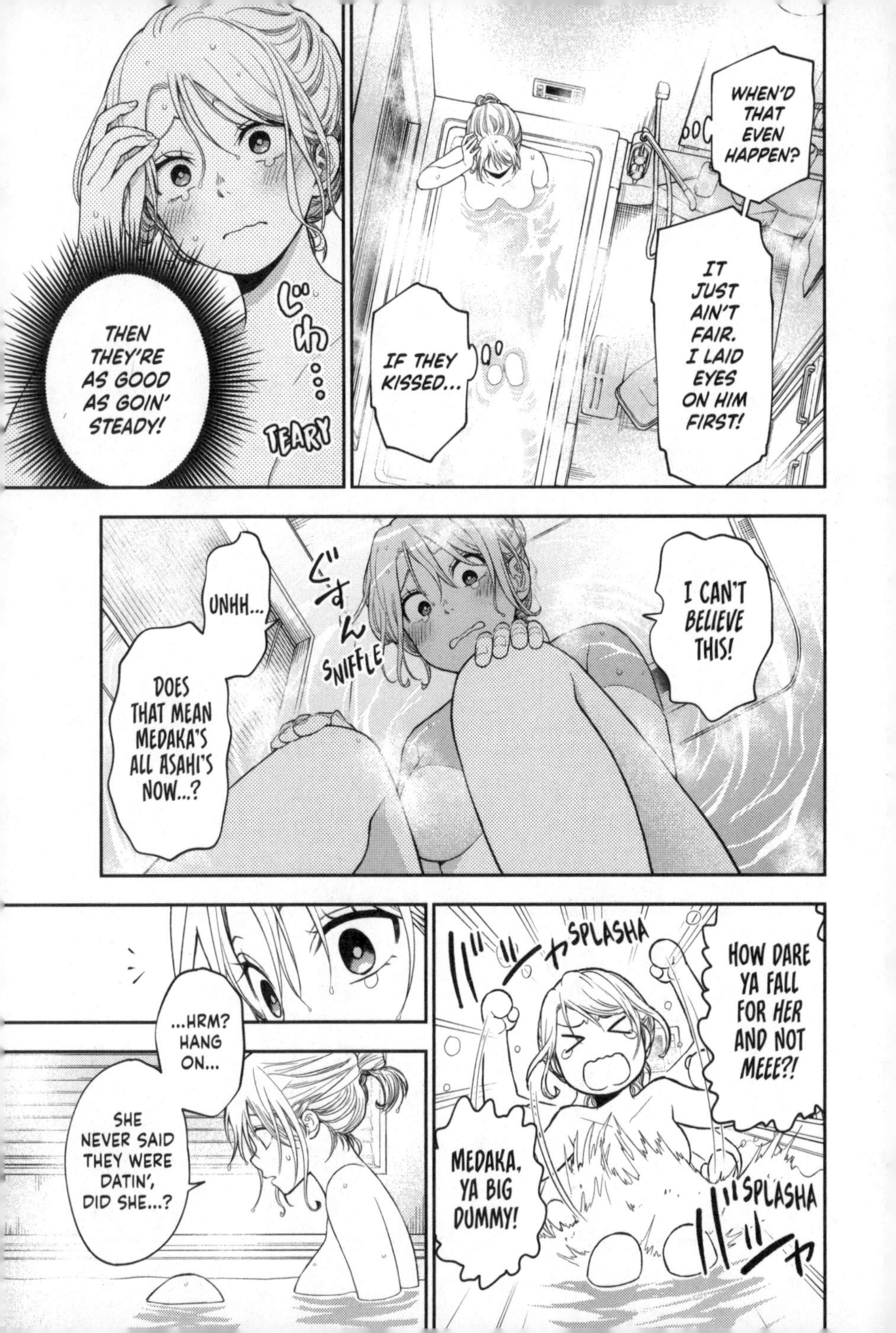
WHEN'D THAT EVEN HAPPEN?
IT JUST AIN'T FAIR. I LAID EYES ON HIM FIRST!
IF THEY KISSED...
THEN THEY'RE AS GOOD AS GOIN' STEADY!
じわ…
TEARY
I CAN'T BELIEVE THIS!
ぐすん
SNIFFLE
UNHH...
DOES THAT MEAN MEDAKA'S ALL ASAHI'S NOW...?
SPLASHA
HOW DARE YA FALL FOR HER AND NOT MEEE?!
MEDAKA, YA BIG DUMMY!
SPLASHA
...HRM? HANG ON...
SHE NEVER SAID THEY WERE DATIN', DID SHE...?

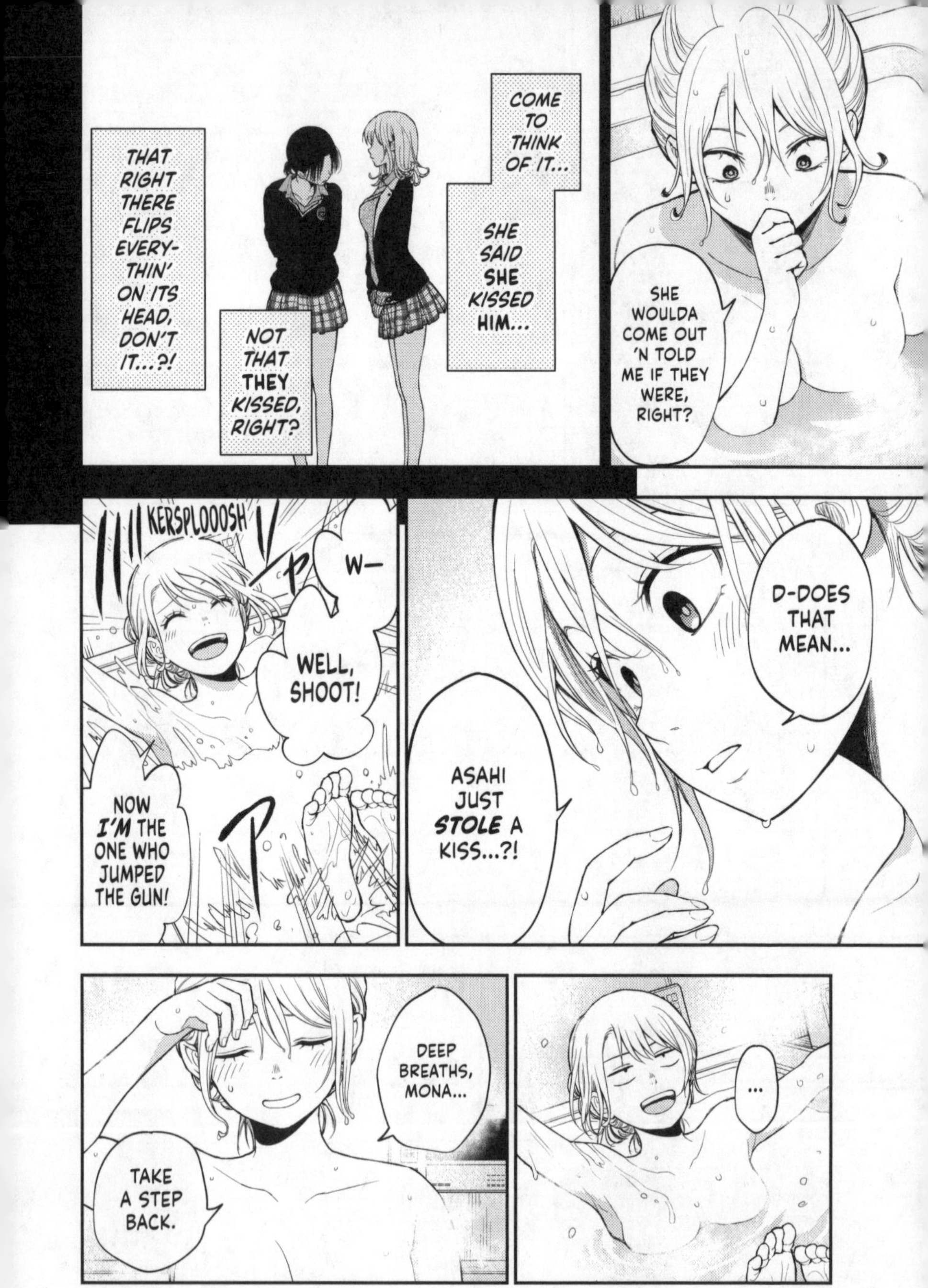
SHE WOULDA COME OUT 'N TOLD ME IF THEY WERE, RIGHT?
COME TO THINK OF IT...
SHE SAID SHE KISSED HIM...
NOT THAT THEY KISSED, RIGHT?
THAT RIGHT THERE FLIPS EVERY-THIN' ON ITS HEAD, DON'T IT...?!
D-DOES THAT MEAN...
ASAHI JUST STOLE A KISS...?!
W—
WELL, SHOOT!
KERSPLOOOSH
NOW I'M THE ONE WHO JUMPED THE GUN!
...
DEEP BREATHS, MONA...
TAKE A STEP BACK.

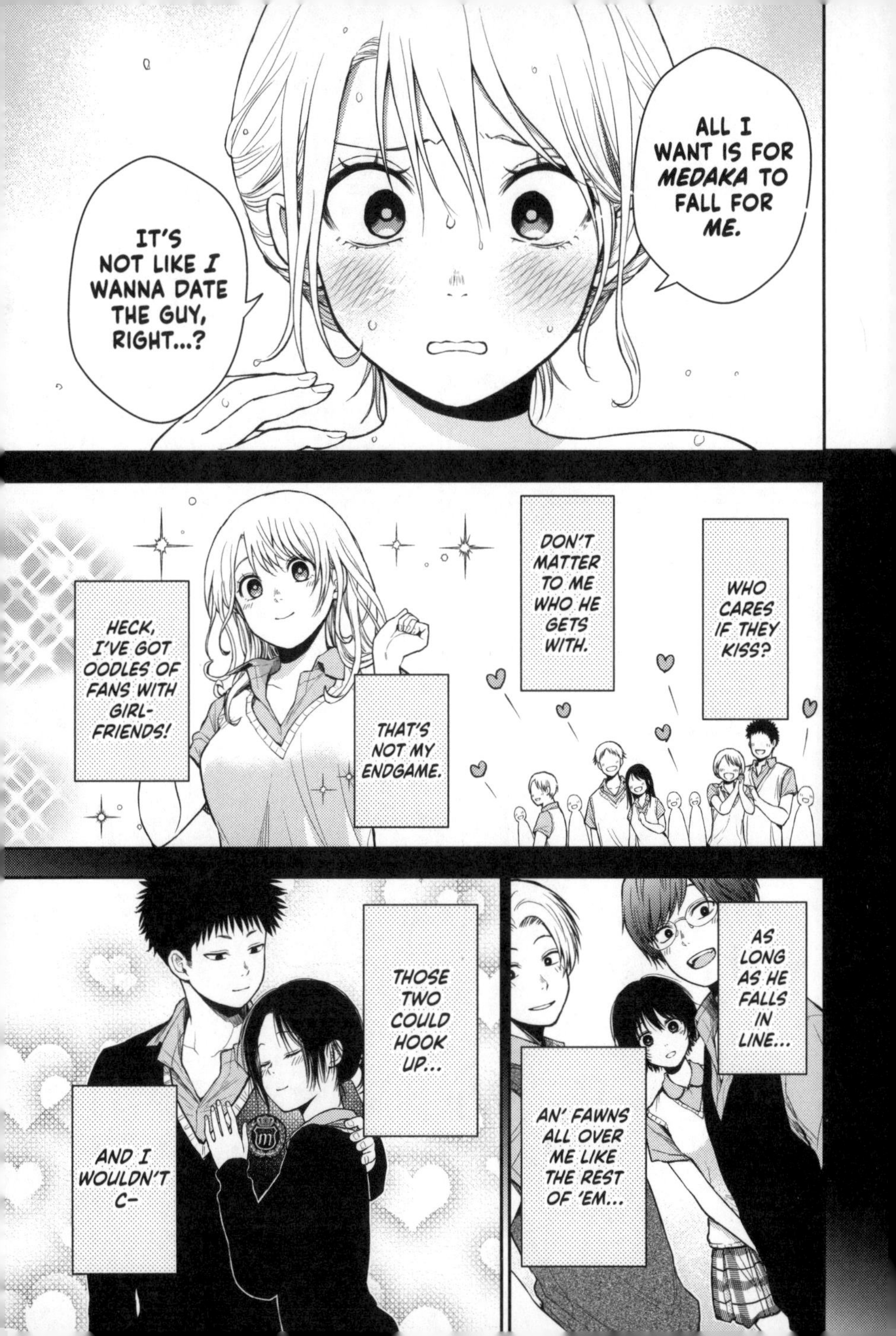
ALL I WANT IS FOR *MEDAKA* TO FALL FOR *ME.*
IT'S NOT LIKE *I* WANNA DATE THE GUY, RIGHT...?
WHO CARES IF THEY KISS?
DON'T MATTER TO ME WHO HE GETS WITH.
THAT'S NOT MY ENDGAME.
HECK, I'VE GOT OODLES OF FANS WITH GIRL-FRIENDS!
AS LONG AS HE FALLS IN LINE...
AN' FAWNS ALL OVER ME LIKE THE REST OF 'EM...
THOSE TWO COULD HOOK UP...
AND I WOULDN'T C–

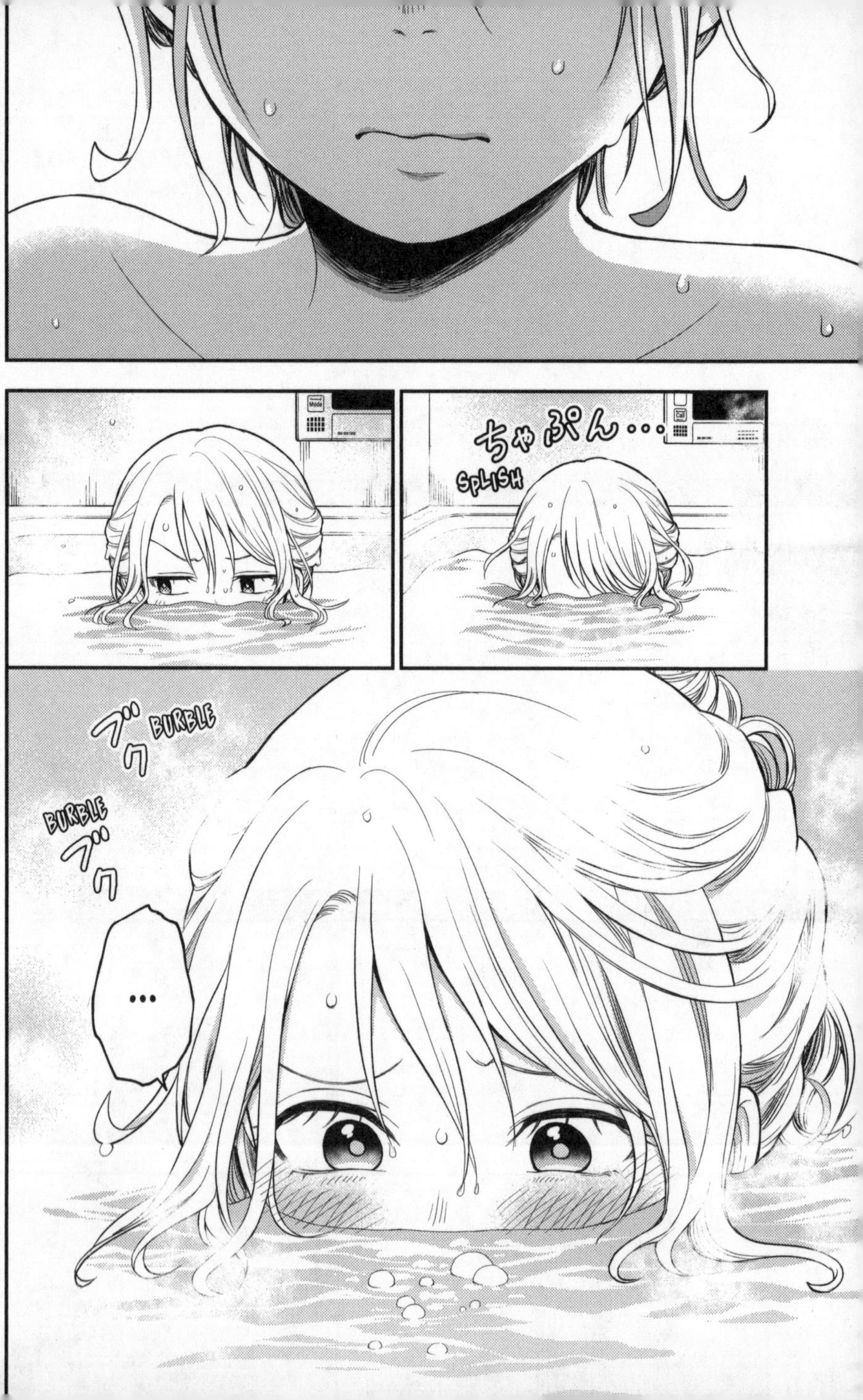
ちゃぷん…
SPLISH
ブク BURBLE
BURBLE ブク
…

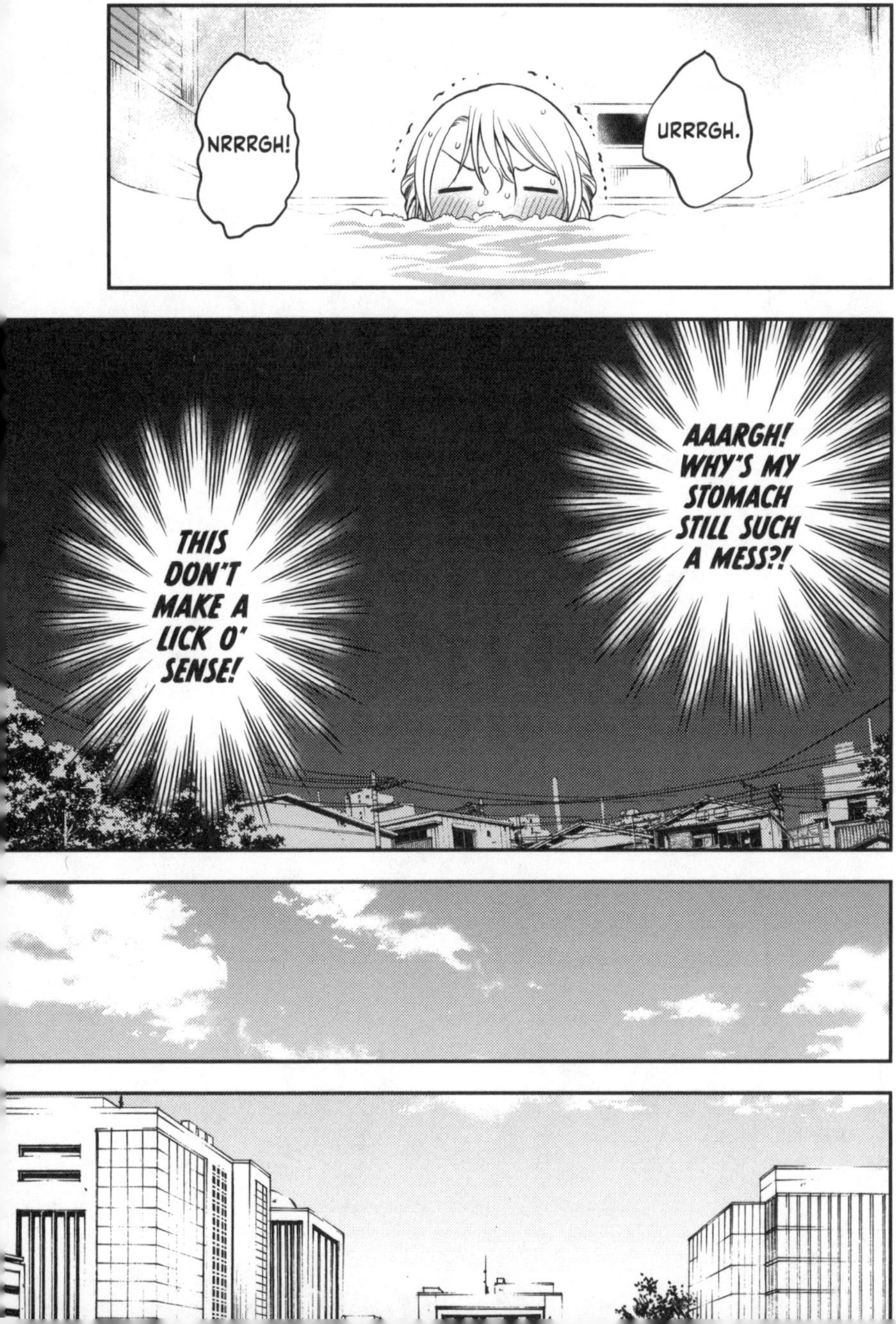
URRRGH.
NRRRGH!
AAARGH! WHY'S MY STOMACH STILL SUCH A MESS?!
THIS DON'T MAKE A LICK O' SENSE!

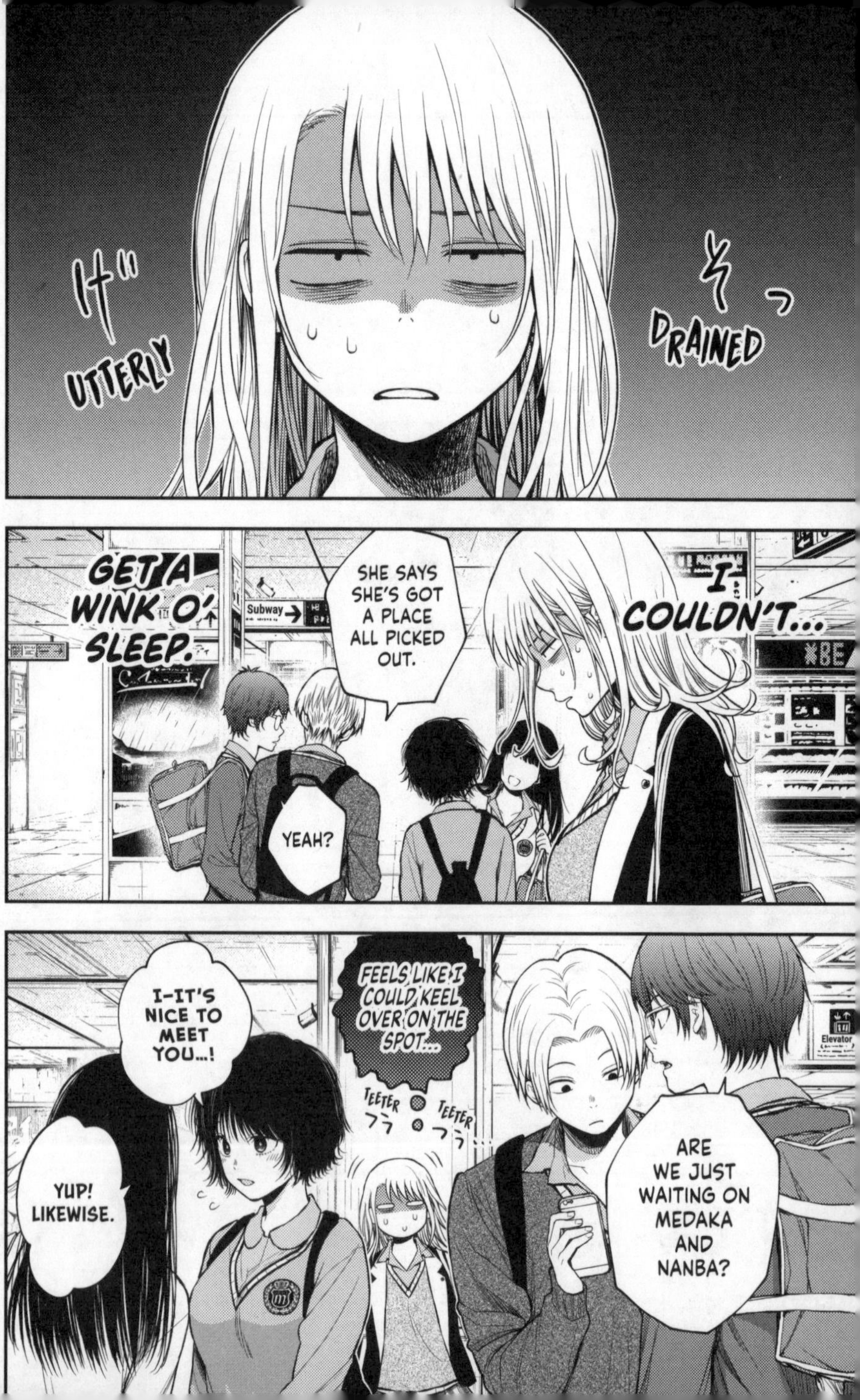
DRAINED
UTTERLY
I COULDN'T...
SHE SAYS SHE'S GOT A PLACE ALL PICKED OUT.
GET A WINK O' SLEEP.
Subway
YEAH?
Elevator
ARE WE JUST WAITING ON MEDAKA AND NANBA?
FEELS LIKE I COULD KEEL OVER ON THE SPOT...
TEETER
TEETER
I-IT'S NICE TO MEET YOU...!
YUP! LIKEWISE.

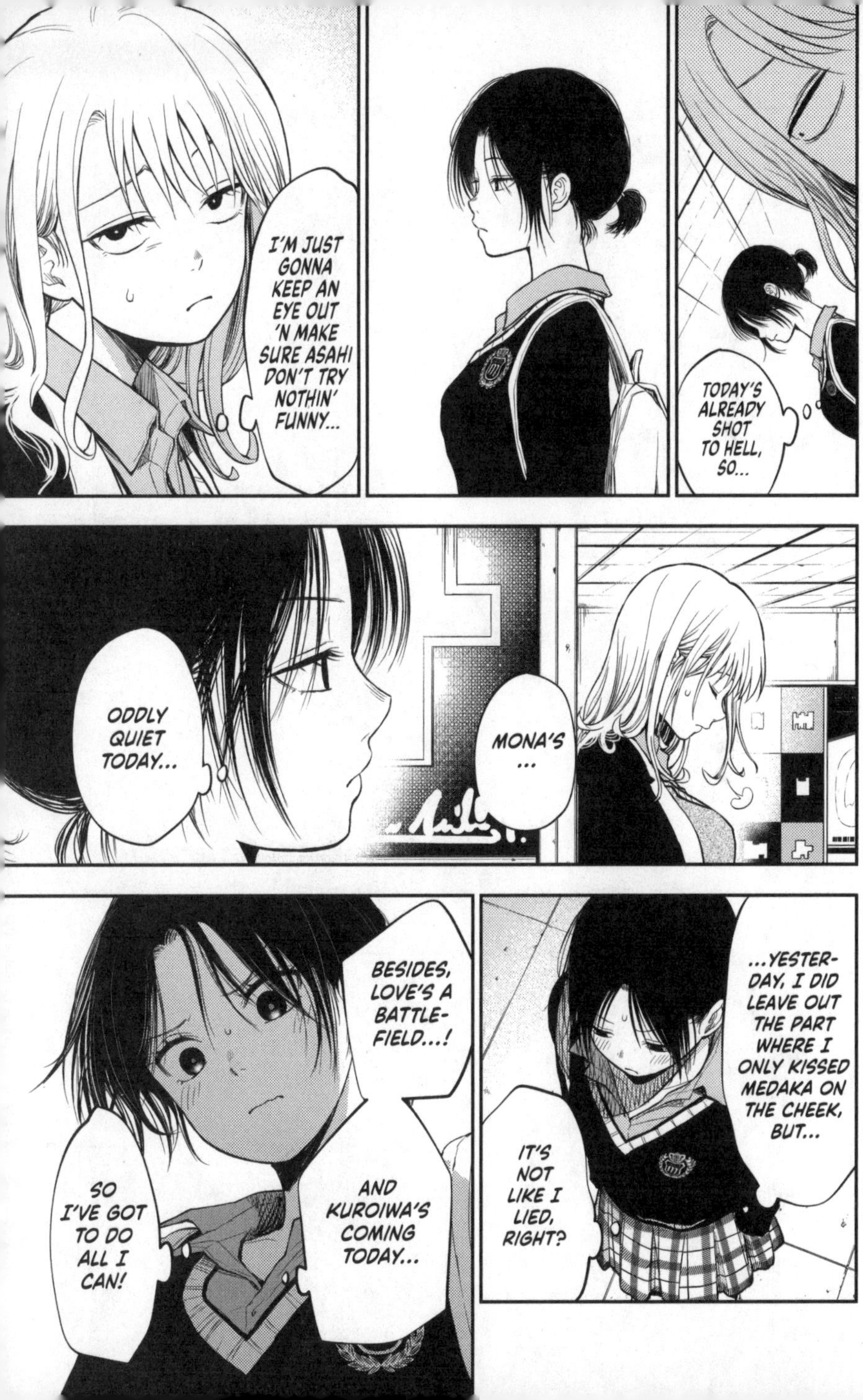
TODAY'S ALREADY SHOT TO HELL, SO...
I'M JUST GONNA KEEP AN EYE OUT 'N MAKE SURE ASAHI DON'T TRY NOTHIN' FUNNY...
MONA'S ...
ODDLY QUIET TODAY...
...YESTER-DAY, I DID LEAVE OUT THE PART WHERE I ONLY KISSED MEDAKA ON THE CHEEK, BUT...
IT'S NOT LIKE I LIED, RIGHT?
BESIDES, LOVE'S A BATTLE-FIELD...!
AND KUROIWA'S COMING TODAY...
SO I'VE GOT TO DO ALL I CAN!

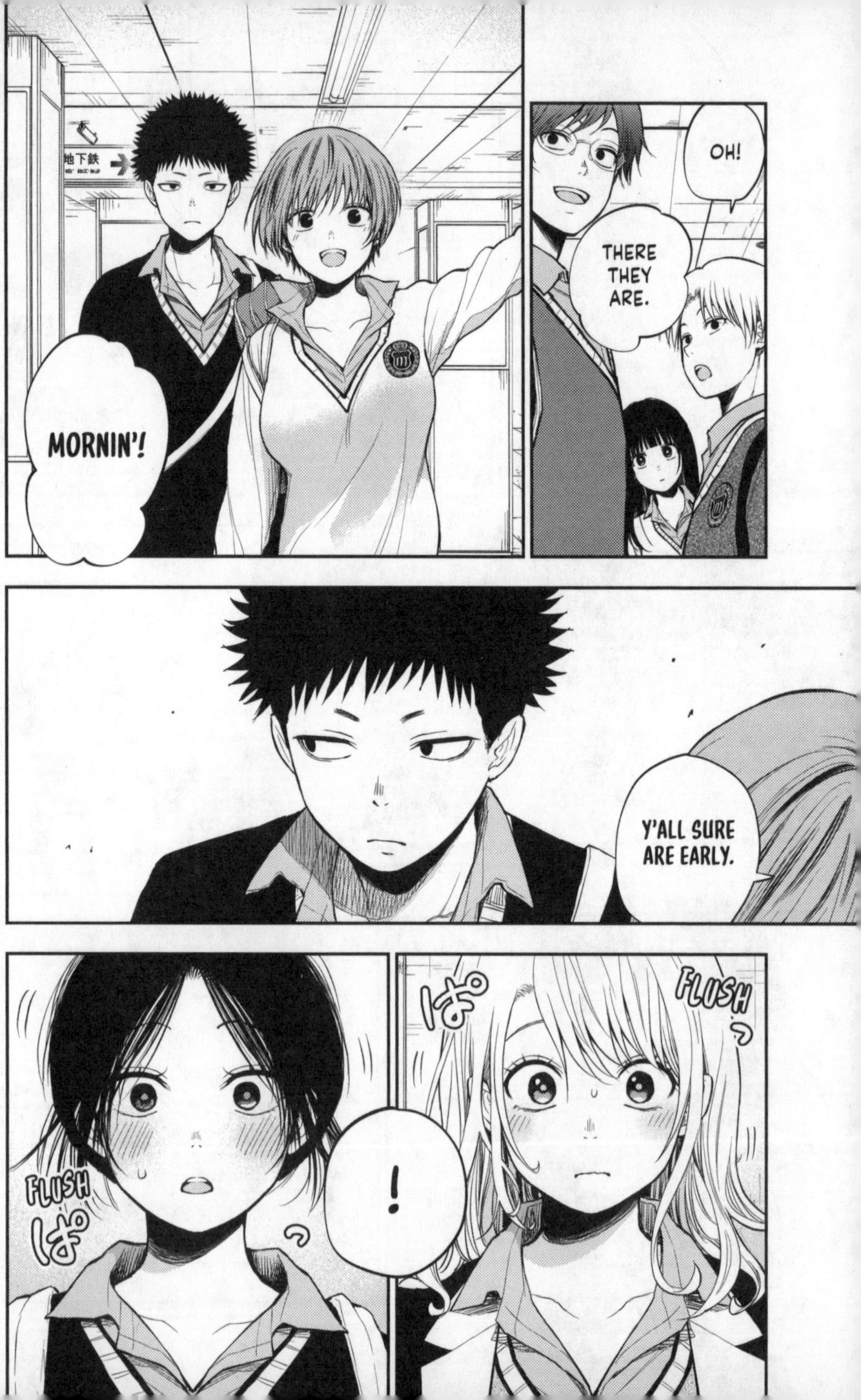
OH!
THERE THEY ARE.
地下鉄
MORNIN'!
Y'ALL SURE ARE EARLY.
ぱ
FLUSH
!
FLUSH
ぱ

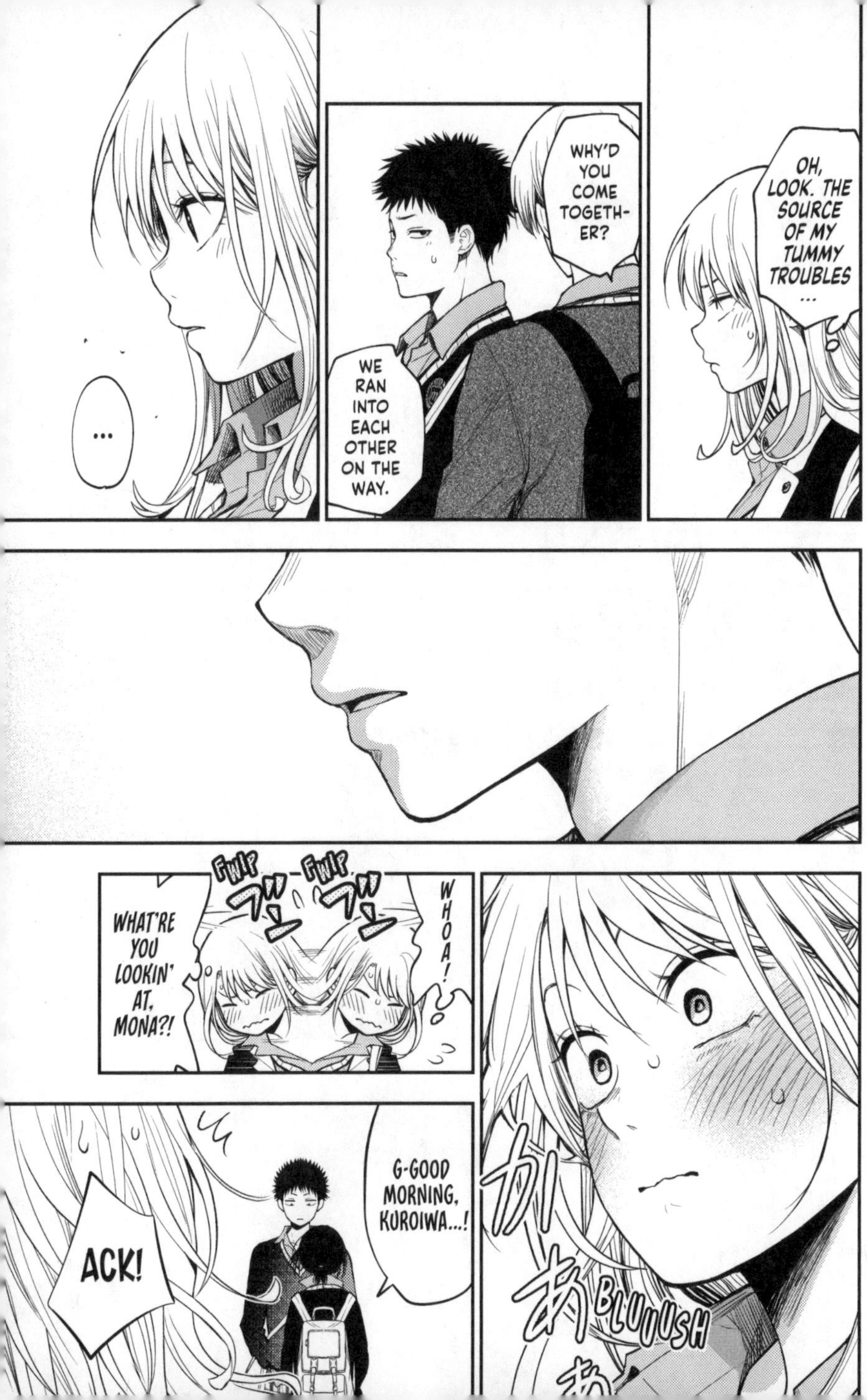
OH, LOOK. THE SOURCE OF MY TUMMY TROUBLES ...
WHY'D YOU COME TOGETH-ER?
WE RAN INTO EACH OTHER ON THE WAY.
...
BLUUUSH
FWIP
FWIP
WHOA!
WHAT'RE YOU LOOKIN' AT, MONA?!
G-GOOD MORNING, KUROIWA...!
ACK!

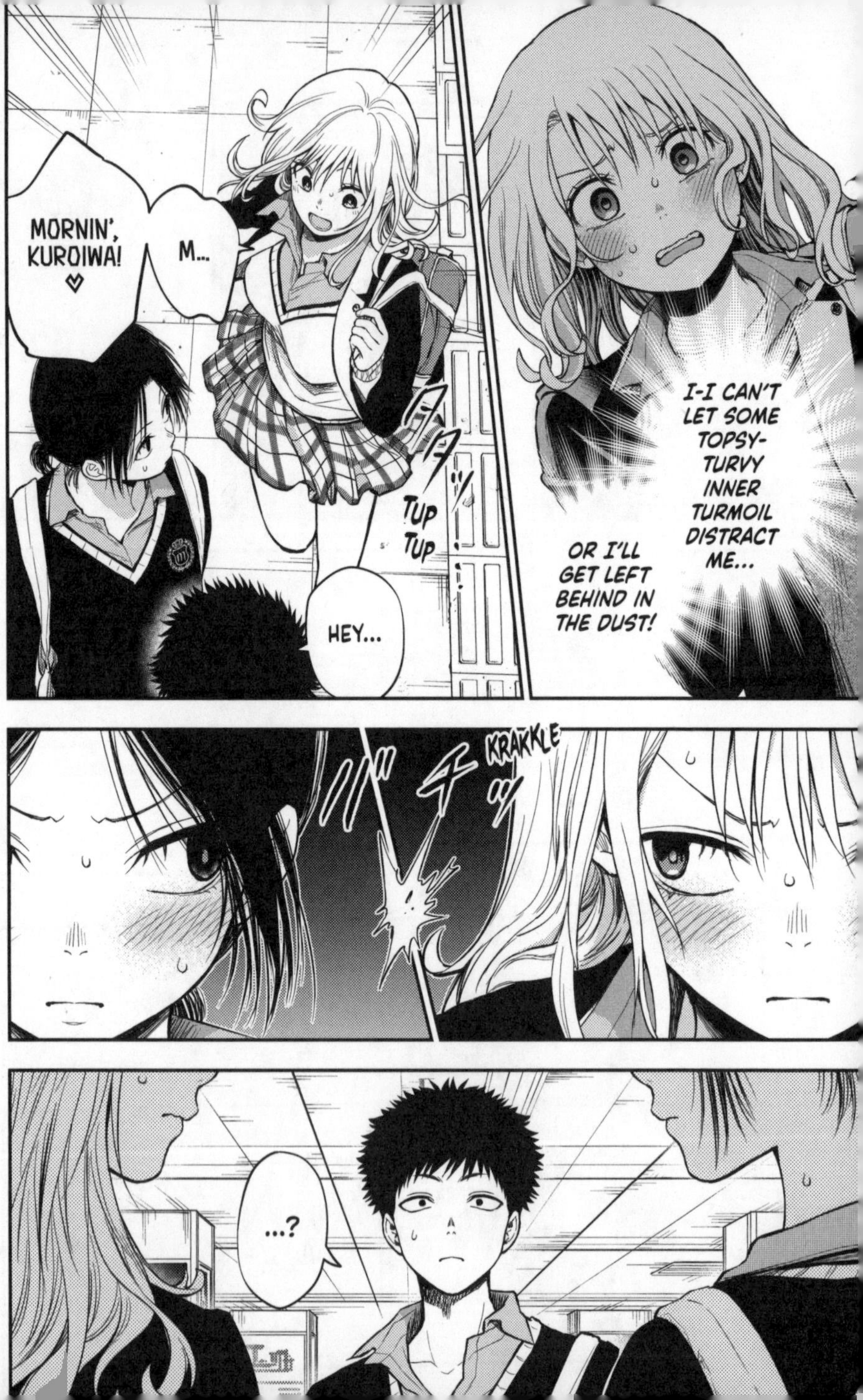
I-I CAN'T LET SOME TOPSY-TURVY INNER TURMOIL DISTRACT ME...
OR I'LL GET LEFT BEHIND IN THE DUST!
MORNIN', KUROIWA! ♡
M...
TUP TUP
HEY...
KRAKKLE
...?

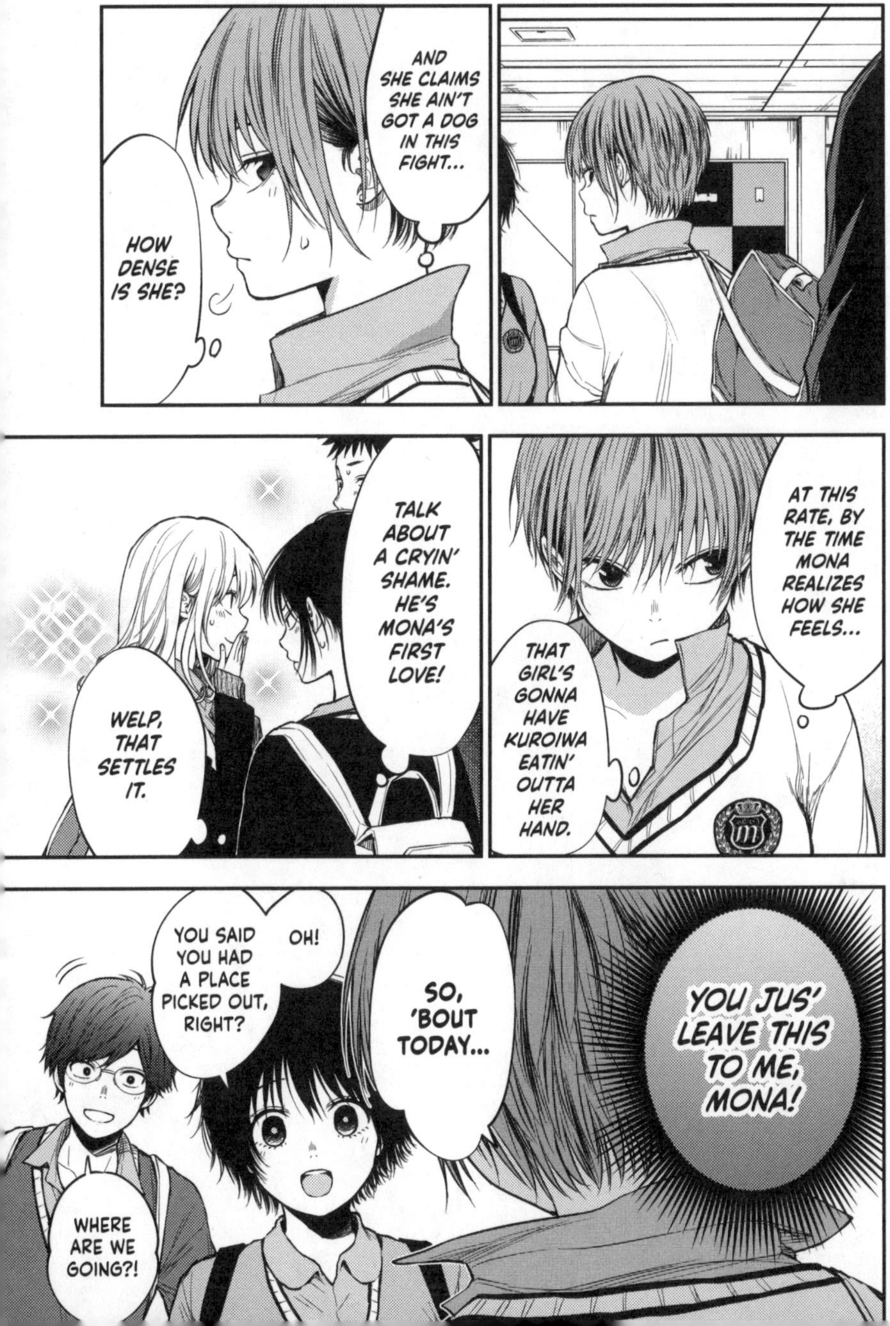
AND SHE CLAIMS SHE AIN'T GOT A DOG IN THIS FIGHT...
HOW DENSE IS SHE?
AT THIS RATE, BY THE TIME MONA REALIZES HOW SHE FEELS...
THAT GIRL'S GONNA HAVE KUROIWA EATIN' OUTTA HER HAND.
TALK ABOUT A CRYIN' SHAME. HE'S MONA'S FIRST LOVE!
WELP, THAT SETTLES IT.
YOU JUS' LEAVE THIS TO ME, MONA!
SO, 'BOUT TODAY...
OH!
YOU SAID YOU HAD A PLACE PICKED OUT, RIGHT?
WHERE ARE WE GOING?!

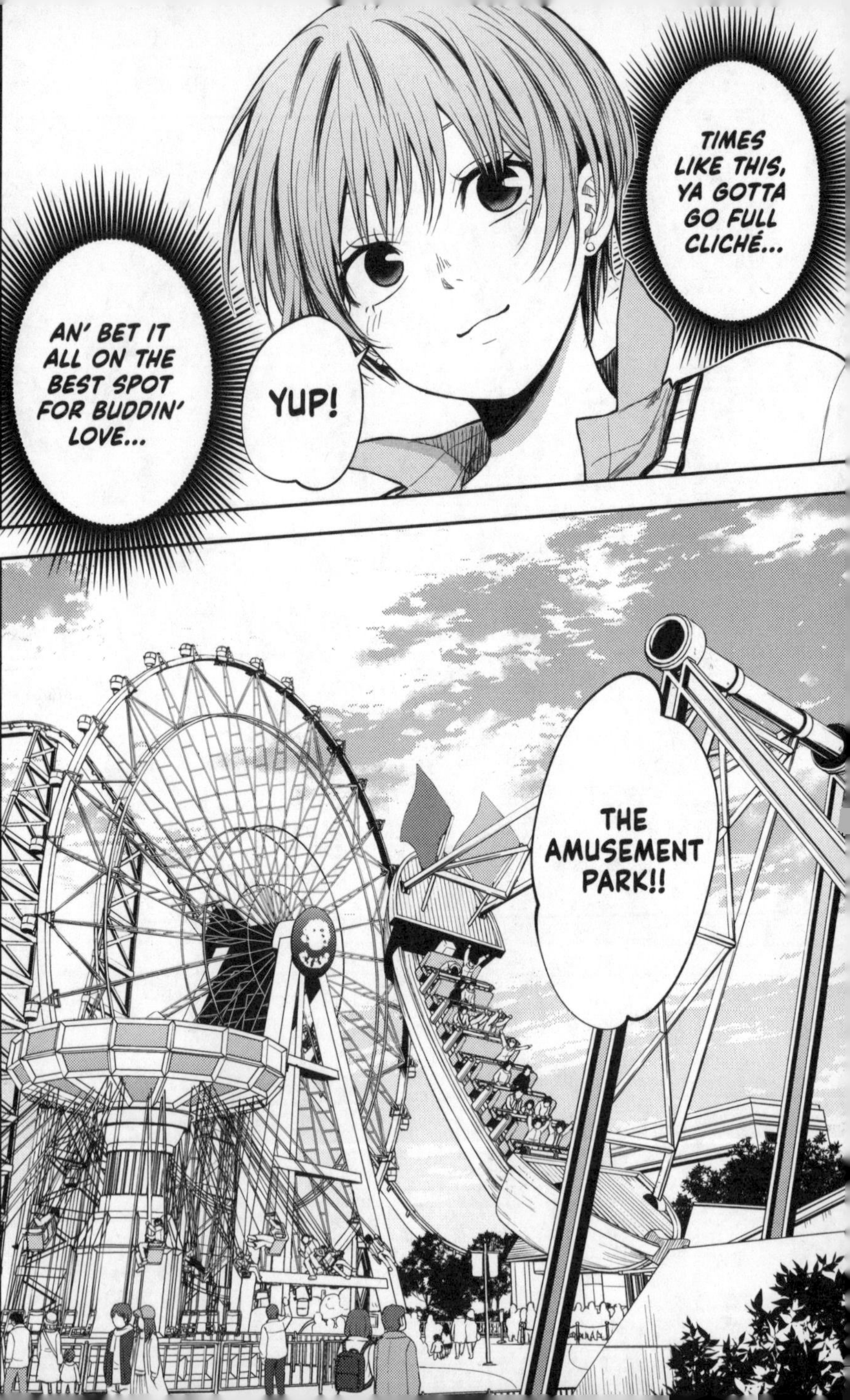
TIMES LIKE THIS, YA GOTTA GO FULL CLICHÉ...
YUP!
AN' BET IT ALL ON THE BEST SPOT FOR BUDDIN' LOVE...
THE AMUSEMENT PARK!!

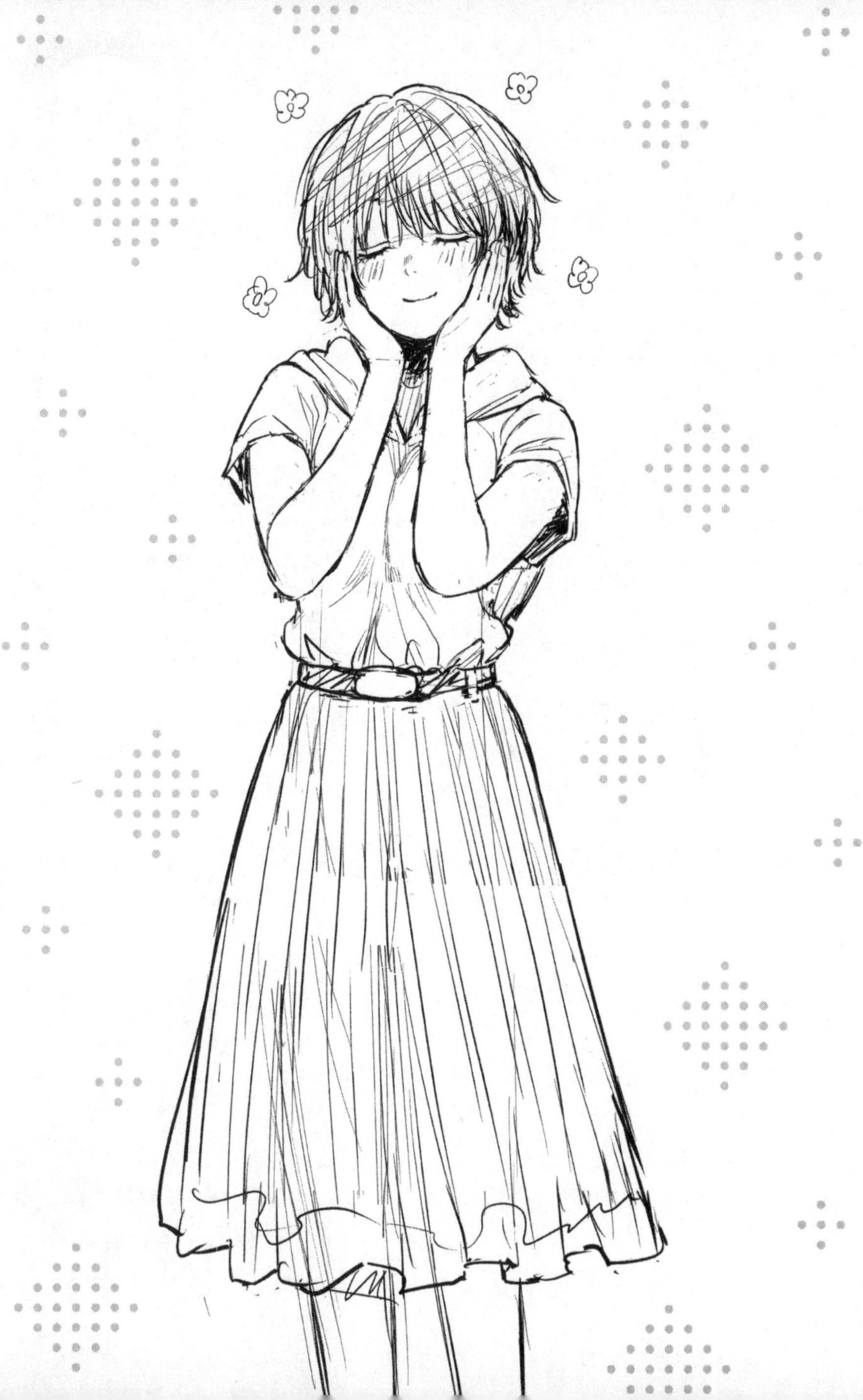

Medaka Kuroiwa is Impervious to My Charms

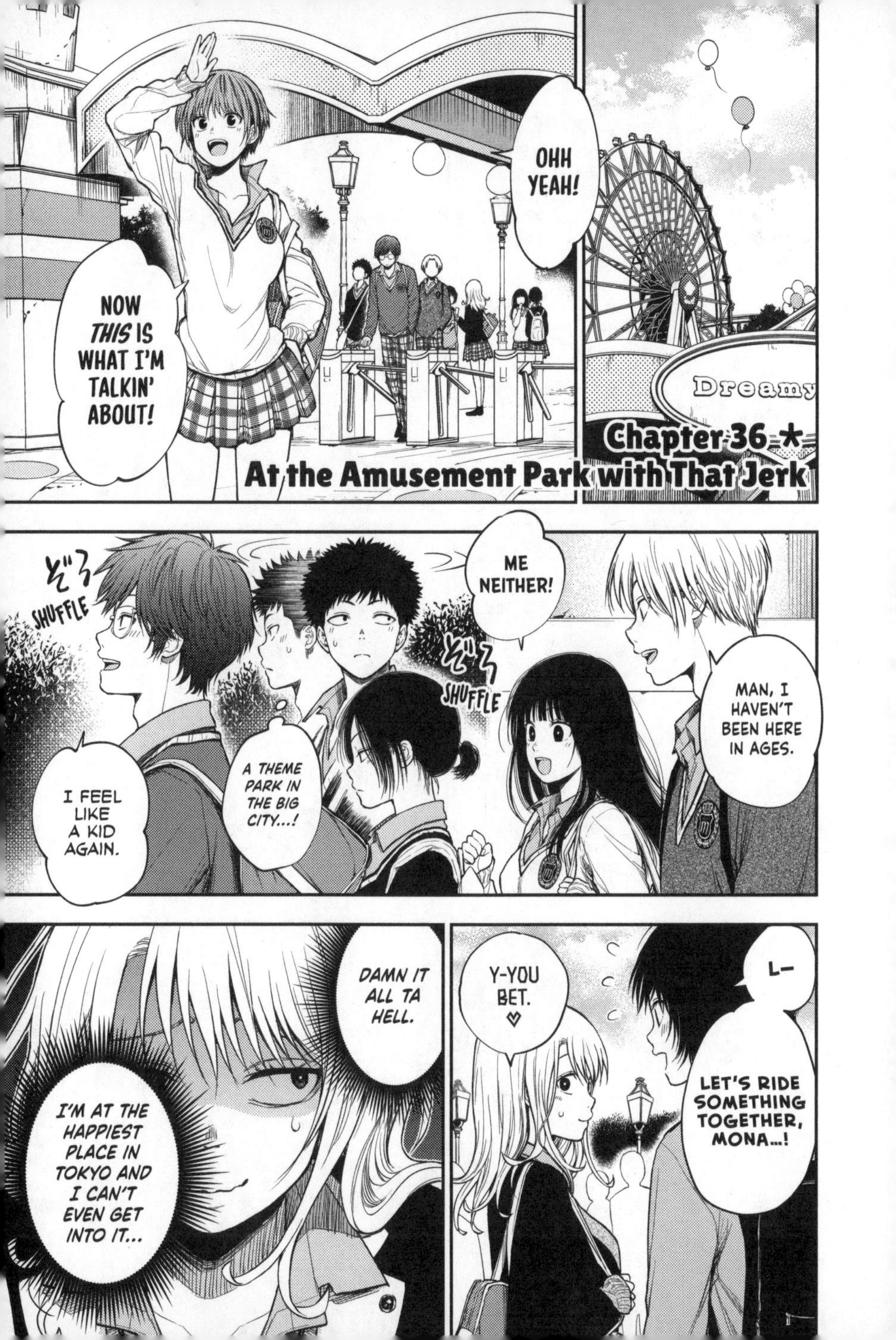
Dreamy
Chapter 36 ★ At the Amusement Park with That Jerk
OHH YEAH!
NOW THIS IS WHAT I'M TALKIN' ABOUT!
MAN, I HAVEN'T BEEN HERE IN AGES.
ME NEITHER!
SHUFFLE
A THEME PARK IN THE BIG CITY...!
SHUFFLE
I FEEL LIKE A KID AGAIN.
L—
LET'S RIDE SOMETHING TOGETHER, MONA...!
Y-YOU BET. ♥
DAMN IT ALL TA HELL.
I'M AT THE HAPPIEST PLACE IN TOKYO AND I CAN'T EVEN GET INTO IT...

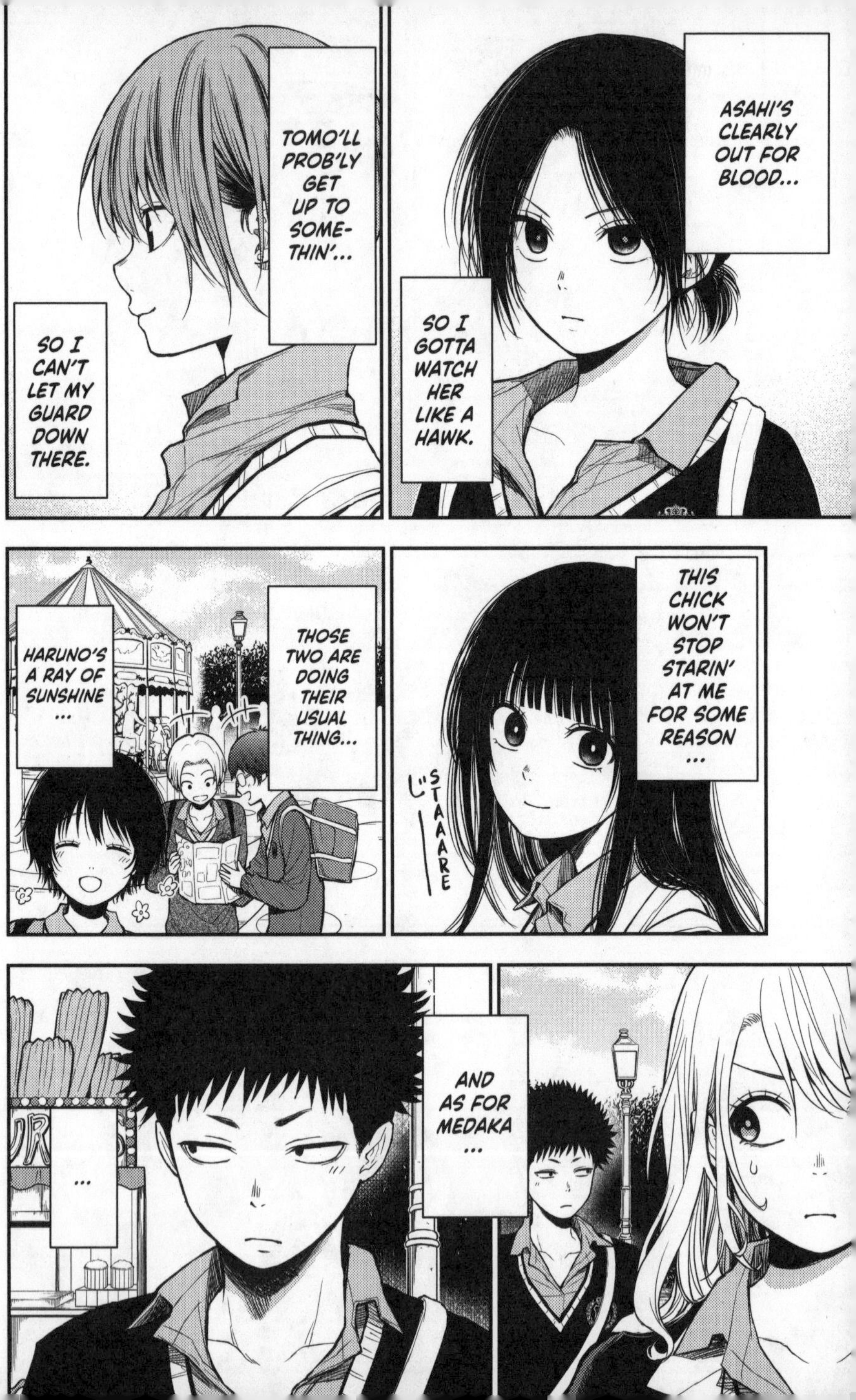
ASAHI'S CLEARLY OUT FOR BLOOD...
SO I GOTTA WATCH HER LIKE A HAWK.
TOMO'LL PROB'LY GET UP TO SOME-THIN'...
SO I CAN'T LET MY GUARD DOWN THERE.
THIS CHICK WON'T STOP STARIN' AT ME FOR SOME REASON ...
じー STAAAARE
THOSE TWO ARE DOING THEIR USUAL THING...
HARUNO'S A RAY OF SUNSHINE ...
AND AS FOR MEDAKA ...
...

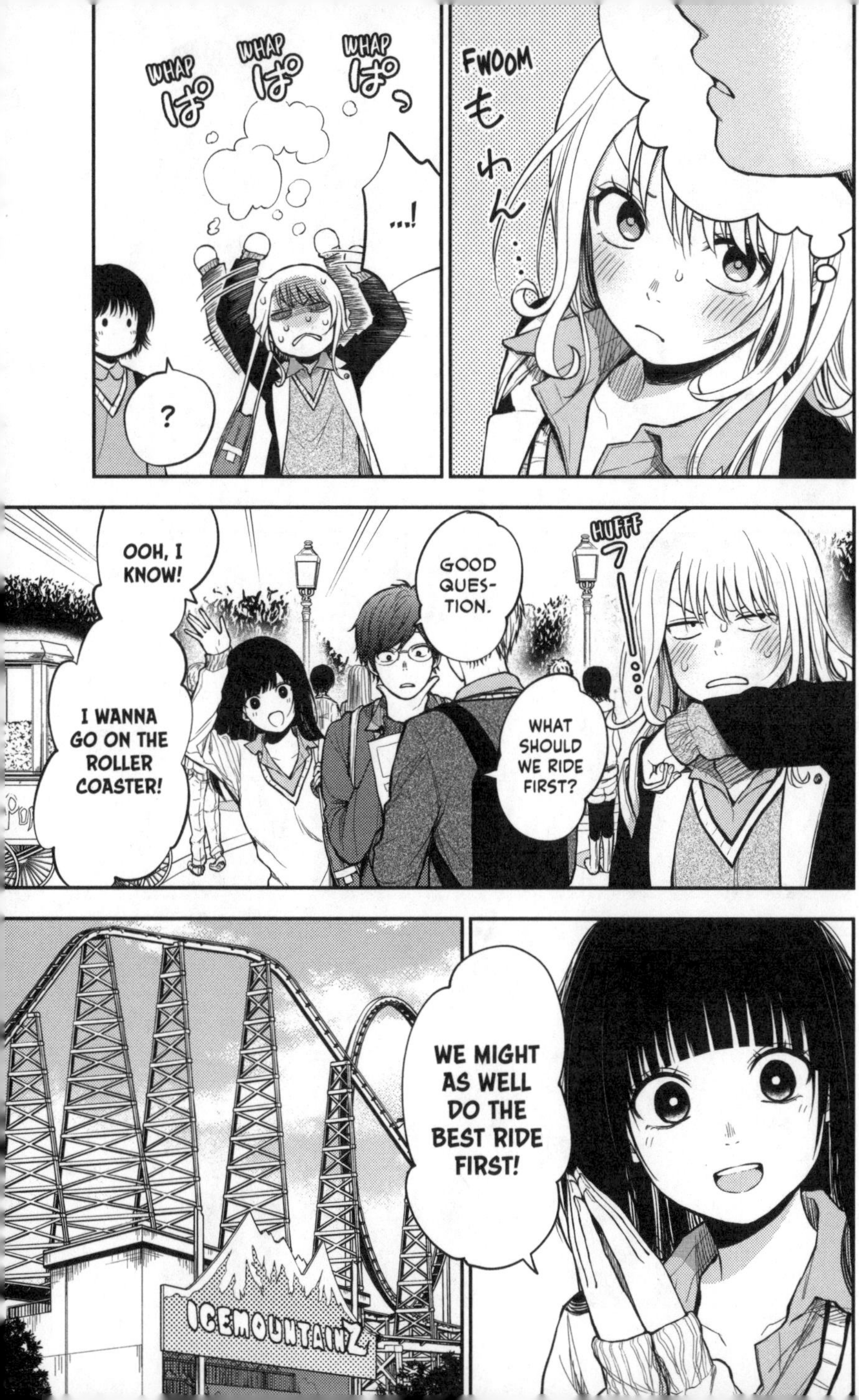
FWOOM
もわん…
WHAP
ぱ
WHAP
ぱ
WHAP
ぱっ
...!
?
HUFFF
フー…
WHAT SHOULD WE RIDE FIRST?
GOOD QUESTION.
OOH, I KNOW!
I WANNA GO ON THE ROLLER COASTER!
WE MIGHT AS WELL DO THE BEST RIDE FIRST!
ICEMOUNTAINZ

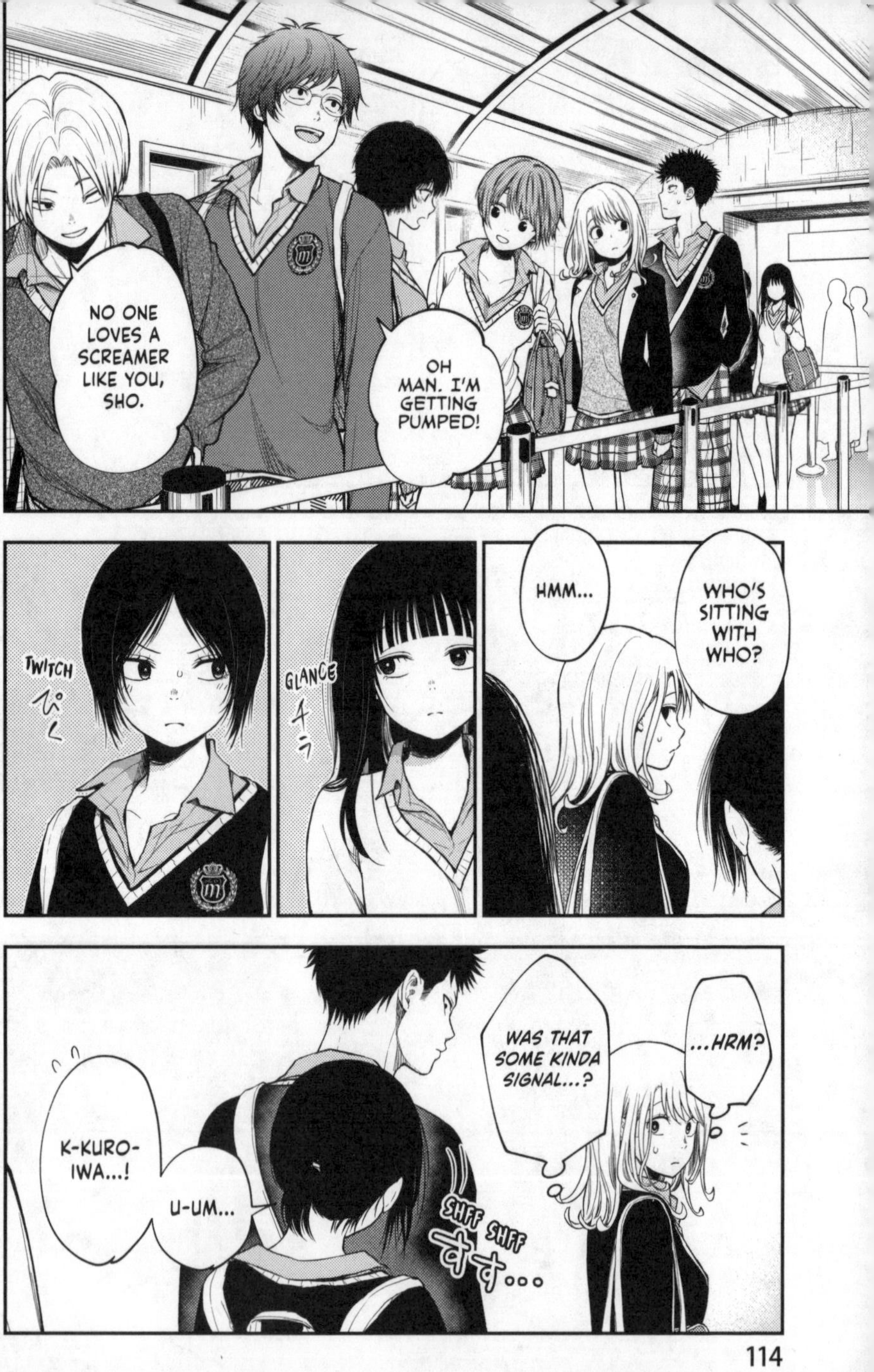
OH MAN. I'M GETTING PUMPED!
NO ONE LOVES A SCREAMER LIKE YOU, SHO.
WHO'S SITTING WITH WHO?
HMM...
GLANCE
チラ
TWITCH
ぴく
...HRM?
WAS THAT SOME KINDA SIGNAL...?
SHFF SHFF
すす...
K-KURO-IWA...!
U-UM...

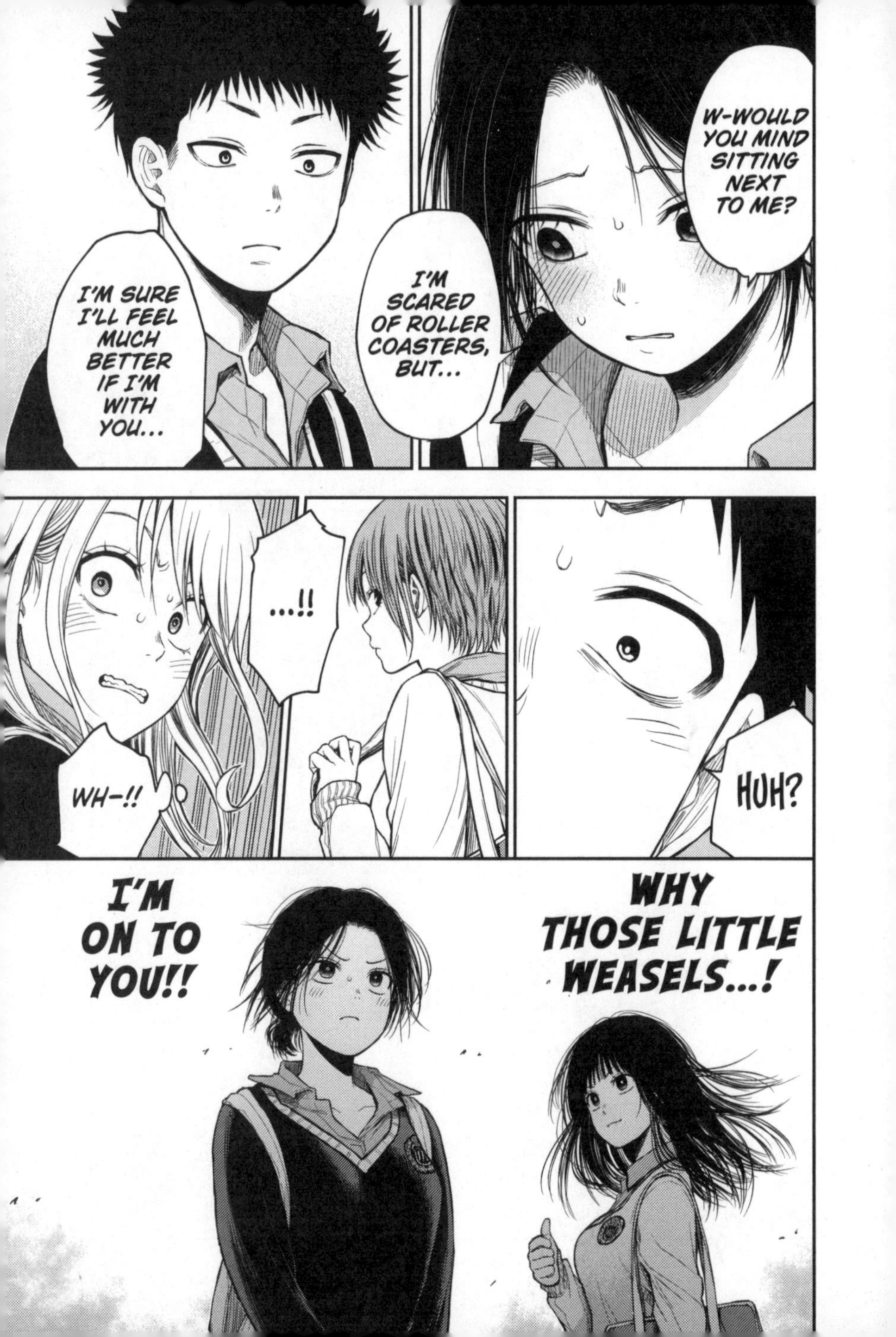
W-WOULD YOU MIND SITTING NEXT TO ME?
I'M SCARED OF ROLLER COASTERS, BUT...
I'M SURE I'LL FEEL MUCH BETTER IF I'M WITH YOU...
HUH?
...!!
WH-!!
WHY THOSE LITTLE WEASELS...!
I'M ON TO YOU!!

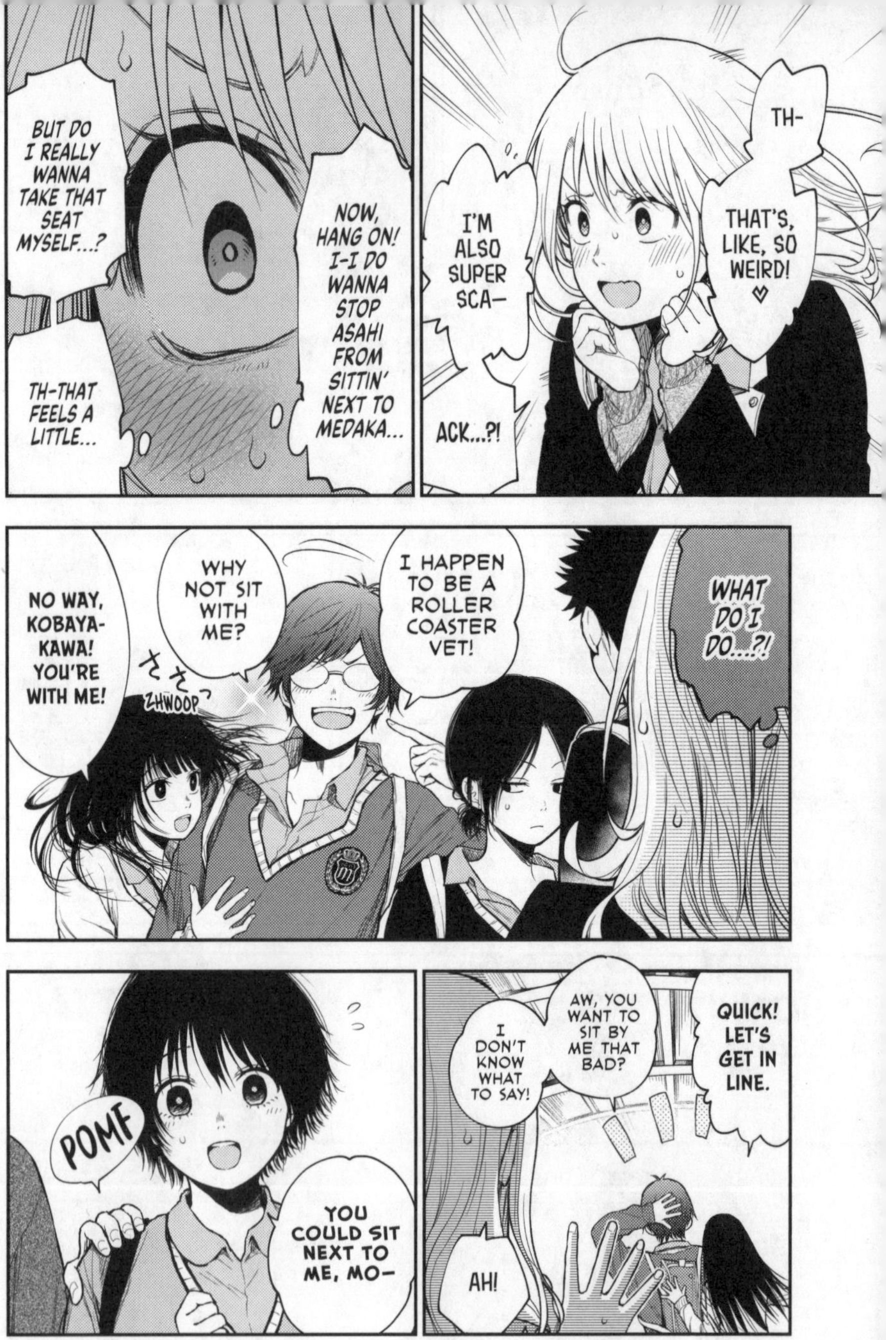
TH-
THAT'S, LIKE, SO WEIRD! ♡
I'M ALSO SUPER SCA-
ACK...?!
NOW, HANG ON! I-I DO WANNA STOP ASAHI FROM SITTIN' NEXT TO MEDAKA...
BUT DO I REALLY WANNA TAKE THAT SEAT MYSELF...?
TH-THAT FEELS A LITTLE...
WHAT DO I DO...?!
I HAPPEN TO BE A ROLLER COASTER VET!
WHY NOT SIT WITH ME?
ZHWOOP
NO WAY, KOBAYAKAWA! YOU'RE WITH ME!
QUICK! LET'S GET IN LINE.
AW, YOU WANT TO SIT BY ME THAT BAD?
I DON'T KNOW WHAT TO SAY!
AH!
POMF
YOU COULD SIT NEXT TO ME, MO-

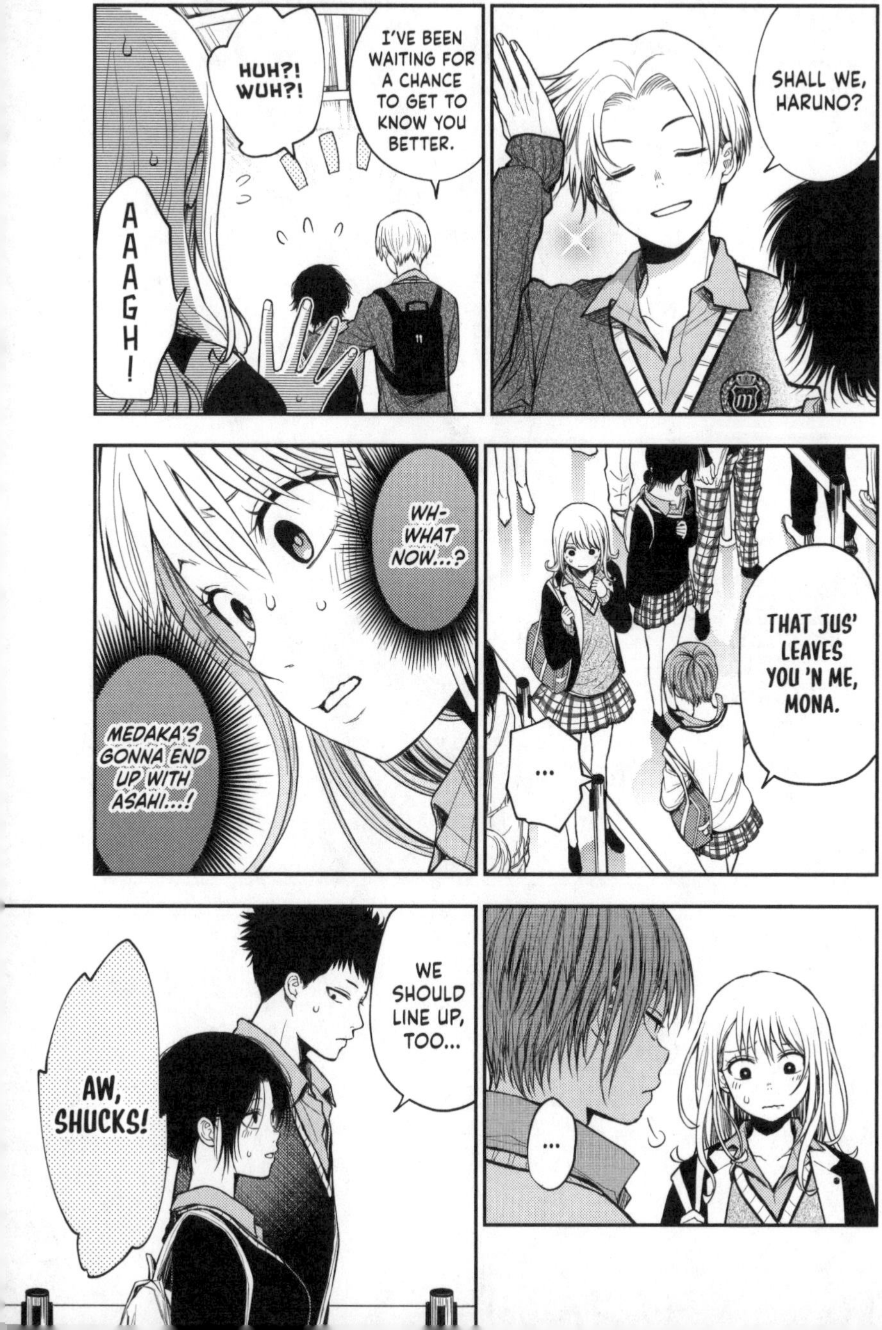
SHALL WE, HARUNO?
I'VE BEEN WAITING FOR A CHANCE TO GET TO KNOW YOU BETTER.
HUH?! WUH?!
AAAGH!
THAT JUS' LEAVES YOU 'N ME, MONA.
...
WH-WHAT NOW...?
MEDAKA'S GONNA END UP WITH ASAHI...!
...
WE SHOULD LINE UP, TOO...
AW, SHUCKS!

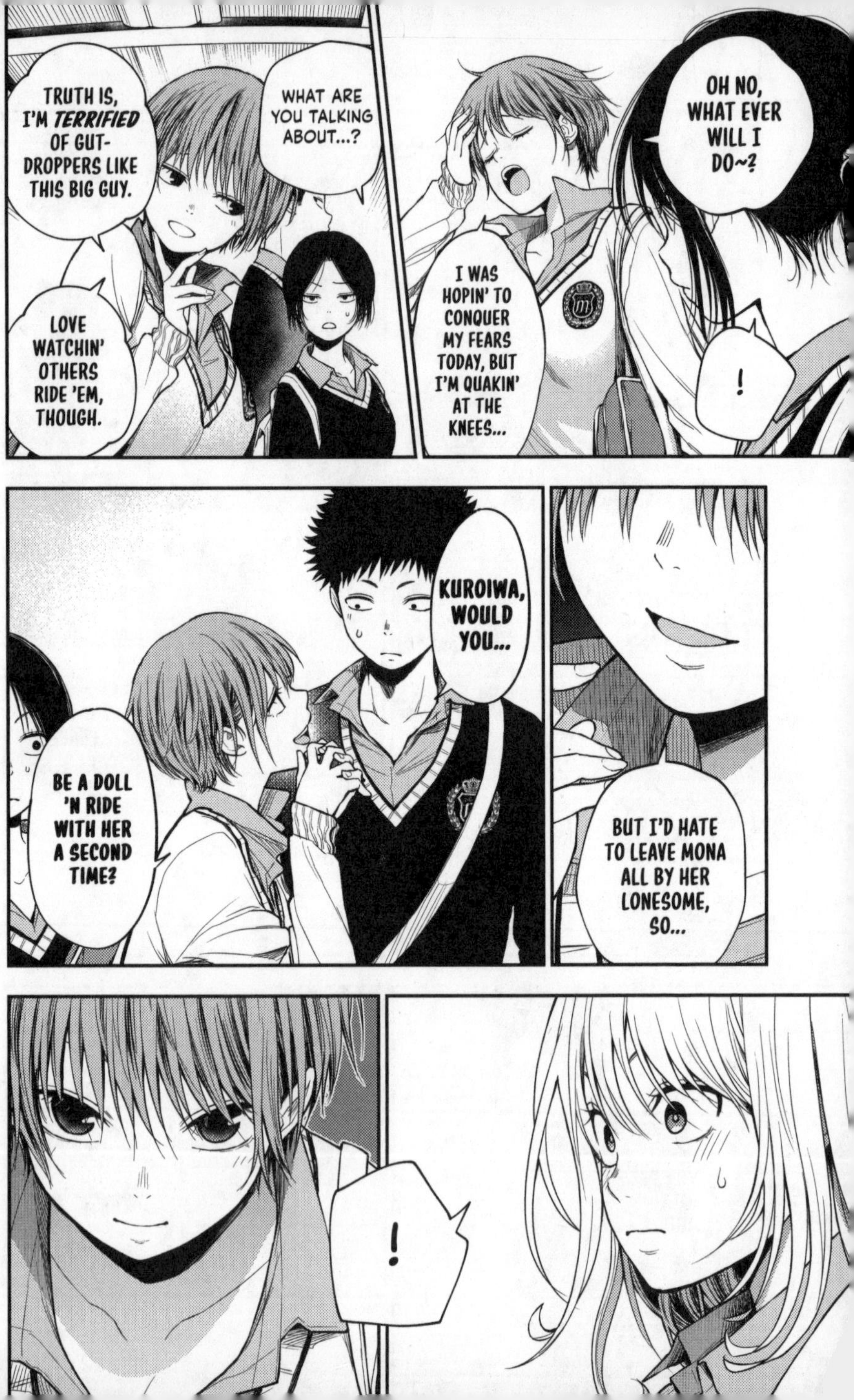
OH NO, WHAT EVER WILL I DO~?
I WAS HOPIN' TO CONQUER MY FEARS TODAY, BUT I'M QUAKIN' AT THE KNEES...
!
WHAT ARE YOU TALKING ABOUT...?
TRUTH IS, I'M *TERRIFIED* OF GUT-DROPPERS LIKE THIS BIG GUY.
LOVE WATCHIN' OTHERS RIDE 'EM, THOUGH.
BUT I'D HATE TO LEAVE MONA ALL BY HER LONESOME, SO...
KUROIWA, WOULD YOU...
BE A DOLL 'N RIDE WITH HER A SECOND TIME?
!

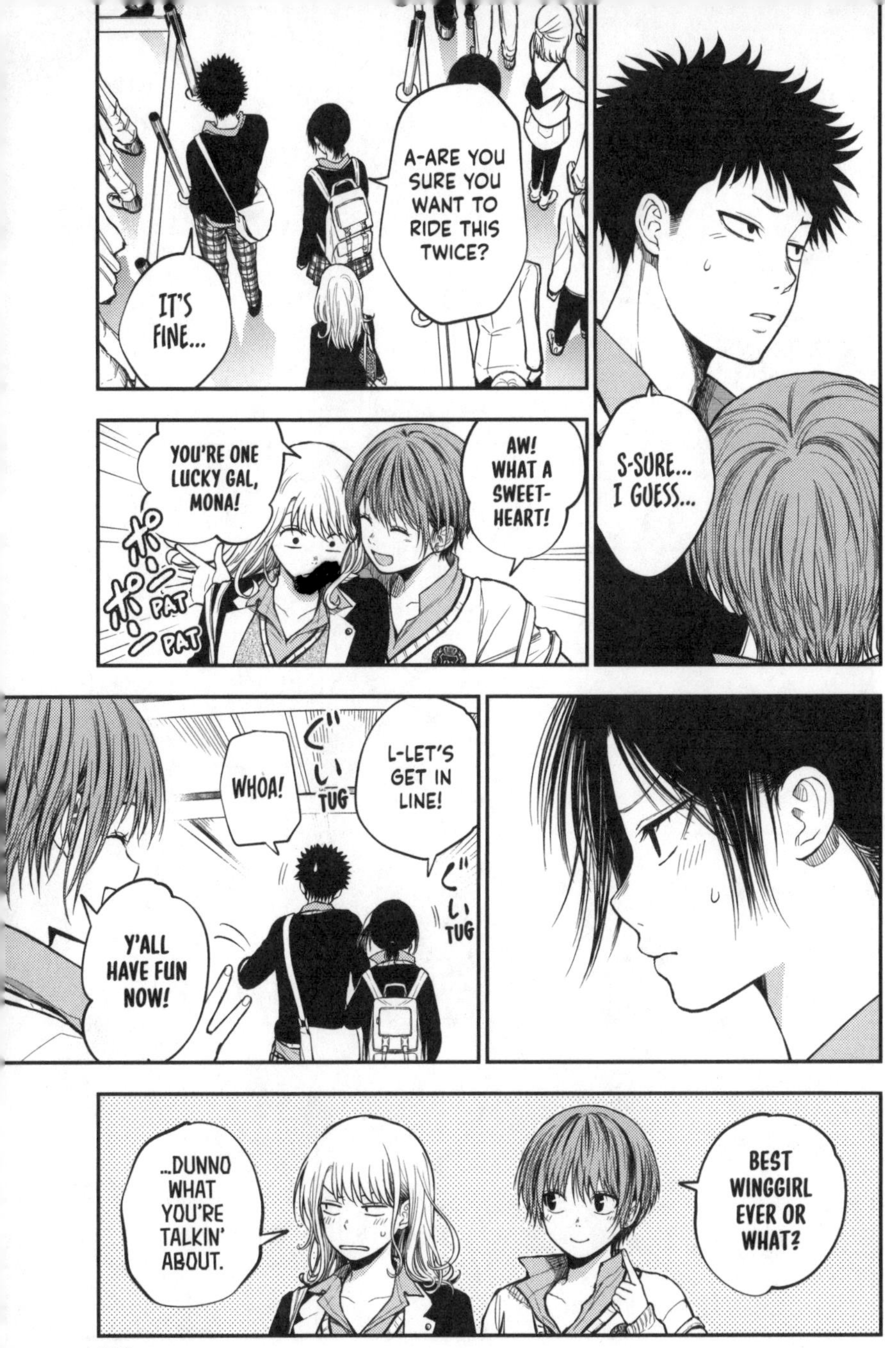
S-SURE... I GUESS...
A-ARE YOU SURE YOU WANT TO RIDE THIS TWICE?
IT'S FINE...
AW! WHAT A SWEET-HEART!
YOU'RE ONE LUCKY GAL, MONA!
PAT PAT
L-LET'S GET IN LINE!
TUG
WHOA!
TUG
Y'ALL HAVE FUN NOW!
BEST WINGGIRL EVER OR WHAT?
...DUNNO WHAT YOU'RE TALKIN' ABOUT.

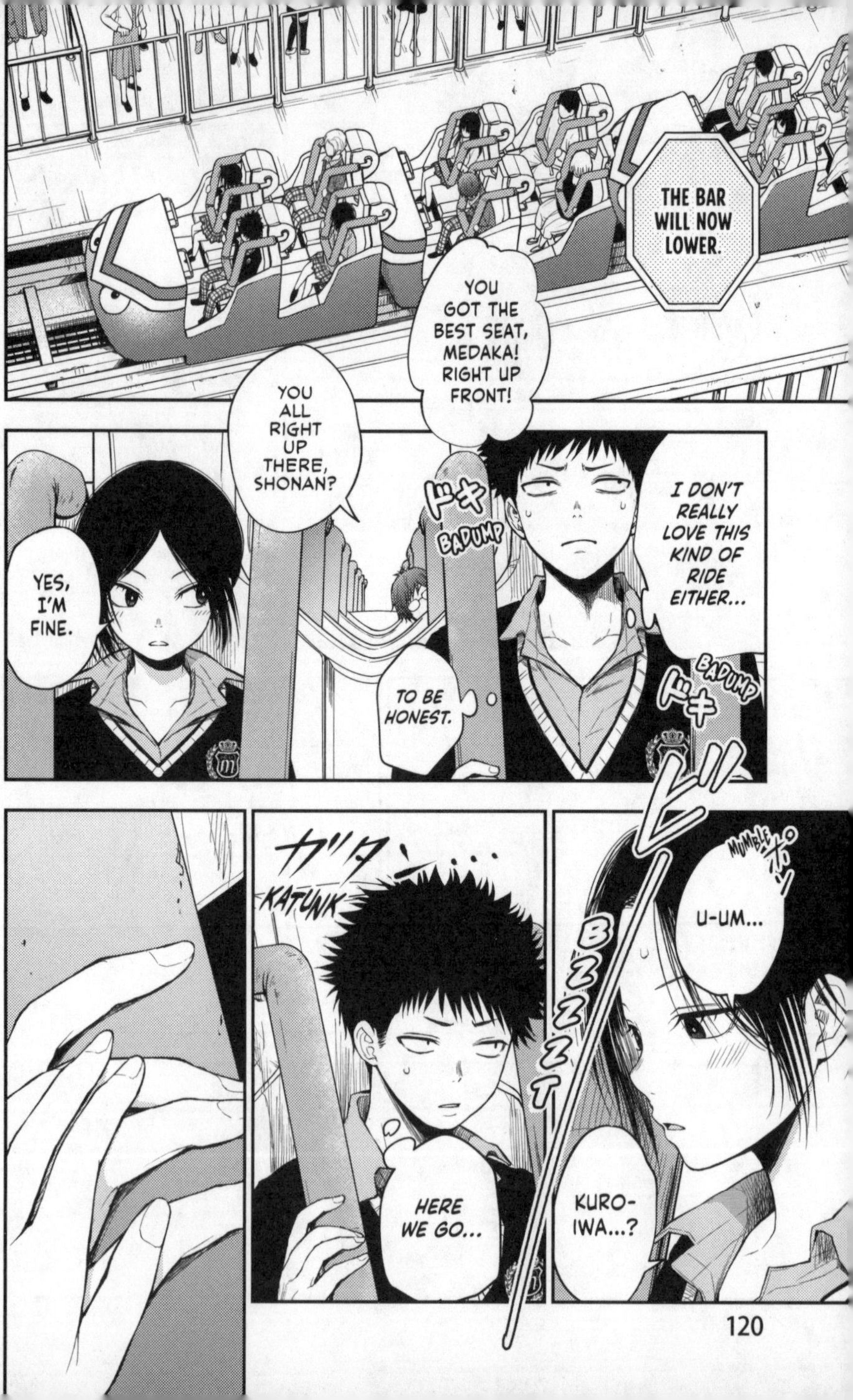
THE BAR WILL NOW LOWER.
YOU GOT THE BEST SEAT, MEDAKA! RIGHT UP FRONT!
YOU ALL RIGHT UP THERE, SHONAN?
I DON'T REALLY LOVE THIS KIND OF RIDE EITHER...
BADUMP
BADUMP
TO BE HONEST.
YES, I'M FINE.
MUMBLE
U-UM...
BZZZZT
KURO-IWA...?
KATUNK
HERE WE GO...

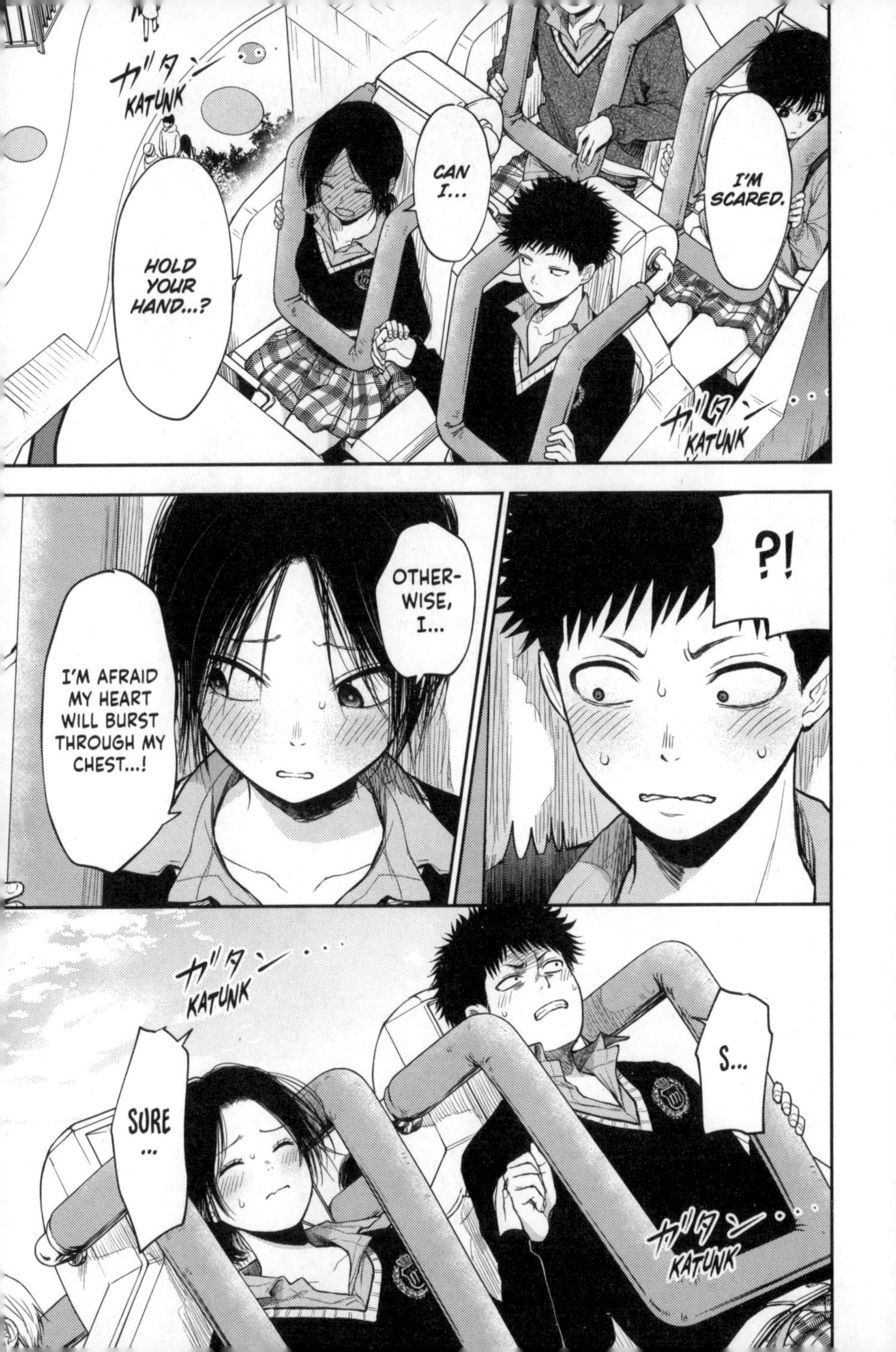
I'M SCARED.
CAN I...
HOLD YOUR HAND...?
ガタン
KATUNK
ガタン
KATUNK
?!
OTHER-WISE, I...
I'M AFRAID MY HEART WILL BURST THROUGH MY CHEST...!
S...
ガタン
KATUNK
SURE ...
ガタン
KATUNK

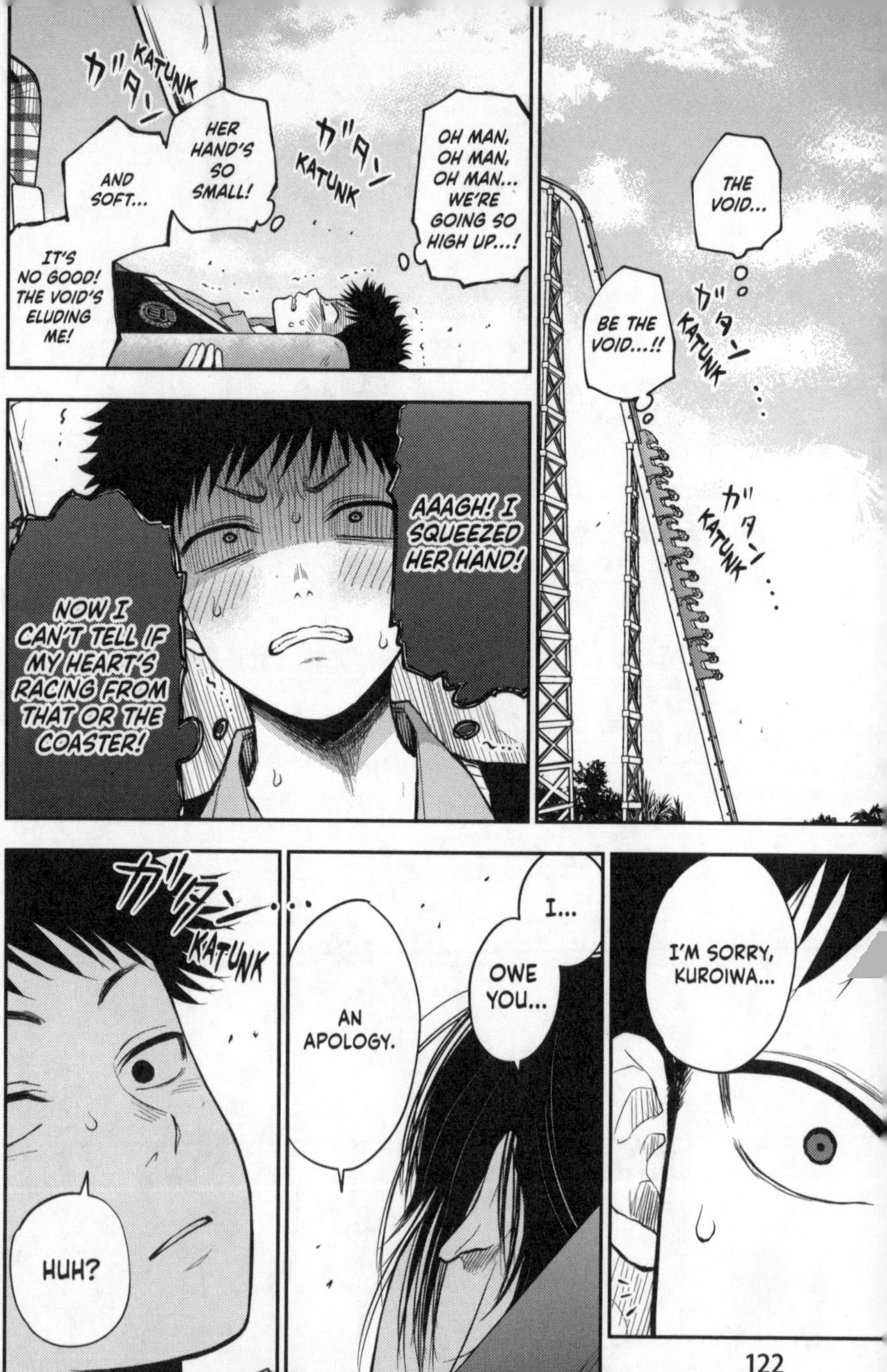
THE VOID...
ガタン
KATUNK
BE THE VOID...!!
ガタン
KATUNK
OH MAN, OH MAN, OH MAN... WE'RE GOING SO HIGH UP...!
ガタン
KATUNK
HER HAND'S SO SMALL!
AND SOFT...
IT'S NO GOOD! THE VOID'S ELUDING ME!
ガタン
KATUNK
AAAGH! I SQUEEZED HER HAND!
NOW I CAN'T TELL IF MY HEART'S RACING FROM THAT OR THE COASTER!
I'M SORRY, KUROIWA...
I...
OWE YOU...
AN APOLOGY.
ガタン
KATUNK
HUH?

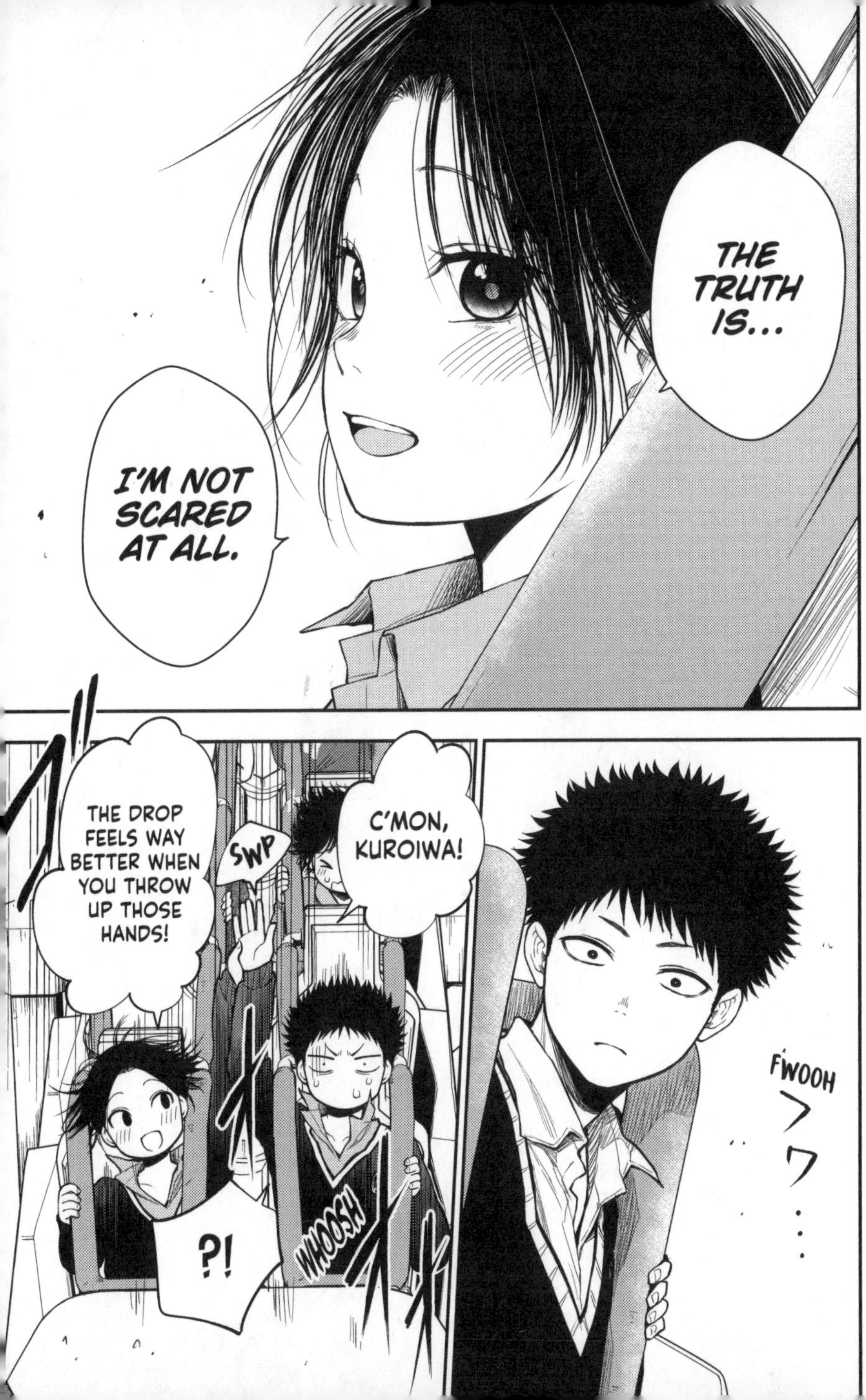
THE TRUTH IS...
I'M NOT SCARED AT ALL.
FWOOH
C'MON, KUROIWA!
SWP
THE DROP FEELS WAY BETTER WHEN YOU THROW UP THOSE HANDS!
WHOOSH
?!

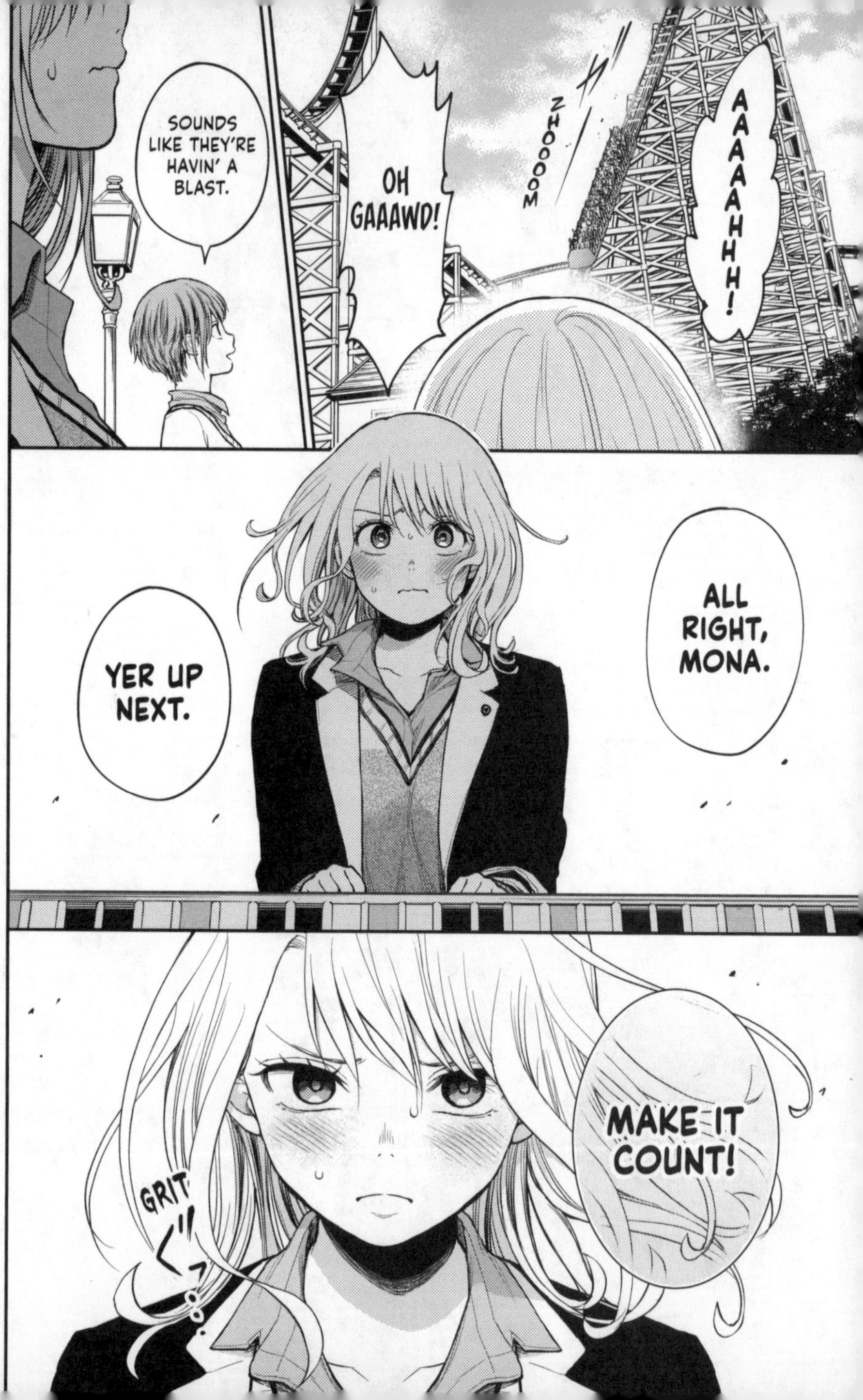
AAAAAHHH!
ZHOOOOOM
OH GAAAWD!
SOUNDS LIKE THEY'RE HAVIN' A BLAST.
ALL RIGHT, MONA.
YER UP NEXT.
MAKE IT COUNT!
GRIT

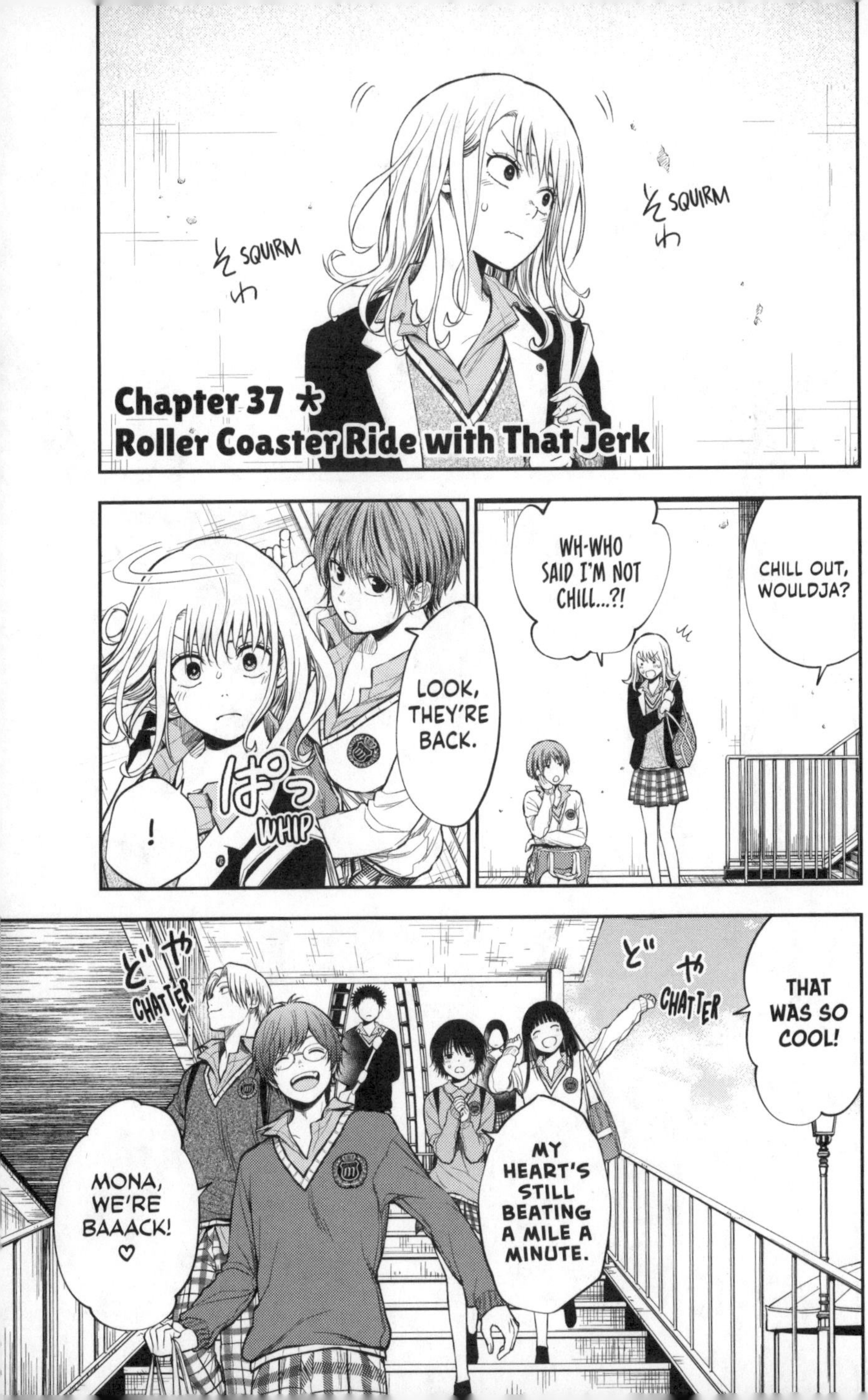
そわ SQUIRM
そわ SQUIRM
Chapter 37 ★
Roller Coaster Ride with That Jerk
CHILL OUT, WOULDJA?
WH-WHO SAID I'M NOT CHILL...?!
LOOK, THEY'RE BACK.
ぱっ WHIP
!
THAT WAS SO COOL!
どや CHATTER
MY HEART'S STILL BEATING A MILE A MINUTE.
どや CHATTER
MONA, WE'RE BAAACK! ♡

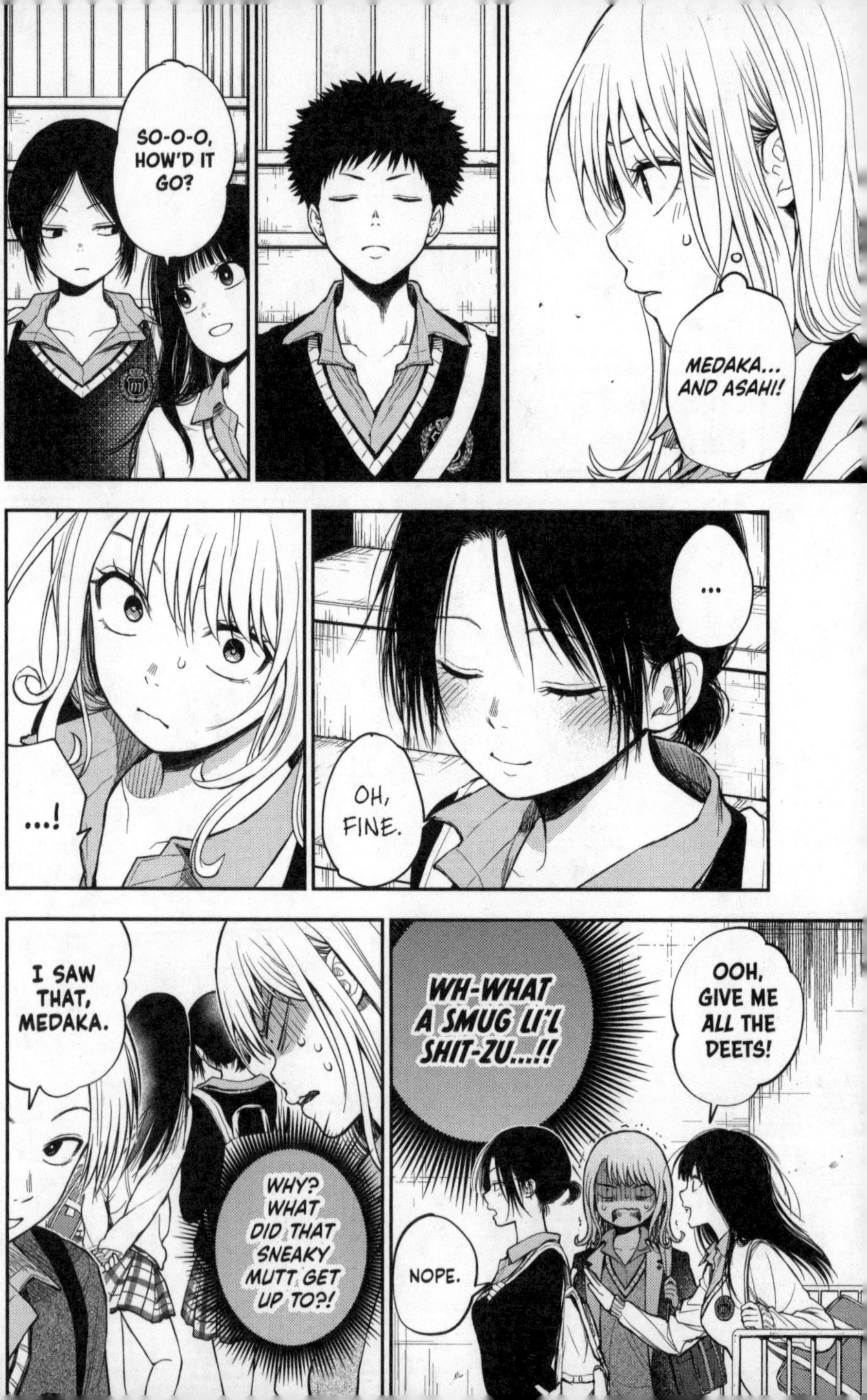
MEDAKA... AND ASAHI!
SO-O-O, HOW'D IT GO?
...
OH, FINE.
...!
OOH, GIVE ME ALL THE DEETS!
WH-WHAT A SMUG LI'L SHIT-ZU...!!
NOPE.
I SAW THAT, MEDAKA.
WHY? WHAT DID THAT SNEAKY MUTT GET UP TO?!

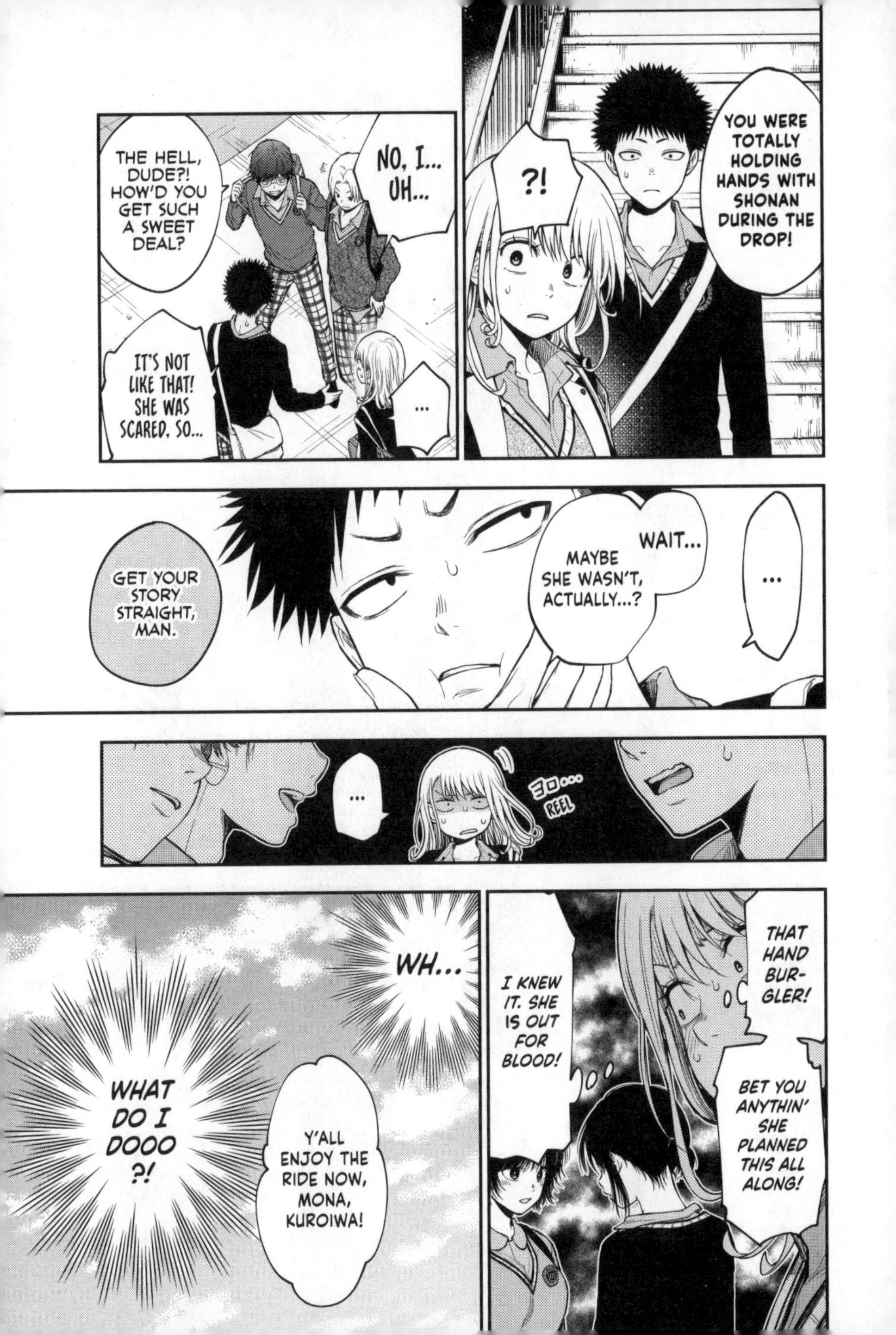
YOU WERE TOTALLY HOLDING HANDS WITH SHONAN DURING THE DROP!
?!
THE HELL, DUDE?! HOW'D YOU GET SUCH A SWEET DEAL?
NO, I... UH...
IT'S NOT LIKE THAT! SHE WAS SCARED, SO...
...
...
WAIT...
MAYBE SHE WASN'T, ACTUALLY...?
GET YOUR STORY STRAIGHT, MAN.
ヨロ•••
REEL
...
THAT HAND BURGLER!
I KNEW IT. SHE IS OUT FOR BLOOD!
BET YOU ANYTHIN' SHE PLANNED THIS ALL ALONG!
WH...
Y'ALL ENJOY THE RIDE NOW, MONA, KUROIWA!
WHAT DO I DOOO?!

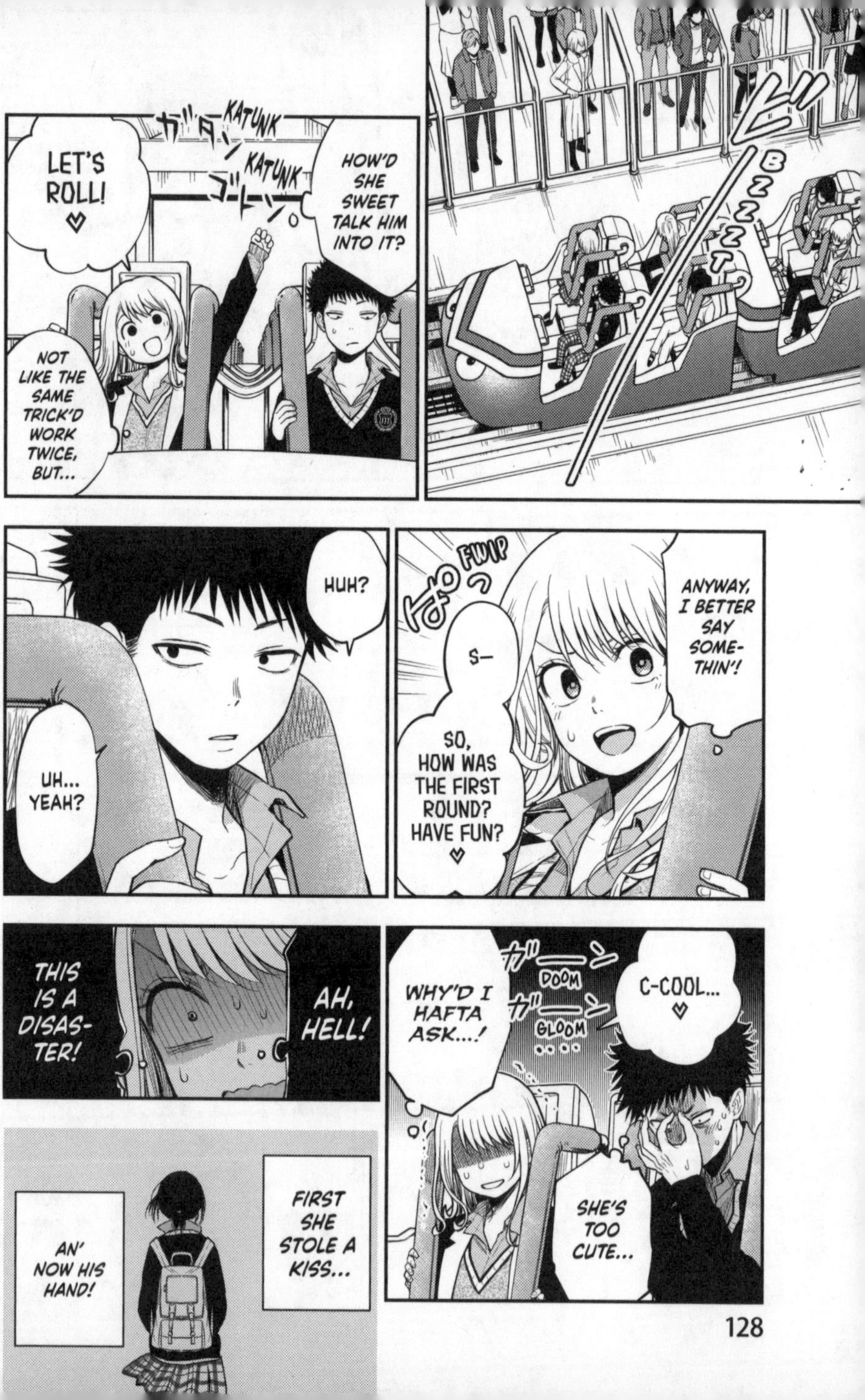
BZZZT
HOW'D SHE SWEET TALK HIM INTO IT?
ガタン KATUNK
ゴトン KATUNK
LET'S ROLL! ♡
NOT LIKE THE SAME TRICK'D WORK TWICE, BUT...
ANYWAY, I BETTER SAY SOME-THIN'!
ぱっ FWIP
S—
SO, HOW WAS THE FIRST ROUND? HAVE FUN? ♡
HUH?
UH... YEAH?
C-COOL... ♡
DOOM
GLOOM
WHY'D I HAFTA ASK...!
SHE'S TOO CUTE...
AH, HELL!
THIS IS A DISAS-TER!
FIRST SHE STOLE A KISS...
AN' NOW HIS HAND!

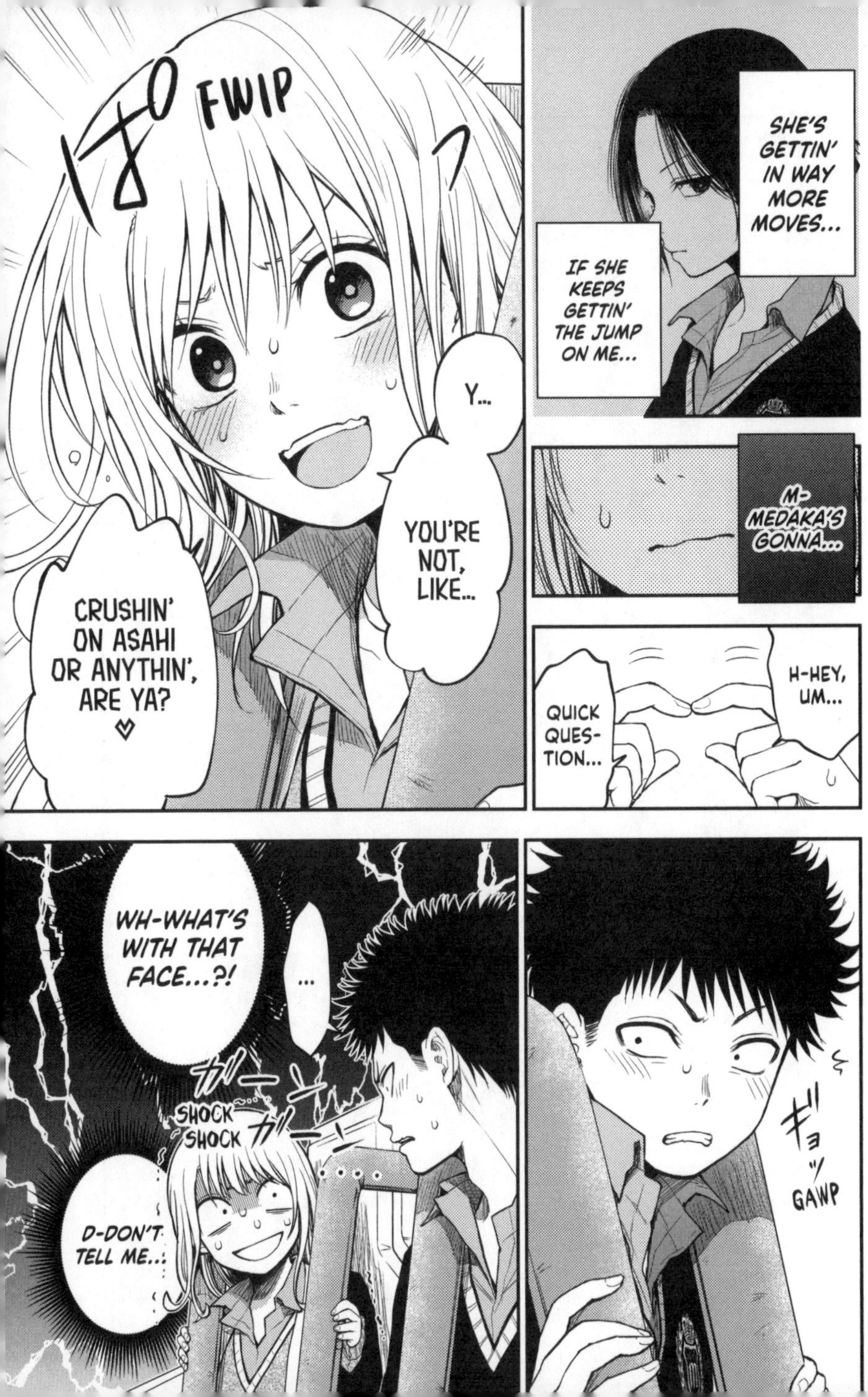
SHE'S GETTIN' IN WAY MORE MOVES...
IF SHE KEEPS GETTIN' THE JUMP ON ME...
M-MEDAKA'S GONNA...
H-HEY, UM...
QUICK QUES-TION...
FWIP
Y...
YOU'RE NOT, LIKE...
CRUSHIN' ON ASAHI OR ANYTHIN', ARE YA? ♡
GAWP
WH-WHAT'S WITH THAT FACE...?!
...
SHOCK SHOCK
D-DON'T TELL ME...

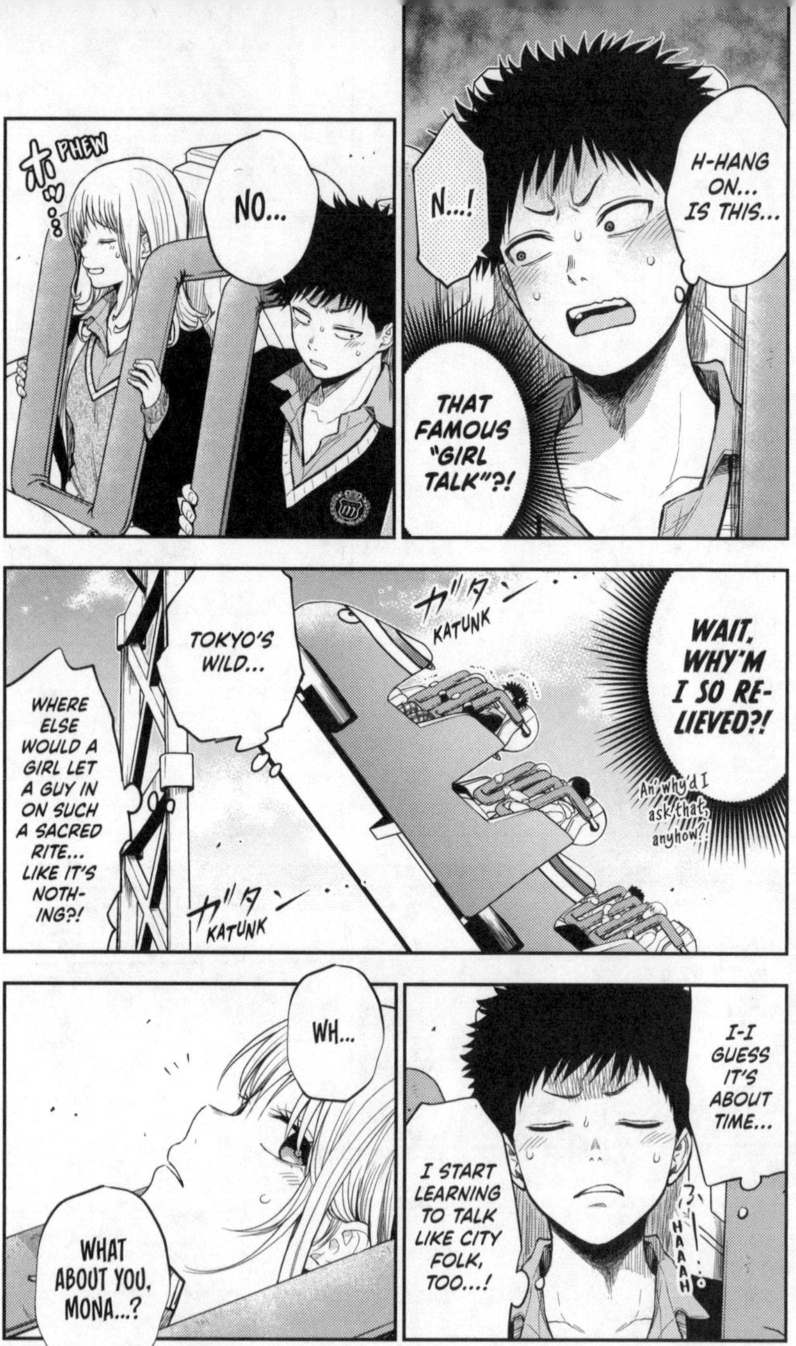
H-HANG ON... IS THIS...
N...!
THAT FAMOUS "GIRL TALK"?!
NO...
PHEW
WAIT, WHY'M I SO RE-LIEVED?!
An' why'd I ask that, anyhow?!
KATUNK
TOKYO'S WILD...
WHERE ELSE WOULD A GIRL LET A GUY IN ON SUCH A SACRED RITE... LIKE IT'S NOTH-ING?!
KATUNK
I-I GUESS IT'S ABOUT TIME...
I START LEARNING TO TALK LIKE CITY FOLK, TOO...!
HAAAH
WH...
WHAT ABOUT YOU, MONA...?

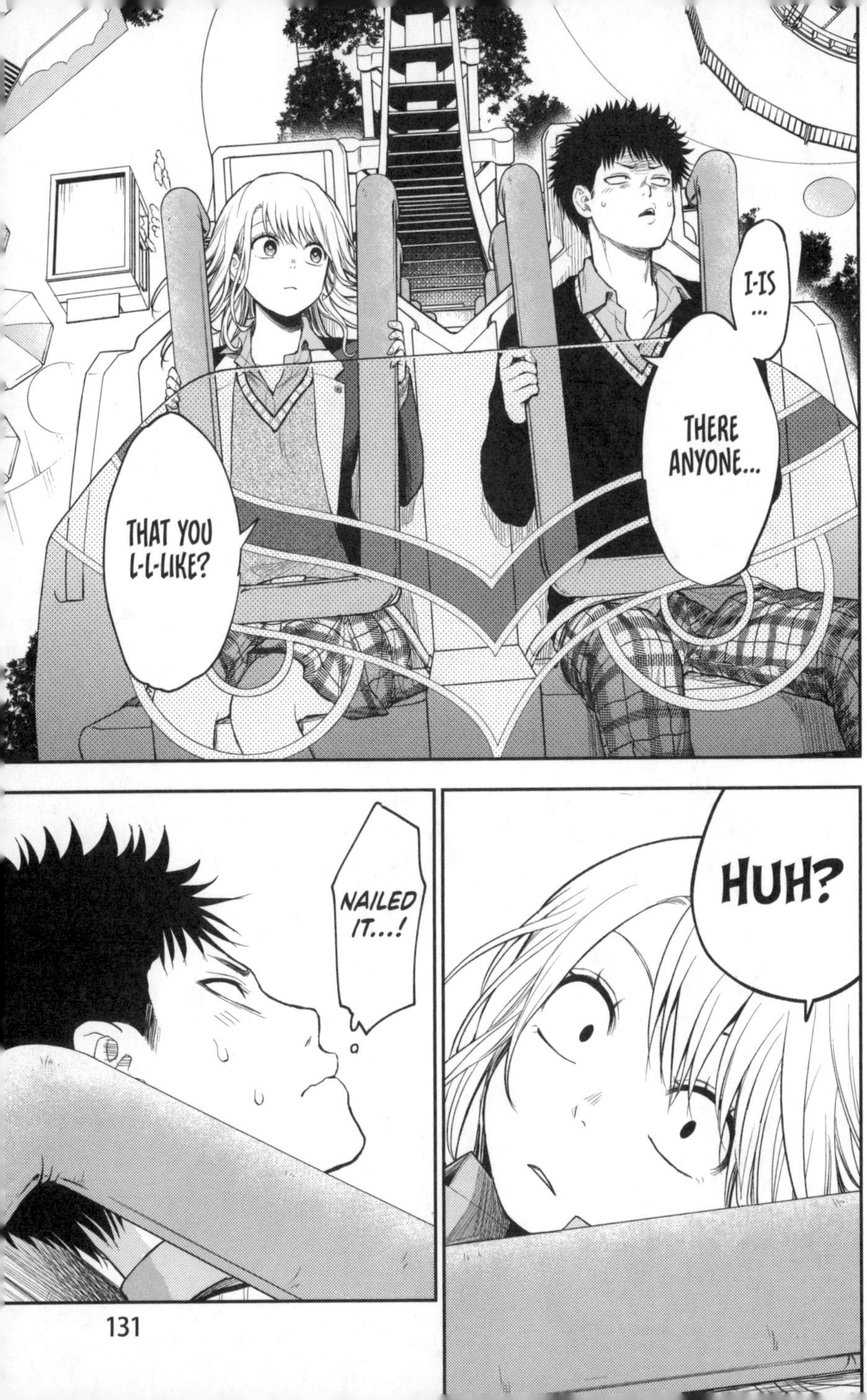
I-IS ...
THERE ANYONE...
THAT YOU L-L-LIKE?
HUH?
NAILED IT...!

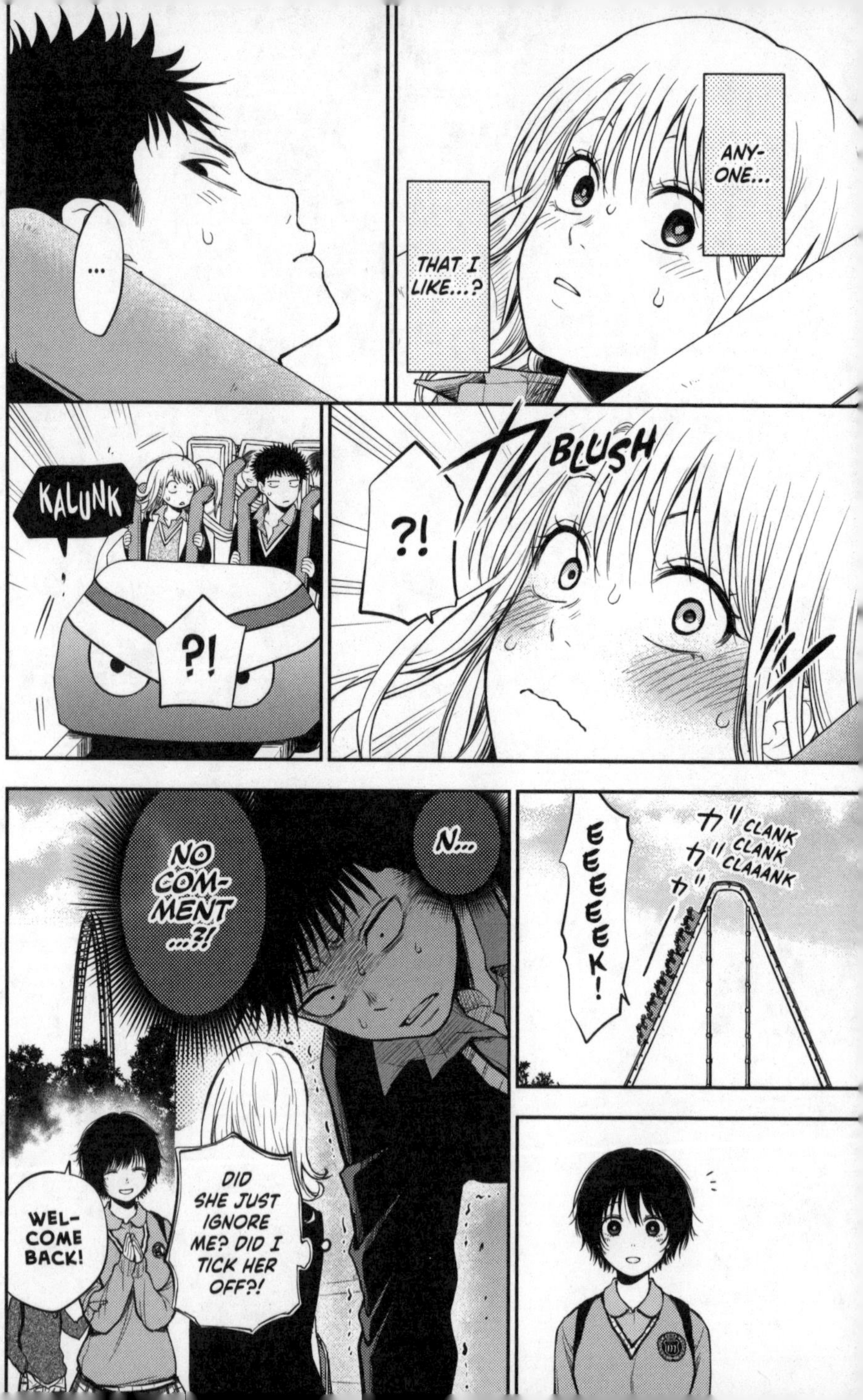
ANY-ONE...
THAT I LIKE...?
...
BLUSH
?!
KALUNK
?!
EEEEEK!
CLANK CLANK CLAAANK
N...
NO COM-MENT ...?!
DID SHE JUST IGNORE ME? DID I TICK HER OFF?!
WEL-COME BACK!

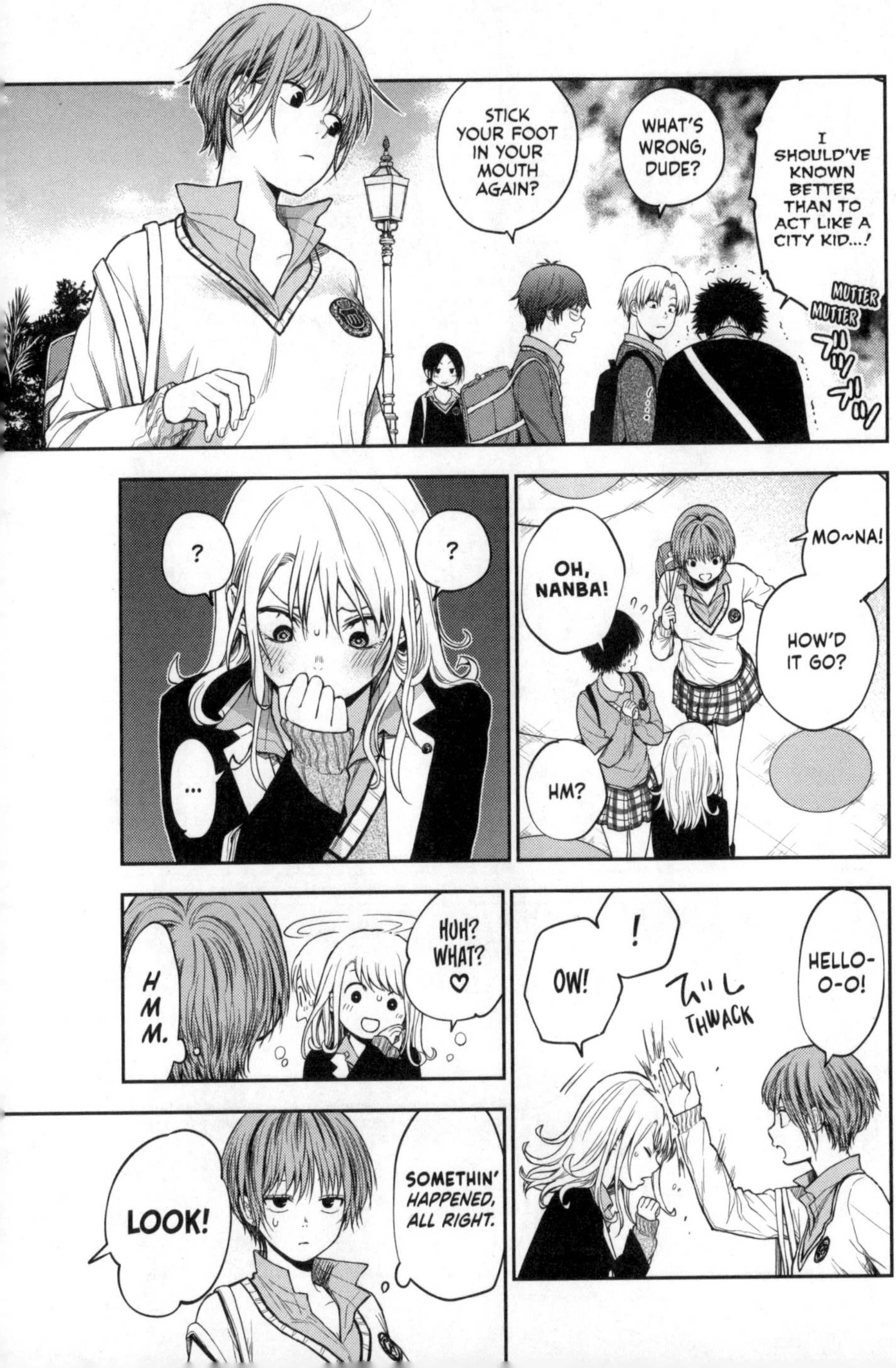
I SHOULD'VE KNOWN BETTER THAN TO ACT LIKE A CITY KID...!
MUTTER MUTTER
WHAT'S WRONG, DUDE?
STICK YOUR FOOT IN YOUR MOUTH AGAIN?
MO~NA!
OH, NANBA!
HOW'D IT GO?
HM?
?
?
...
HELLO-O-O!
!
OW!
THWACK
HUH? WHAT? ♡
HMM.
SOMETHIN' HAPPENED, ALL RIGHT.
LOOK!

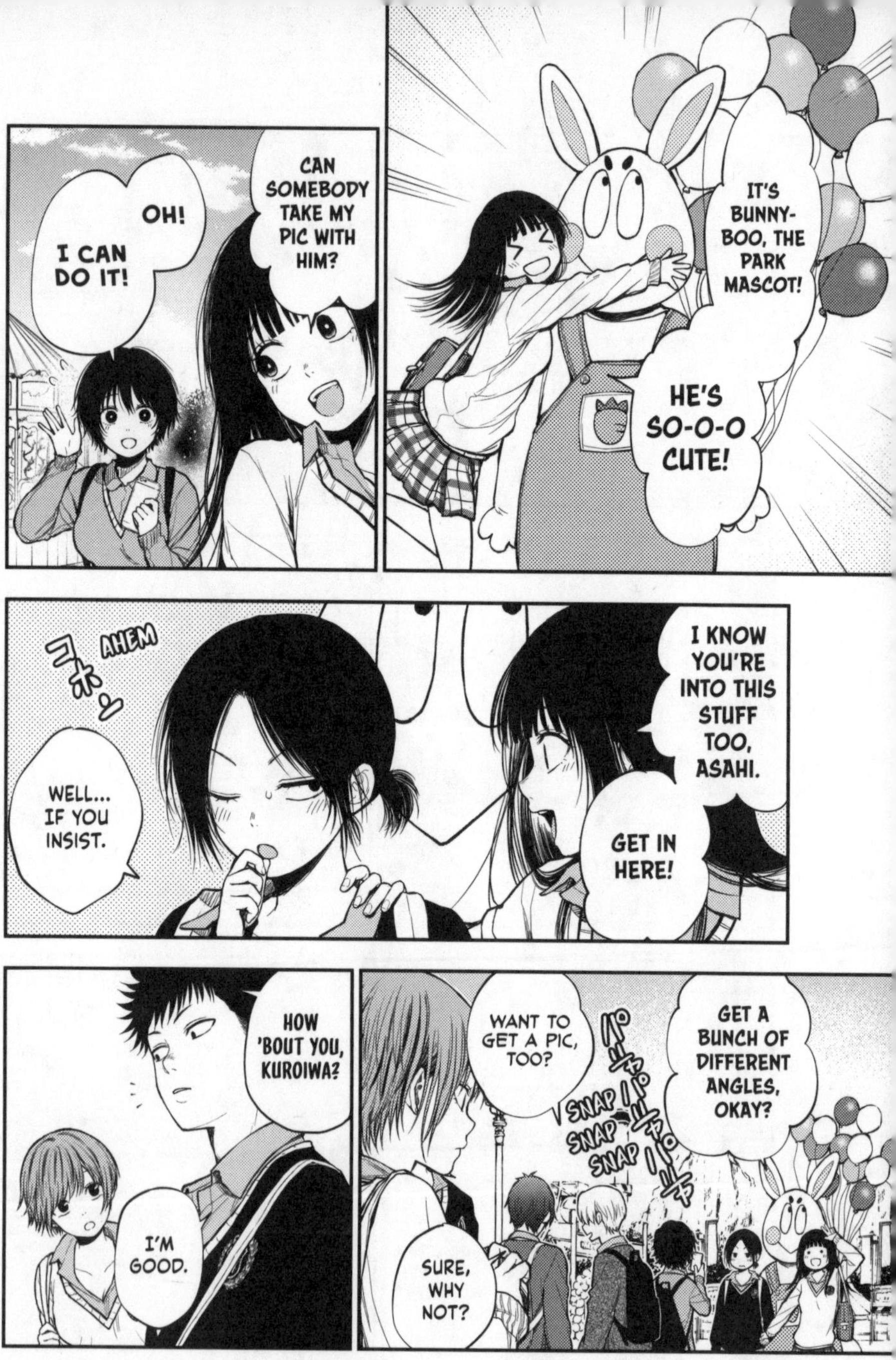

IT'S BUNNY-BOO, THE PARK MASCOT!
HE'S SO-O-O CUTE!
CAN SOMEBODY TAKE MY PIC WITH HIM?
OH! I CAN DO IT!
I KNOW YOU'RE INTO THIS STUFF TOO, ASAHI.
GET IN HERE!
コホン
AHEM
WELL... IF YOU INSIST.
GET A BUNCH OF DIFFERENT ANGLES, OKAY?
パシャパシャパシャ
SNAP SNAP SNAP
WANT TO GET A PIC, TOO?
SURE, WHY NOT?
HOW 'BOUT YOU, KUROIWA?
I'M GOOD.

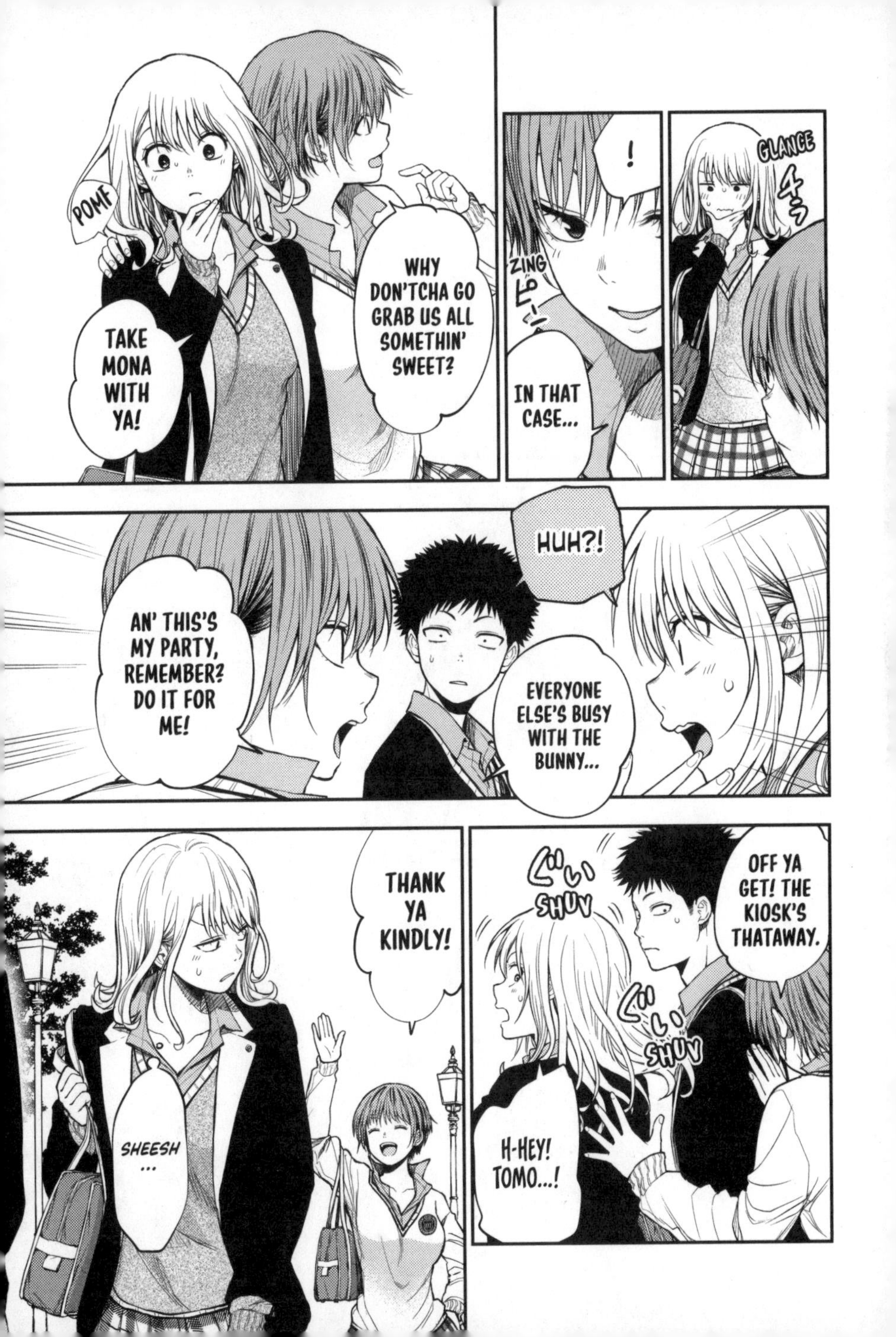
GLANCE
!
ZING
IN THAT CASE...
WHY DON'TCHA GO GRAB US ALL SOMETHIN' SWEET?
POMF
TAKE MONA WITH YA!
HUH?!
EVERYONE ELSE'S BUSY WITH THE BUNNY...
AN' THIS'S MY PARTY, REMEMBER? DO IT FOR ME!
OFF YA GET! THE KIOSK'S THATAWAY.
SHUV
SHUV
H-HEY! TOMO...!
THANK YA KINDLY!
SHEESH ...

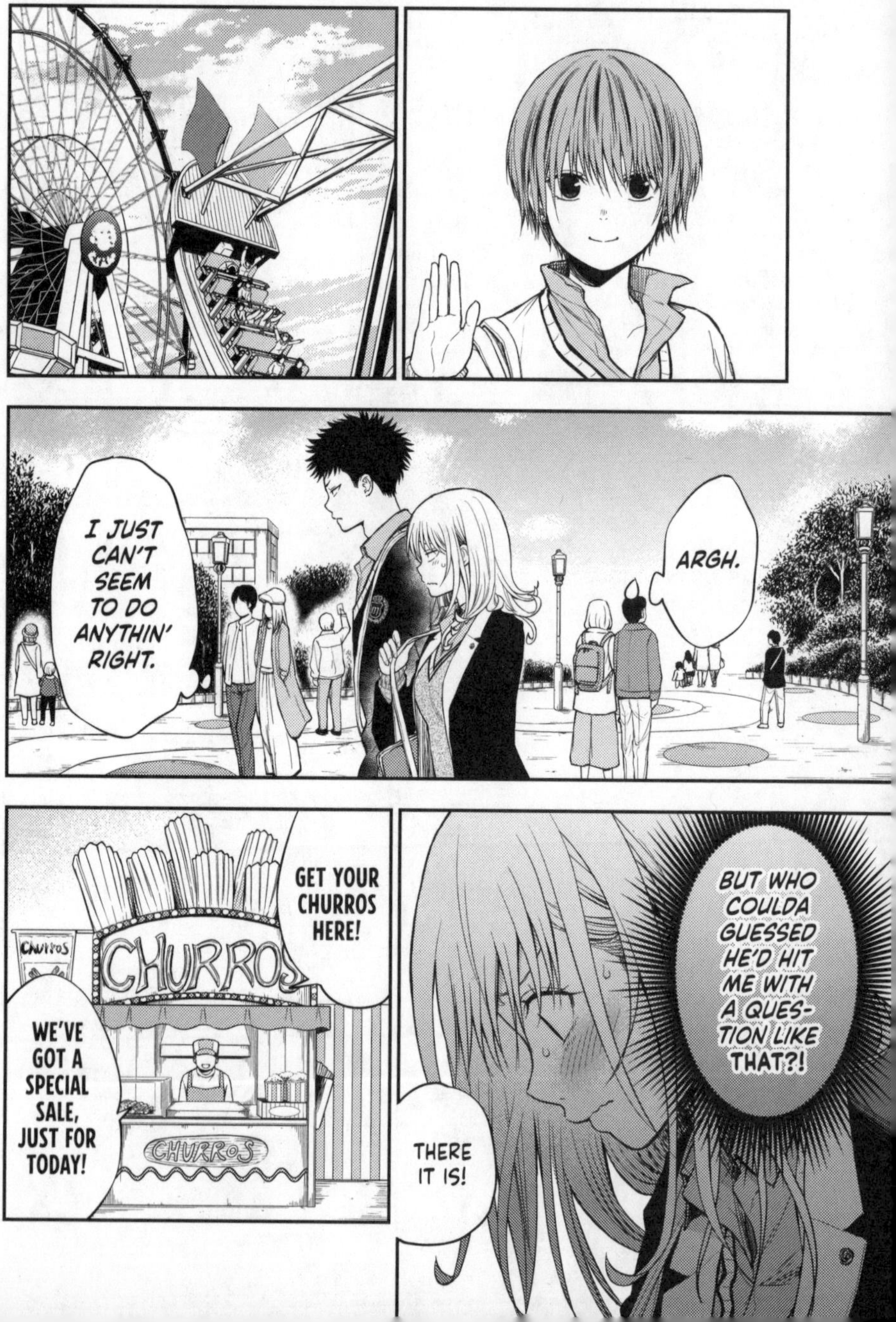
ARGH.
I JUST CAN'T SEEM TO DO ANYTHIN' RIGHT.
BUT WHO COULDA GUESSED HE'D HIT ME WITH A QUES-TION LIKE THAT?!
THERE IT IS!
GET YOUR CHURROS HERE!
CHURROS
CHURROS
CHURROS
WE'VE GOT A SPECIAL SALE, JUST FOR TODAY!

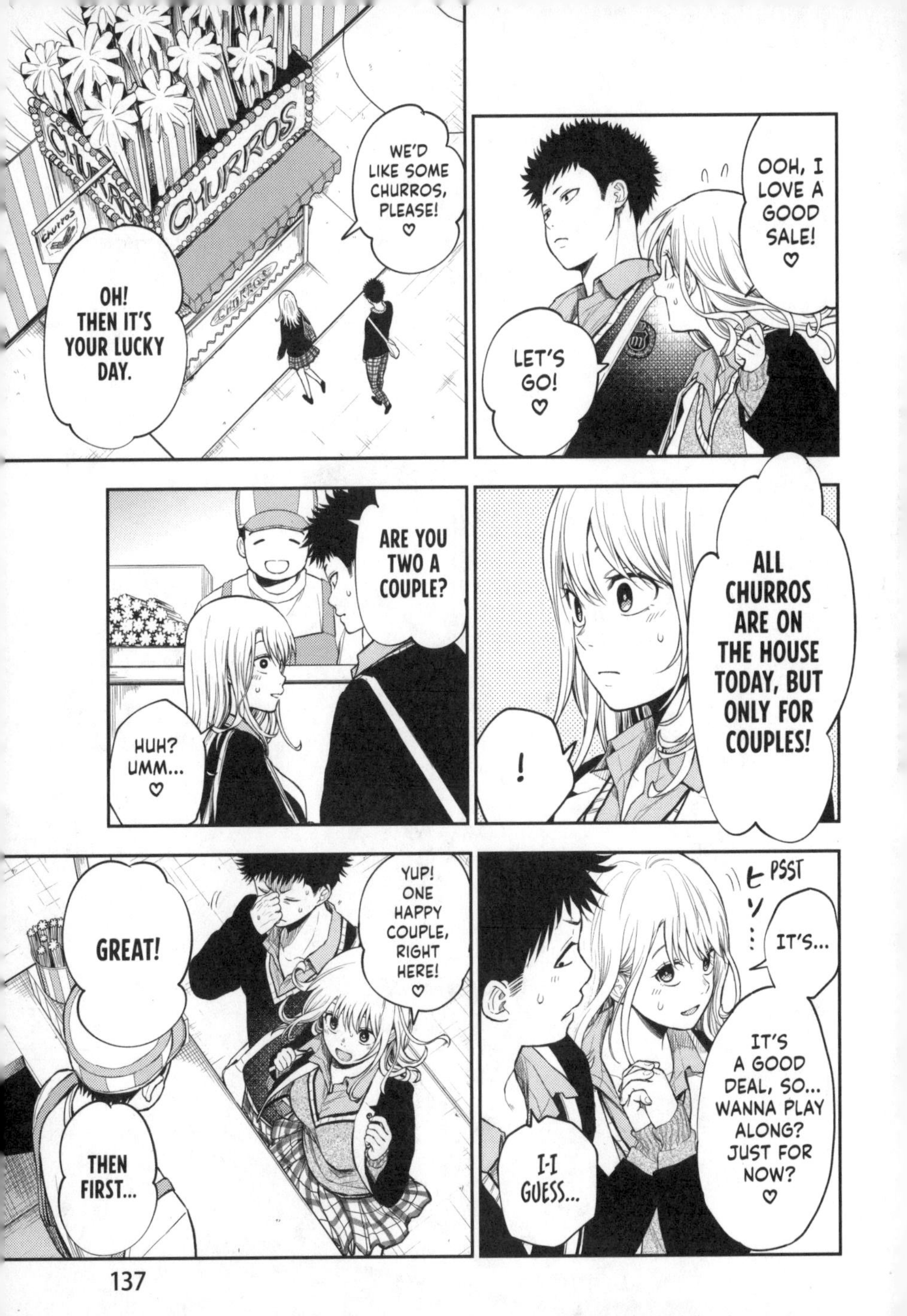
OOH, I LOVE A GOOD SALE! ♡
LET'S GO! ♡
CHURROS
CHURROS
WE'D LIKE SOME CHURROS, PLEASE! ♡
OH! THEN IT'S YOUR LUCKY DAY.
ALL CHURROS ARE ON THE HOUSE TODAY, BUT ONLY FOR COUPLES!
!
ARE YOU TWO A COUPLE?
HUH? UMM... ♡
ヒソ… PSST
IT'S...
IT'S A GOOD DEAL, SO... WANNA PLAY ALONG? JUST FOR NOW? ♡
I-I GUESS...
YUP! ONE HAPPY COUPLE, RIGHT HERE! ♡
GREAT!
THEN FIRST...

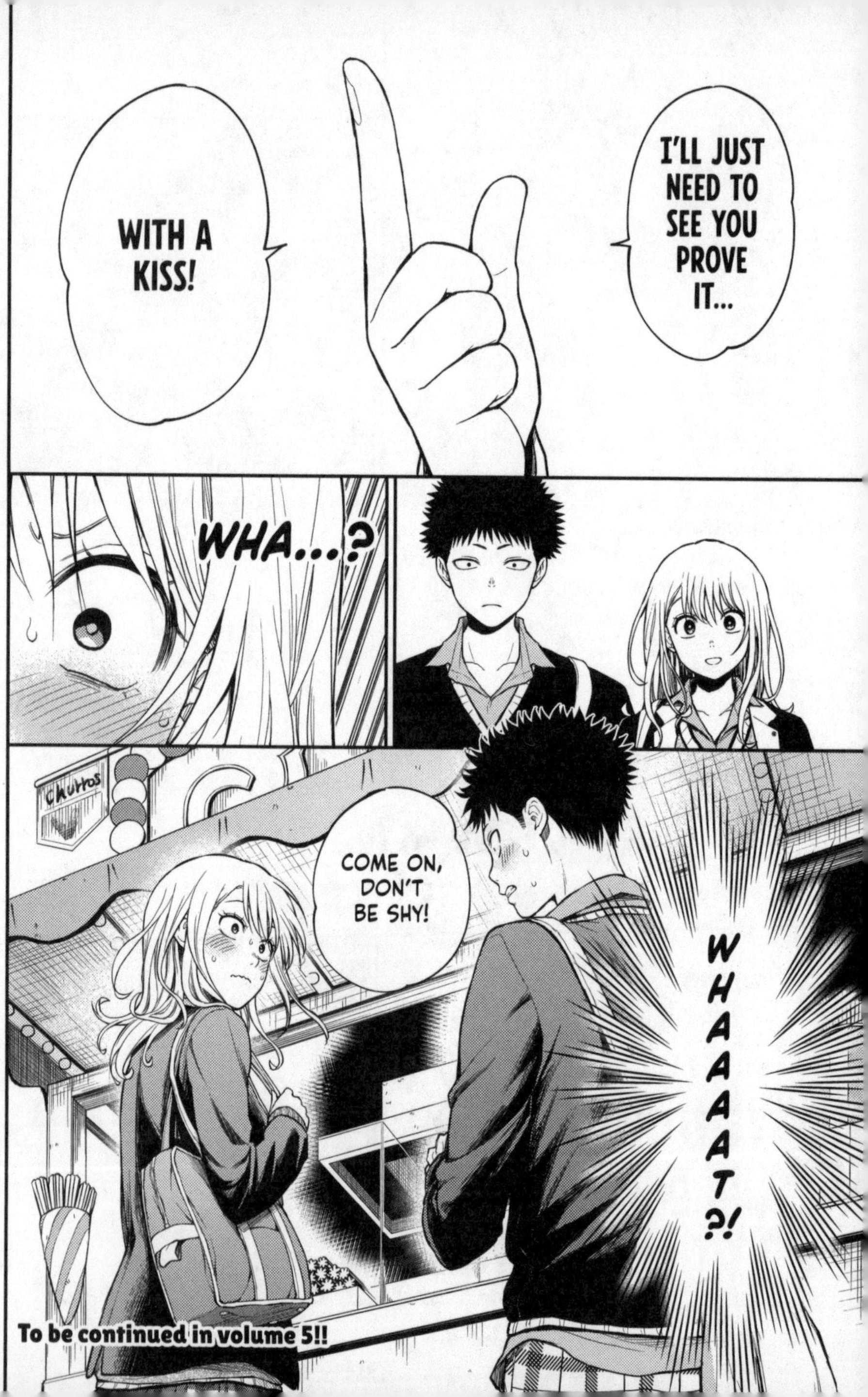
I'LL JUST NEED TO SEE YOU PROVE IT...
WITH A KISS!
WHA...?
COME ON, DON'T BE SHY!
Churros
WHAAAAAT?!
To be continued in volume 5!!

Medaka Kuroiwa is Impervious to My Charms

PREVIEW

CAN SHE DO IT?! WILL SHE GO IN FOR THE K-K-K-KISS?!

MOVES ARE MADE AND MINDS ARE CHANGED AS THE "THEME PARK DATE" ARC KICKS IT INTO HIGH GEAR!

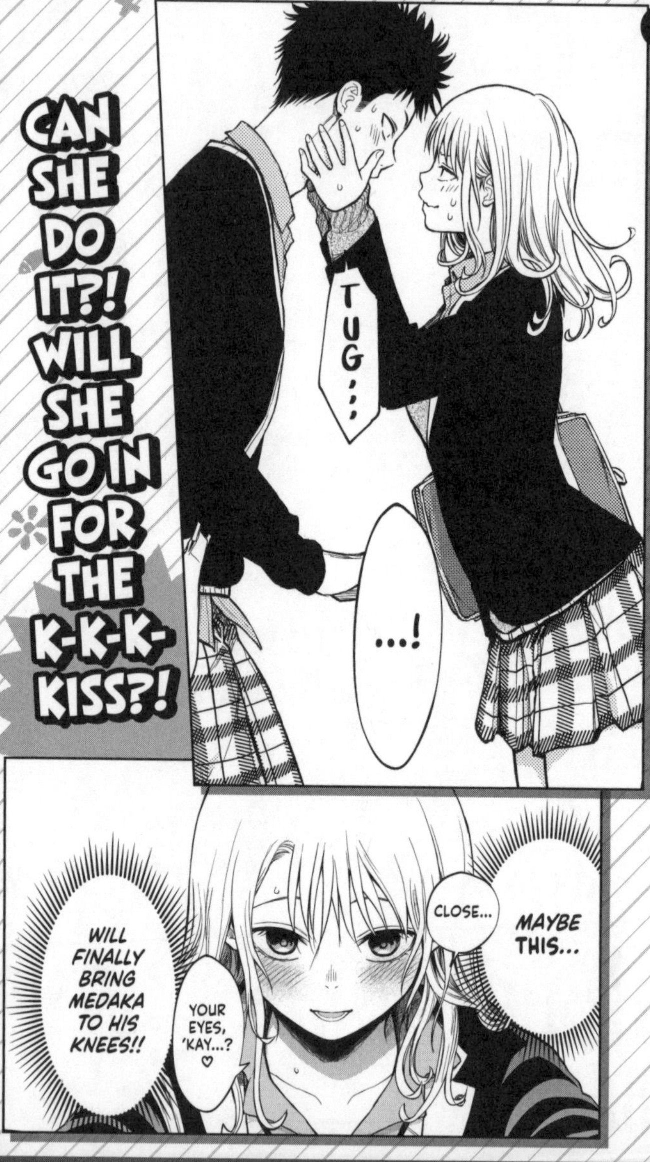
TUG;;
...!
MAYBE THIS...
CLOSE...
WILL FINALLY BRING MEDAKA TO HIS KNEES!!
YOUR EYES, 'KAY...? ♡

ervious to My Charms

Spring 2024!!

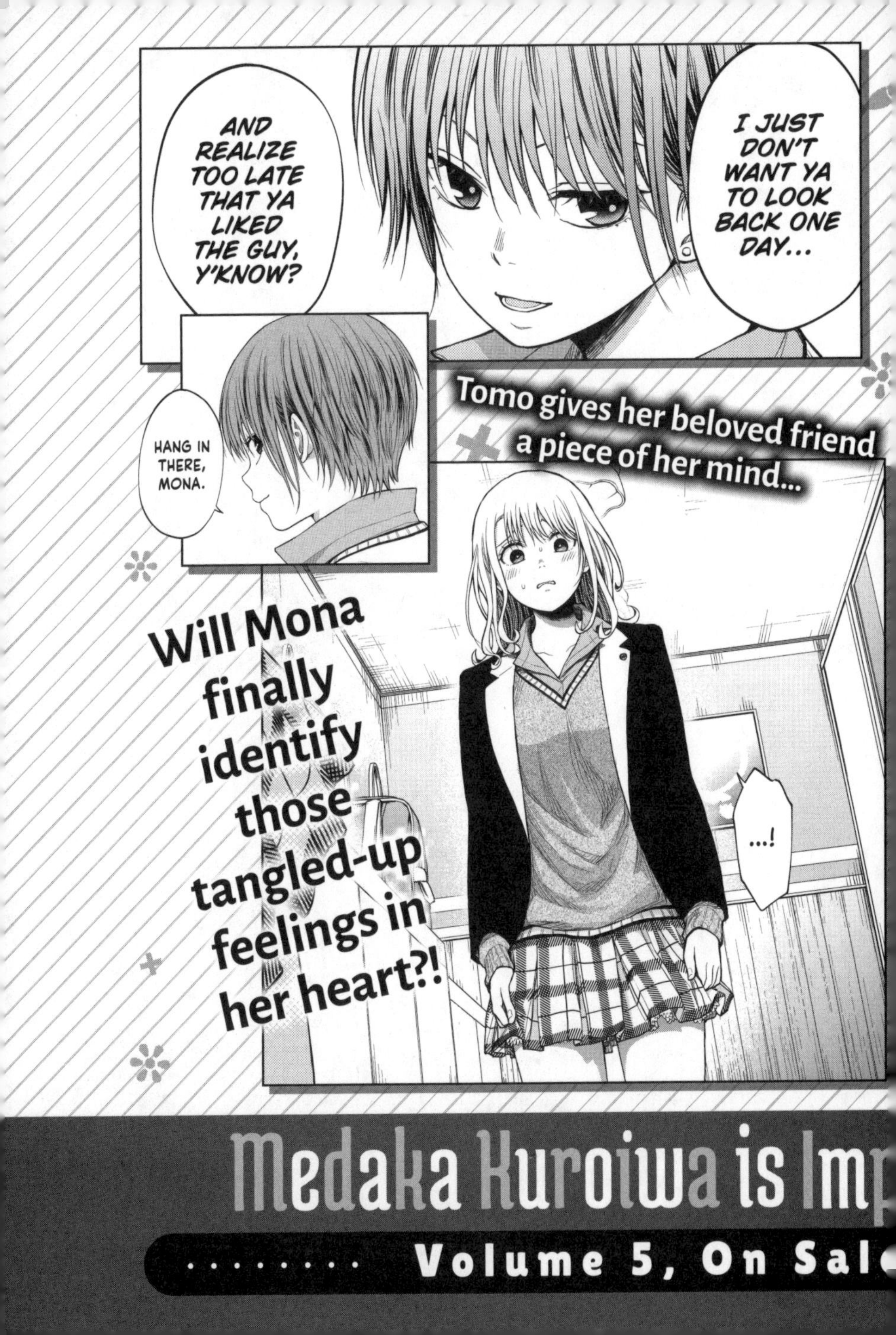
I JUST DON'T WANT YA TO LOOK BACK ONE DAY...
AND REALIZE TOO LATE THAT YA LIKED THE GUY, Y'KNOW?
HANG IN THERE, MONA.
Tomo gives her beloved friend a piece of her mind...
Will Mona finally identify those tangled-up feelings in her heart?!
...!
Medaka Kuroiwa is Imp
Volume 5, On Sal

THE DARWIN INCIDENT

SHUN UMEZAWA

IT'S **THE** HUMANZEE VERSUS **THE TERRORISTS,**

WITH ALL HUMANKIND

CAUGHT **IN THE** MIDDLE!!

The Animal Liberation Alliance, an eco-terrorist organization, rescues a pregnant chimpanzee from an animal testing lab—only for it to give birth to a half-human, half-chimpanzee "humanzee" named Charlie! Fifteen years later, Charlie's human foster parents are finally ready to send him to a normal high school, where he makes his first friend: a human girl named Lucy. In the meantime, however, the ALA's stance has become ever more extreme, and now they're here to drag Charlie into their terrorist plot...

VOLUME 1 AVAILABLE NOW!

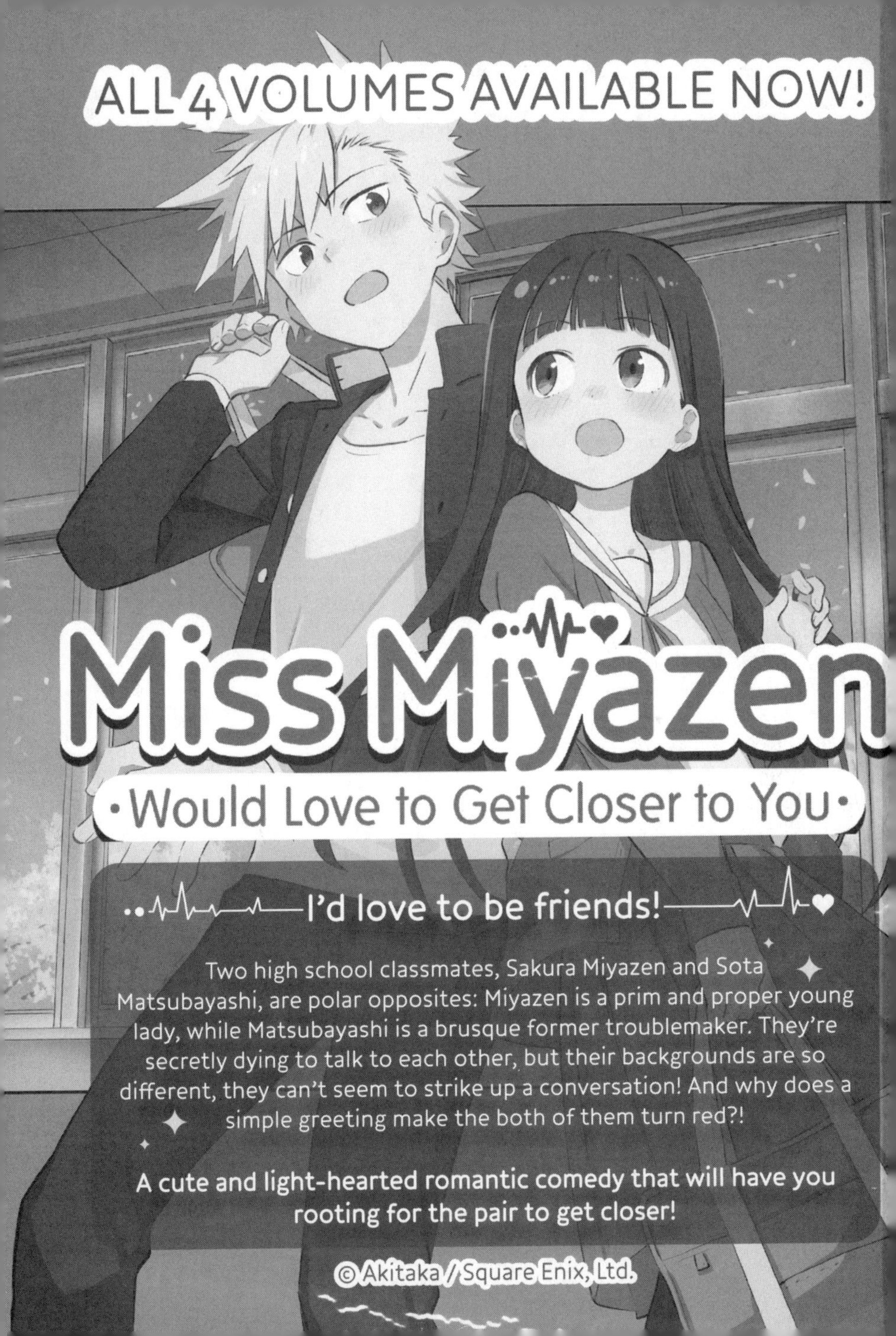
ALL 4 VOLUMES AVAILABLE NOW!
Miss Miyazen
•Would Love to Get Closer to You•
I'd love to be friends!
Two high school classmates, Sakura Miyazen and Sota Matsubayashi, are polar opposites: Miyazen is a prim and proper young lady, while Matsubayashi is a brusque former troublemaker. They're secretly dying to talk to each other, but their backgrounds are so different, they can't seem to strike up a conversation! And why does a simple greeting make the both of them turn red?!
A cute and light-hearted romantic comedy that will have you rooting for the pair to get closer!
© Akitaka / Square Enix, Ltd.

Medaka Kuroiwa is Impervious to My Charms 4

A VERTICAL Book

Translation (Original Digital): Anh Kiet Pham Ngo
Translation (Print): Nicole Frasik
Editor (Original Digital): Thalia Sutton
Editor (Print): Alexandra McCullough-Garcia
Production: Risa Cho, Pei Ann Yeap (print)
Letterer: Arbash Mughal
Proofreading: Kevin Luo (print)
YKS Services LLC/SKY JAPAN, Inc. (original digital)

First published in Japan in 2022 by Kodansha, Ltd., Tokyo
Publication rights for this English edition arranged through Kodansha, Ltd., Tokyo
English language version produced by Kodansha USA Publishing, LLC, 2023

Originally published in Japanese as *Kuroiwa Medaka ni Watashi no Kawaii ga Tsūjinai 4* by Kodansha, Ltd.
Kuroiwa Medaka ni Watashi no Kawaii ga Tsūjinai first serialized in *Weekly Shonen Magazine*, Kodansha, Ltd., 2021-

This is a work of fiction.

ISBN: 978-1-64729-308-6

Printed in the United States of America

First Edition

Kodansha USA Publishing, LLC
451 Park Avenue South
7th Floor
New York, NY 10016
www.kodansha.us

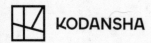